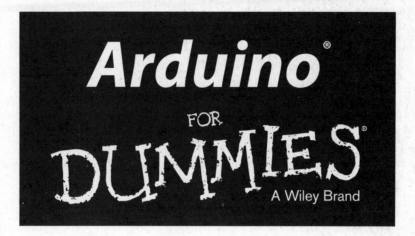

Arduino®

FOR

DUMMIES

A Wiley Brand

by John Nussey

FOR

DUMMIES

A Wiley Brand

Arduino® For Dummies®

Published by
John Wiley & Sons, Ltd
The Atrium
Southern Gate
Chichester
West Sussex
PO19 8SQ
England

Email (for orders and customer service enquires): cs-books@wiley.co.uk

Visit our home page on www.wiley.com

For general information on our other products and services, please contact our Customer Care Department within the U.S. at 877-762-2974, outside the U.S. at 317-572-3993, or fax 317-572-4002.

For technical support, please visit www.wiley.com/techsupport.

Wiley also publishes its books in a variety of electronic formats and by print-on-demand. Some content that appears in standard print versions of this book may not be available in other formats. For more information about Wiley products, visit us at www.wiley.com.

British Library Cataloguing in Publication Data: A catalogue record for this book is available from the British Library.

ISBN 978-1-118-44637-9 (paperback); ISBN 978-1-118-44643-0 (ebook); 978-1-118-44644-7 (ebook); 978-1-118-44642-3 (ebook)

Printed and bound in the United States by Bind-Rite

10 9 8 7 6 5 4 3 2 1

About the Author

John Nussey is a creative technologist based in London. His work involves using technology in new and interesting ways and covers many areas, including physical computing, creative coding, interaction design, and product prototyping.

During his career, he has worked on many varied projects with clients such as ARUP, the BBC, the Museum of Science and Industry, the National Maritime Museum, Nokia, and the Southbank Centre.

He is a proud advocate of the Arduino prototyping platform and has taught the craft of interaction design and prototyping to people of all ages, competencies, and abilities at a variety of establishments, including Goldsmiths College, the Bartlett School of Architecture, the Royal College of Art, and OneDotZero.

Dedication

To Avril, the love of my life (and only person I trust with a soldering iron), for providing encouragement when I was writing and distraction when I wished I wasn't; to Roanne and Oliver for our stimulating literary chats; to Craig for helping me bridge the trans-Atlantic gap; to all the guys and girls at Kin for still feigning interest and asking "How's the books going?" after 6 months; and to Alexandra for all the guidance that led me to such an enjoyable and inspiring career.

Author's Acknowledgments

John would like to thank the folks at Wiley, especially Craig Smith for always being upbeat and his gentle reminders, and Susan Christophersen for her hard work and support throughout.

Many thanks to Andy Huntington for his excellent technical editing and occasional humorous comments that helped me through the long nights.

A big thanks to all my friends, family, and loved ones for their encouragement and enthusiasm. I love making things, and I hope that this book inspires you to make things of your own and find the same enjoyment I have.

Publisher's Acknowledgments

We're proud of this book; please send us your comments at http://dummies.custhelp.com. For other comments, please contact our Customer Care Department within the U.S. at 877-762-2974, outside the U.S. at 317-572-3993, or fax 317-572-4002.

Some of the people who helped bring this book to market include the following:

Acquisitions, Editorial

Project and Copy Editor:
Susan Christophersen

Executive Commissioning Editor: Craig Smith

Development Editors: Susan Christophersen,
Susannah Gardner

Technical Editor: Andy Huntington

Editorial Manager: Jodi Jensen

Senior Project Editor: Sara Shlaer

Editorial Assistant: Leslie Saxman

Cover Photo: © John Nussey

Cartoons: Rich Tennant (www.the5thwave.com)

Marketing

Associate Marketing Director: Louise Breinholt

Marketing Manager: Lorna Mein

Senior Marketing Executive: Kate Parrett

Composition Services

Senior Project Coordinator: Kristie Rees

Layout and Graphics: Melanee Habig,
Joyce Haughey, Andrea Hornberger,
Christin Swinford

Proofreader: Wordsmith Editorial

Indexer: Potomac Indexing, LLC

UK Tech Publishing

    Michelle Leete, VP Consumer and Technology Publishing Director

    Martin Tribe, Associate Director–Book Content Management

    Chris Webb, Associate Publisher

Publishing and Editorial for Technology Dummies

    Richard Swadley, Vice President and Executive Group Publisher

    Andy Cummings, Vice President and Publisher

    Mary Bednarek, Executive Acquisitions Director

    Mary C. Corder, Editorial Director

Publishing for Consumer Dummies

    Kathleen Nebenhaus, Vice President and Executive Publisher

Composition Services

    Debbie Stailey, Director of Composition Services

Contents at a Glance

Table of Contents

Foreword

The moment a *For Dummies* book comes out, it's definitely a milestone in the history of a product.

Programming embedded computers used to be a very difficult task, reserved only to experienced engineers willing to master the obscure assembly language. In recent years, however, many platforms have tried to make this task simpler and more accessible to everyday people. Arduino is one of the latest attempts at making technology less scary and more creative.

With John, this book's author, we watched this creative tool being adopted by designers and artists in London, making its way into many memorable projects. Now Arduino has escaped the lab of Arts & Design and spread like a virus, becoming the tool of choice for all kinds of people who have great ideas they want to realize.

I'm really glad that John decided to write this book, because he's an early user of the Arduino platform from back in the days when it was still quite experimental. Having taught Arduino classes for many years, he has the ability to introduce the subject to all audiences.

Any newcomer to Arduino will, with the right tools and teaching — such as those found in this book — show true genius in no time.

Massimo Banzi

Introduction

● ●

Arduino is a tool, a community, and a way of thinking that is affecting how we use and understand technology. It has rekindled a love and understanding for electronics for many people, including myself, who felt that electronics was something that they had left behind at school.

Arduino is tiny circuit board that has huge potential. It can be used to blink a Morse-code signal using a single LED or to control every light in a building, depending on how far you take it. Its capabilities are limited only by your imagination.

Arduino is also providing a new, practical approach to technical education, lowering the entry level for those wanting to use electronics to complete small projects and, I hope, encouraging you to read further to take on big ones.

A huge and ever-growing community of Arduin-ists has emerged — users and developers who learn from each other and contribute to the open source philosophy by sharing the details of their projects. Arduin-ists and their supporters with their open source attitude are responsible for the huge popularity of Arduino.

Arduino is more than just a "bit of kit"; it's a tool. A piece of technology that makes understanding and using today's technology easier.

So if the prospect of understanding the limitless possibilities of technology doesn't sound interesting to you, please put this book down and back away.

Otherwise, read on!

About This Book

This is a technical book, but it's not for technical people only. Arduino is designed to be usable by anyone, whether they're technical, creative, crafty, or just curious. All you need is an open mind or a problem to fix and you'll soon find ways that using Arduino can benefit you.

Arduino has rekindled my love of electronics and opened many avenues for my career. I wrote this book to share that experience. When I first went to an Arduino workshop, I had no experience in programming and could only vaguely remember which end of a soldering iron to hold (don't worry, I cover soldering, too). Now the mainstay of my work involves building interactive installations, prototyping products, and generally finding new ways to play with technology using Arduino.

I think it is an excellent platform that lowers the entry level into electronics and coding, allowing people who may not have had the attention span or interest at school to dive straight into the areas that interest them and explore them from there.

Foolish Assumptions

This book assumes nothing about your technical knowledge. Arduino is an easy-to-use platform for learning about electronics and programming. It is for people from all walks of life, whether you're a designer, an artist, or a hobbyist.

It can also be a great platform for people who are already technical. Maybe you've done a bit of coding but want to bring your projects into the physical world in some way, or maybe you've worked with electronics and want to see what Arduino can bring to the table.

But whoever you are, you'll find that Arduino has great potential. It's really up to you to decide what to make of it.

This book starts on the most basic level to get you started with using and understanding Arduino. At times throughout the book, I may refer to a number of very technical things that will, like anything, take time to understand. I guide you through all the basics and then on to more advanced activities.

Much of what is in this book is based on my learning and teaching experiences. I learned all about Arduino from scratch, but have always found that the best way to learn is in practice, by making your own projects. The key is to learn the basics that I cover in this book and then build on that knowledge by thinking about how you can apply it to solve problems, create things, or just entertain yourself.

How This Book Is Organized

Arduino For Dummies is organized in a way that allows you to jump around the book as you like. If you've dabbled in Arduino before, you might want to skip to the later chapters, or if you've forgotten some of the basics, consider starting at the beginning.

Part I: Getting to Know Arduino

In Part I, I introduce you to Arduino, outlining a variety of other practices and circumstances that created a need for Arduino and that have influenced its development. Then I look at Arduino in more detail, both as a physical board and software environment, and I walk you through uploading your first sketch.

Part II: Getting Physical with Arduino

In this part, you find out how to do some basic prototyping using bread-boards and other components to give your Arduino more reach into the physical world. Using just a few simple components, you can explore a variety of applications for Arduino and form a base on which you can build your own projects. The chapters in this part cover a variety of inputs and outputs, including light, motion, and sound that you can build on and combine to form your own projects.

Part III: Building on the Basics

After you have covered the basics, you'll be itching to do more. In Part III, I tell you about some real-world projects and how they work. You find out how to solder your own circuit board to get your project out into the world for others to see. You also learn how to choose the correct sensor for the job and how to use code to fine-tune or change the behavior of your circuits.

Part IV: Unlocking Your Arduino's Potential

This part pushes the possibilities of your Arduino project further. You learn about using shields to add specific functionality to your Arduino, using hardware and techniques to allow you project to grow, and hacking existing hardware. You also find out how to communicate with Processing, Arduino's sister project, to combine open source hardware with software.

Part V: Sussing Out Software

If you work through the book to this part, you should have a good understanding of how you can use electronics and hardware in your own projects. In this part, you learn how to combine this knowledge of the physical world with the digital world of software. I introduce you to a few open source programming environments and then more specifically to Processing, which is a digital sketchbook that you can use for a huge variety of applications to enhance your Arduino project.

Part VI: The Part of Tens

The Part of Tens is a *For Dummies* standard that breaks down useful information into groups of ten bite-sized chunks. This part covers where to learn more about Arduino, where to shop for Arduino-specific parts, and where to shop for electronics in general.

Icons Used in This Book

Arduino For Dummies uses icons to highlight important points for you. Keep an eye out for these:

This icon highlights a bit of helpful information. That info may be a technique to help you complete a project more easily or the answer to common problems.

Arduinos aren't dangerous on their own; indeed, they're made to be extremely safe and easy to use. But if they are used in a circuit without proper planning as well as care and attention, they can damage your circuit, your computer, and yourself. When you see a Warning icon, please take special note.

There are often points that must be considered before proceeding with a task. I use Remember icons to remind you of such points.

Some information is more technical than others and is not for the faint hearted. The joy of Arduino is that you don't need to fully understand the technical details immediately. You can skip anything that's marked with this icon if it's more complicated than you want to deal with at the moment; you can always return to it when you're ready.

Where to Go from Here

If you're uncertain about where to start, I suggest the beginning. By the end of Chapter 2, you'll have acquired a simple understanding of Arduino and will know where you can get a kit to continue learning.

If you've used Arduino before, you may want to jump straight to Chapter 4 to cover the basics again, or head straight to the area that interests you.

Part I
Getting to Know Arduino

The 5th Wave   By Rich Tennant

"So I guess you forgot to tell me to strip out the components before drilling for blowholes."

In this part . . .

So what is an Arduino, anyway? In the chapters ahead, you find out all about this little blue circuit board, how it came into being, and what it can be used for. After a brief introduction, I talk you through all the things you need to get started with Arduino and where to get them. Next, you learn how to wield the awesome power of an LED, blinking it on command with a few simple lines of code.

Chapter 1

What Is Arduino and Where Did It Come From?

In This Chapter

▶ Discovering Arduino

▶ Learning where Arduino came from and why it's so important

▶ Introducing the basic principles

Arduino is made up of both hardware and software.

The Arduino board is a printed circuit board (PCB) that is specifically designed to use a microcontroller chip as well as other input and outputs. It also has many other electronic components that are needed for the microcontroller to function or to extend its capabilities.

Microcontrollers are small computers contained within a single, integrated circuit or computer chip, and they are an excellent way to program and control electronics. Many devices, referred to as microcontroller boards, have a microcontroller chip and other useful connectors and components that allow a user to attach inputs and outputs. Some examples of devices with microcontroller boards are the Wiring board, the PIC, and the Basic Stamp.

You write code in the Arduino software to tell the microcontroller what to do. For example, by writing a line of code, you can tell an LED to blink on and off. If you connect a pushbutton and add another line of code, you can tell the LED to turn on only when the button is pressed. Next, you may want to tell the LED to blink only when the pushbutton is held down. In this way, you can quickly build a behavior for a system that would be difficult to achieve without a microcontroller.

Similarly to a conventional computer, an Arduino can perform a multitude of functions, but it's not much use on its own. It requires other inputs or outputs to make it useful. These inputs and outputs allow a computer to sense objects in the world and to affect the world.

Before you move forward, it might help you to understand a bit of the history of Arduino.

Where Did Arduino Come From?

Arduino started its life in Italy, at Interaction Design Institute Ivera (IDII), a graduate school for interaction design. This is a specific school of design education that focuses on how people interact with digital products, systems, and environments and how they in turn influence us.

The term *interaction design* was coined by Bill Verplank and Bill Moggridge in the mid-1980s. The sketch in Figure 1-1 by Verplank illustrates the basic premise of interaction design. This diagram is an excellent illustration of how the process of interaction works: If you do something, you feel a change, and from that you can know something about the world.

Although it is a general principle, interaction design more commonly refers to how we interact with conventional computers by using peripherals, such as mice, keyboards, and touchscreens, to navigate a digital environment that is graphically displayed on a screen.

Figure 1-1: The principle of interaction design, illustrated by Bill Verplank.

Courtesy of Bill Verplank

There is another avenue, referred to as physical computing, which is about extending the range of these computer programs, software, or systems. Through electronics, computers can sense more about the world and have a physical impact on the world themselves.

Both of these areas — interaction design and physical computing — require prototypes to fully understand and explore the interactions, which presented a hurdle for nontechnical design students.

In 2001, a project called Processing that was started by Casey Reas and Benjamin Fry aimed to get nonprogrammers into programming by making it quick and easy to produce onscreen visualizations and graphics. The project gave the user a digital sketchbook on which to try ideas and experiment with a very small investment of time. This project in turn inspired a similar project for experimenting in the physical world.

Building on the same principles as Processing, in 2003 Hernando Barragán started developing a microcontroller board called Wiring. This board was the predecessor to Arduino.

In common with the Processing project, the Wiring project also aimed to involve artists, designers, and other nontechnical people, but Wiring was designed to get people into electronics rather than programming. The Wiring board (shown in Figure 1-2) was less expensive than some other microcontrollers, such as the PIC and the Basic Stamp, but it was still a sizable investment for students to make.

Figure 1-2:
An early
Wiring
board.

In 2005, the Arduino project began in response to the need for affordable and easy-to-use devices for Interaction Design students to use in their projects. It is said that Massimo Banzi and David Cuartielles named the project after Arduin of Ivera, an Italian king, but I've heard from reliable sources that it also happens to be the name of the local pub near the university, which may have been of more significance to the project.

The Arduino project drew from many of the experiences of both Wiring and Processing. For example, an obvious influence from Processing is the *graphic user interface* (GUI) that is used in the Arduino software. This GUI was initially "borrowed" from Processing, and even though it still looks similar, it has since been refined to be more specific to Arduino. I cover the Arduino interface in more depth in Chapter 4.

Arduino also kept the naming convention from Processing, naming its programs *sketches*. In the same way that Processing gives people a digital sketchbook to create and test programs quickly, Arduino gives people a way to sketch out their hardware ideas as well. Throughout this book, I show many sketches that allow your Arduino to perform a huge variety of tasks. By using and editing the example sketches in this book, you can quickly build up your understanding of how they work and will be writing your own in no time. Each sketch is followed with a line-by-line explanation of how it works to ensure that no stone is left unturned.

The Arduino board, shown in Figure 1-3, was made to be more robust and forgiving than Wiring or other earlier microcontrollers. It was not uncommon for students and professions, especially those from a design or arts background, to break their microcontroller within minutes of using it, simply by getting the wires the wrong way around. This fragility was a huge problem, not only financially but also for the success of the boards outside technical circles.

It is also possible to change the microcontroller chip on an Arduino, so if it is damaged, you can just replace the chip rather than the whole board.

Another important difference between Arduino and other microcontroller boards is the cost. In 2006, another popular microcontroller, the Basic Stamp, cost nearly four times as much (http://blog.makezine.com/2006/09/25/arduino-the-basic-stamp-k/) as an Arduino, and even today, a Wiring board still costs nearly double the price of an Arduino.

In one of my first Arduino workshops, I was told that the price was intended to be affordable for students. The price of a nice meal and a glass of wine at that time was about 30 euros, so if you had a project deadline, you could choose to skip a nice meal that week and make your project instead.

The range of Arduino boards on the market is a lot bigger than it was back in 2006. In Chapter 2, you learn about just a few of the most useful Arduino and Arduino-compatible boards and how they differ to provide you with a variety of solutions for your own projects. Also, in Chapter 13 you learn all about a special type of circuit board called a shield, which can add useful, and in some cases phenomenal, features to your Arduino, turning it into a GPS receiver, a Geiger counter, or even a mobile phone, to name just a few.

Figure 1-3: The original Arduino Serial board.

Learning by Doing

People have used technology in many ways to achieve their own goals without needing to delve into the details of electronics. Following are just a few related schools of thought that have allowed people to play with electronics.

Patching

Patching isn't just a town in West Sussex; it is also a technique for experimenting with systems. The earliest popular example of patching is in phone switchboards. For an operator to put you through to another line they had to physically attach a cable. This was also a popular technique for synthesizing music, such as with the Moog synthesizer.

When an electronic instrument generates a sound, it is really generating a voltage. Different collections of components in the instrument manipulate that voltage before it is outputted as an audible sound. The Moog synthesizer works by changing the path that that voltage takes, sending it through a number of different components to apply different effects.

Because so many combinations are possible, for the musician the experience is largely based on trial and error. But the simple interface means that this process is extremely quick and requires very little preparation to get going.

Hacking

Hacking is popular term and is commonly used to refer to subversive people on the Internet. More generally, though, it refers to exploring systems and making full use of them or repurposing them to suit your needs.

Hacking in this sense is possible in hardware as well as software. A great example of hardware hacking is a keyboard hack. Say that you want to use a big, red button to move through a slideshow. Most software has keyboard shortcuts, and most PDF viewers move to the next page when the user presses the spacebar. If you know this, then you ideally want a keyboard with only a spacebar.

Keyboards have been refined so much that inside a standard keyboard is a small circuit board, a bit smaller than a credit card (see Figure 1-4). On it are lots of contacts that are connected when you press different keys. If you can find the correct combination, you can connect a couple of wires to the contacts and the other ends to a pushbutton. Now every time you hit that button, you send a space to your computer.

This technique is great for sidestepping the intricacies of hardware and getting the results you want. In the bonus chapter (www.dummies.com/go/arduinofd), you learn more about the joy of hacking and how you can weave hacked pieces of hardware into your Arduino project to control remote devices, cameras, and even computers with ease.

Figure 1-4:
The insides
of a key-
board,
ready to be
hacked.

Circuit bending

Circuit bending flies in the face of traditional education and is all about spon-
taneous experimentation. Children's toys are the staple diet of circuit benders,
but really any electronic device has the potential to be experimented with.

By opening a toy or device and revealing the circuitry, you can alter the path
of the current to affect its behavior. Although this technique is similar to
patching, it's a lot more unpredictable. However, after you find the combinations, you can also add or replace components, such as resistors or switches,
to give the user more control over the instrument.

Most commonly, circuit bending is about sound, and the finished instrument
becomes a rudimentary synthesizer or drum machine. Two of the most popular devices are the *Speak & Spell* (see Figure 1-5) and the *Nintendo GameBoy*.
Musicians such as the Modified Toy Orchestra (modifiedtoyorchestra.
com), in their own words, "explore the hidden potential and surplus value
latent inside redundant technology." So think twice before putting your old
toys on eBay!

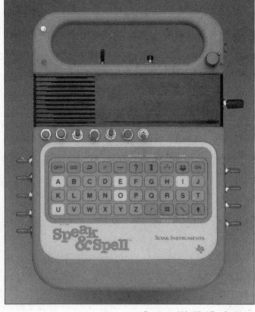

Figure 1-5:
A Modified
Toy
Orchestra
Speak &
Spell after
circuit
bending.

Courtesy of Modified Toy Orchestra

Electronics

Although there are many ways to work around technology, eventually you'll want more of everything: more precision, more complexity, and more control.

If you learned about electronics at school, you were most likely taught how to build circuits using specific components. These circuits are based solely on the chemical properties of the components and need to be calculated in detail to make sure that the correct amount of current is going to the correct components.

These are the kind of circuits you find as kits at Radio Shack (or Maplin, in the United Kingdom) that do a specific job, such as an egg timer or a security buzzer that goes off when you open a cookie jar. These are very good at their specific job, but they can't do much else.

This is where microcontrollers come in. Microcontrollers are tiny computers, and if used in conjunction with analog circuitry, can give that circuitry a more advanced behavior. They can also be reprogrammed to perform different functions as needed. Your Arduino is actually designed around one of these microcontrollers and helps you get the most out of it. In Chapter 2, you look closely at an Arduino Uno to see exactly how it is designed and what it is capable of.

The microcontroller is the brains of a system, but it needs data to either sense things about or affect things in its environment. It uses inputs and outputs to do so.

Inputs

Inputs are senses for your Arduino. They tell it what is going on in the world. At its most basic, an input could be a switch, such as a light switch in your home. At the other end of the spectrum, it could be a gyroscope, telling the Arduino the exact direction it's facing in three dimensions. You learn all about basic inputs in Chapter 7, and more about the variety of sensors and when to use them in Chapter 12.

Outputs

Outputs allow your Arduino to affect the real world in some way. An output could be very subtle and discreet, such as in the same way that a mobile phone vibrates, or it could be a huge visual display on the side of a building that can be seen for miles around. The first sketch in the book walks you through "blinking" an LED (see Chapter 4). From there you can go on to motor control (Chapter 8) and even controlling huge numbers of outputs (see Chapters 14 and 15) to discover a variety of outputs for your Arduino project.

Open Source

Open source software, in particular Processing, has had a huge influence on the development of Arduino. In the world of computer software, open source is a philosophy involving sharing the details of a program and encouraging others to use, remix, and redistribute them, as they like.

Just as the Processing software is open source, so are Arduino software and hardware. This means that the Arduino software and hardware are both released freely to be adapted as needed. Possibly because of this openness on the part of the Arduino team, you find the same open source community spirit in the Arduino forums.

On the official Arduino forums (www.arduino.cc/forum/) and many other ones around the world, people have shared their code, projects, and questions for an informal peer review. This sharing allows all sorts of people, including experienced engineers, talented developers, practiced designers, and innovative artists, to lend their expertise to complete novices in some or all of these areas. It also provides a means to gauge people's areas of interest, which then occasionally filters into the official release of Arduino software or board design with new refinements or additions. The Arduino website has an area known as the Playground (www.playground.arduino.cc) where people are free to upload their code for the community to use, share, and edit.

This kind of philosophy has encouraged the relatively small community to pool knowledge on forums, blogs, and websites, thereby creating a vast resource for new Arduin-ists to tap into.

There is also a strange paradox that despite the open source nature of Arduino, a huge loyalty to Arduino as a brand exists — so much so that there is an Arduino naming convention of adding -duino or -ino to the name of boards and accessories (much to the disgust of Italian members of the Arduino team)!

Chapter 2

Finding Your Board and Your Way Around It

*I*n Chapter 1, I describe Arduino in general terms, but now it's time to look a little closer. The name *Arduino* encompasses a host of concepts. It can refer to an Arduino board, the physical hardware, the Arduino environment — that is, a piece of software that runs on your computer — and, finally, Arduino as a subject in its own right, as in this book: how the hardware and software can be combined with related craft and electronics knowledge to create a toolkit for any situation.

This chapter is relatively short and provides an overview of what you need to get started with Arduino. You may be eager to dive in, so you may want to quickly scan through this chapter, stopping at any areas of uncertainty and referring back to it later as needed.

In this chapter, you learn about the components used on the Arduino Uno R3 board, which is the stating point for most Arduin-ists. Beyond that, you learn about the other available Arduino boards, how they differ, and what uses they have. The chapter lists a few suppliers that can equip you with all the parts you need and examines some of the starter kits that are ideal for beginners and for accompanying this book. When you have the kit, all you need is a workspace and then you're ready to start.

Getting to Know the Arduino Uno R3

No one definitive Arduino board exists; many types of Arduino boards are available, each with its own design to suit various applications. Deciding what board to use can be a daunting prospect because the number of boards is increasing, each with new and exciting prospects. However, one board can be considered the backbone of the Arduino hardware; this is the one that almost all people start with and that is suitable for most applications. It's the Arduino Uno.

The most recent main board to date is the Arduino Uno R3 (released in 2011). Think of it as the plain-vanilla of Arduino boards. It's a good and reliable workhorse that is suitable for a variety of projects. If you're just starting out, this is the board for you (see Figures 2-1 and 2-2).

Uno is Italian for the number one, named for the release of version 1.0 of the Arduino software. Predecessors to this had a variety of names, such as Serial, NG, Diecimila (10,000 in Italian, to mark that 10,000 boards have been sold) and Duemilanove (2009 in Italian, the release date of the board), so the Uno has ushered in some much needed order to the naming of the boards. R3 relates to the revision of the features on the board, which includes updates, refinements, and fixes. In this case, it is the third revision.

Figure 2-1:
The front of an Arduino Uno R3.

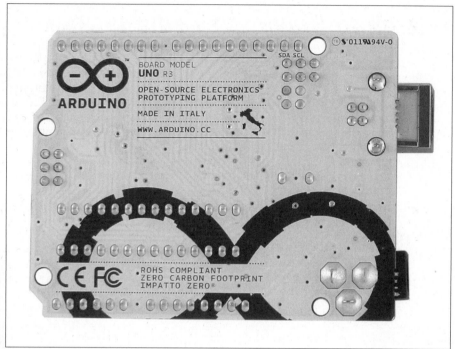

Figure 2-2:
The back of
an Arduino
Uno R3.

The board has many small components, described throughout much of this chapter.

The Brains: ATmega328 microcontroller chip

You can think of the microcontroller chip itself as the "brains" of the board. The chip used in the Arduino Uno is the ATmega328, made by Atmel. It's the large, black component in the center of the board. This chip is known as an integrated circuit, or IC. It's actually not alone but rather sits in a socket. If you were to remove it, it would look like the one shown in Figure 2-3.

This same chip can come in different forms, referred to as *packages*. The one in a regular Arduino Uno R3 is in a plated-through hole, or PTH, package, named because of the way it makes contact with the board. Another variation you may find is the Arduino Uno R3 SMD, where SMD stands for surface mount device, mounted on the surface of the board rather than in holes that go through it. This is a much smaller chip but is not replaceable, as the PTH chip is. Apart from that, as long as the name of the chip is the same, the chips function exactly the same and differ only in looks. You see another example of this kind of chip in Chapter 14 when you learn about the Arduino Mega 2560.

Figure 2-3:
An
ATmega328
microcon-
troller all
by itself.

Header sockets

The microcontroller socket connects all the legs of the ATmega328 microcontroller chip to other sockets, referred to as header sockets, which have been arranged around the board and labeled for ease of use. They are the black sockets that go around the edge of the Arduino board. These are divided up into three main groups: digital pins, analog input pins, and power pins.

All these pins transfer a voltage, which can either be sent as output or received as an input. Why are these pins important? They allow additional circuitry to be connected to the board quickly and easily when prototyping with a breadboard (described in Chapter 7) and allow additional boards, called *shields*, to be designed that will fit neatly on top of your Arduino board (see Chapter 13 for more on shields).

This same process of sending and receiving electrical signals is going on inside modern computers, but because they are so advanced and refined compared to a humble Arduino, it is difficult to directly link a computer that is accustomed to digital signals (0s and 1s) to an electronic circuit that deals with a range of voltages (in the ATmega328's case 0v to 5v).

The Arduino (see the sketch in Figure 2-4) is so special because it is able to interpret these electric signals and convert them to digital signals that your computer can understand — and vice versa. It also allows you to write a program using software on a conventional computer that is converted or compiled using the Arduino Software (IDE) to electrical signals that your circuit can understand.

By bridging this gap, it is possible to use the benefits of a conventional computer — ease of use, user-friendly interfaces, and code that is easy for humans to understand — to control a wide range of electronic circuits and even give them complex behaviors with relative ease.

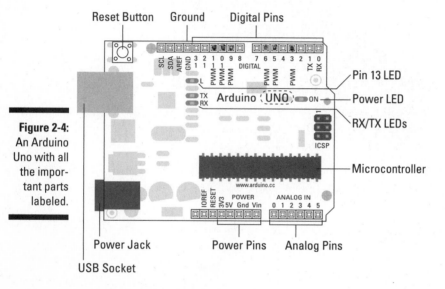

Figure 2-4:
An Arduino Uno with all the important parts labeled.

Digital pins

You use the *digital pins*, which run across the top of the board in Figure 2-1 (shown previously), to send and receive digital signals. Digital implies that they have two states: off or on. In electrical terms, this would mean a value of 0 or 5 volts, but no values in between.

Analog in pins

You use the *analog in* pins, which can be seen in the bottom left of the board in Figure 2-1, to receive an analog value. An analog value is taken from a range of values. In this case, the range is the same 0 to 5V as with the digital pins, but the value can be at any point — 0.1, 0.2, 0.3, and so on.

What about analog out?

The very shrewd ones among you may have noticed that there seem to be no *analog out* pins. In fact, there are, but they're hidden among the digital pins marked as PWM using the "~" symbol. PWM stands for Pulse Width Modulation, which is a technique you can use to give the impression of an analog output using digital pins. I explain how PWM works in Chapter 7. The ~ symbol appears next to digital pins 3, 5, 6, 9, 10, and 11, showing that you have 6 pins that are capable of PWM.

Power pins

You use the power pins to distribute power to inputs and outputs wherever it's needed.

Vin, which stands for *voltage in,* can be used to source a voltage (V) equal to the one that is supplied by the external supply jack (for example, 12V). You can also use this pin to supply power to the Arduino from another source.

GND marks the ground pins, which are essential to complete circuits. There is also a third ground by pin 13. All these pins are linked and share the same (called *common*) ground.

You can use 5V to supply a 5 volt power supply to components or circuits.

And finally, you can use 3.3V to supply a 3.3 volt power supply to components or circuits.

USB socket

To tell the microcontroller on the Arduino board what to do, you need to send a program to it. On the Uno, you send programs primarily by a USB connection. The large, metallic socket is a USB port for a USB A-B cable. This cable is similar to the one used on your home printer or scanner, so you may find a few around the house that can serve as handy spares. The Arduino uses the USB both for power and to transfer data. Using a USB cable is perfect for low-power applications and when data is being sent to or received from a computer.

External power jack

Next to the USB socket is another socket; this one is for power. This socket allows you to power your Arduino from an external power supply. The supply could be from an AC-to-DC adaptor (similar to those used on other consumer electronics), a battery, or even a solar panel.

The connector needed is a 2.1 mm center positive plug. Center positive simply means that the plug has an outside and an inside that fit the socket and that, in this case, the inside of the plug must be positive. You should be able to find this plug among the standard connectors that come with most power supplies; otherwise, you can buy the connector yourself and attach it to bare wires.

If you connect a power supply that is the opposite (center negative), it is known as having a "reverse polarity." There are components on the Arduino Uno R3 to resist your attempts to send voltage the wrong way around the board, but those components can melt in the progress of saving your board, depending on how much power you are sending and how long it takes you to notice the burning smell! If you reverse the polarity when using the Vin, 5V, or 3.3V pins, you bypass this protection and almost instantly destroy several parts of your board and the ATmega 328 chip.

The recommended voltage for the Uno R3 board is 7-12V. If you supply too little power, your board might not function correctly. Or if you provide too much power you can cause your board to overheat and potentially damage it.

LEDs

The components described in this section are tiny. The Uno board has four light-emitting diodes (LEDs), labeled L, RX, TX, and ON. An LED is a component that produces light when electrical current flows through it.

LEDs come in a variety of shapes and sizes and are found in almost every modern piece of consumer electronics, from your bike lights to your TV to your washing machine. They're almost unavoidable. They are the future, and you see a lot more of them in numerous examples throughout the book.

These four LEDs are all used to indicate activity on the board, as follows:

✔ ON is green and signifies that your Arduino is powered.

✔ RX and TX tell you that data is being received or transmitted by the board.

✔ L is a very special LED that's connected to digital pin 13. This is great for testing to see whether your board is functioning as you want.

If your Arduino is plugged in but you don't see any lights, you should double-check that:

✔ Your USB cable is plugged in

✔ Your USB port is working — try another device in the port

✔ Your cable is okay — try another cable, if possible

If none of these steps makes the LED illuminate, something is probably wrong with your Arduino. Your first destination should be the Arduino trouble-shooting page at `http://arduino.cc/en/Guide/troubleshooting`. If you still have no luck, request a replacement Arduino from where you purchased the device.

Reset button

The Uno board also has a button next to the USB socket. This is the reset button. It resets the program on the Arduino or stops it completely when held down for a time. Connecting a wire between GND and the reset pin, which is located next to the 3.3V, achieves the same results.

The board has many other components, all of which perform important jobs, but the ones described in this section are the key ones for you to know for now.

Discovering Other Arduino Boards

The preceding section describes the standard USB Arduino board, but you should be aware that many others exist, all designed with different needs in mind. Some offer more functionality, and others are designed to be more minimal, but generally they follow a design that is similar to that of the Arduino Uno R3. For this reason, all examples in this book are based on the Uno R3 (with a brief mention of the Arduino Mega 2560 in Chapter 14). Previous revisions of the Uno should work without any changes, but if you are using an older or more specialized board, be sure to follow instructions that are specific to it. This section gives you a brief rundown of other available boards.

Official Arduino boards

Although Arduino is open source, it is also a trademarked brand, so to guarantee the quality and consistency of its products, new boards must be properly approved by the Arduino team before they are officially recognized and can bear the name Arduino. You can recognize official boards first by the name — Arduino Pro, Fio, or Lilypad, for example. Other nonofficial boards often include "Arduino compatible" or "for Arduino" in the name. The other way to recognize an official Arduino, made by the Arduino team, is by the branding (in the most recent versions): they are turquoise and display the infinity symbol somewhere on the board, along with a link to Arduino.cc. Some other companies also have their boards accepted as official boards, so you may find other company names printed on them, such as Adafruit Industries and Sparkfun.

You can find more details on the naming guidelines at `http://arduino.cc/en/Main/FAQ#naming`.

Because the schematics for the Arduino board are open source, there is a lot of variation in unofficial Arduino boards, which people have made for their own needs. These are usually based on the same microcontroller chips because the official Arduinos and are compatible with the Arduino software, but they require extra consideration and reading to be sure that they will work as expected. The Seeeduino (by Seeed Studio), for example, is based on the Arduino Duemilanove and is 100 percent compatible but adds various extra connections, switches, and sockets, which may be of more use to you in certain situations than an official Arduino board might be.

Official boards are the safe option for beginners to choose because the majority of Arduino examples online are based around these boards. Because of this official boards are more widely used and because of *that,* any errors or 'bugs' in the board design are likely to be remedied with the next revision or at least well documented.

Arduino Leonardo

The Leonardo is one of the newest boards in the official Arduino range. It has the same footprint (shape of circuit board), but the microcontroller used is different, giving it the benefit of being recognized as a keyboard or mouse by a computer. I provide more detail about the difference of this board to the Uno and how to use it in the bonus chapter at `www.dummies.com/go/arduinofd`.

Arduino Mega 2560 R3

As the name suggests, the Mega 2560 is a bigger board than the Uno. It is for people who want more: more inputs, more outputs, and more processing power! The Mega has 54 digital pins and 16 analog pins compared to the Uno's measly 15 digital and 6 analog pins. This board is introduced further in Chapter 14.

Arduino Mega ADK

The Arduino Mega ADK is essentially the same board as the Mega 2560 but is designed to interface with Android phones. This means that you can share data between your Android mobile or tablet and an Arduino to broaden the range of either.

Arduino Nano 3.0

The Arduino Nano is a condensed Arduino that measures just 0.70" x 1.70". This size is perfect for making your project smaller. The Nano has all the power of an Arduino UNO, using the same ATmega328 microcontroller, but is a fraction of the size. It is also handily fits into a breadboard, making it ideal for prototyping as well.

Arduino Mini R5

Despite what the names suggest, the Arduino Mini is smaller than the Nano. This board also uses the same ATmega328 microcontroller chip but is condensed further, removing all header pins and the Mini-USB connector of the Nano. This board is great if space is at a premium, but it does require great care when connecting because an incorrect connection can easily destroy the board.

Arduino Ethernet

This Arduino has the same footprint as the Uno but is specifically for communicating with the Internet. Rather than access the abundant amounts of data available to you through a computer, you can tell your Arduino Ethernet to access it directly. A web browser on your computer is really just interpreting text that is telling it what to display on your screen: aligning, formatting, and displaying images, for example. If the correct commands are known, the Arduino Ethernet can access this text directly and it can be used for other purposes. A favorite purpose is accessing Twitter so that you can perhaps display Tweets on an LCD display or have a bell ring every time you're mentioned. Some basic examples are included in the Arduino software, but beyond that, you will require a more advanced knowledge of web development to use this board.

Arduino BT

The Arduino BT allows your Arduino to talk with Bluetooth devices in the surrounding area. This is great for interfacing with mobile phones, tablets, or anything with Bluetooth!

Contributed (Approved) Arduinos

Many of the Arduino boards are now standardised and designed by the Arduino team, but some have been contributed by other companies, such as Adafruit Industries and SparkFun, over the years and are recognised as official boards. I list a few of the best ones here.

Arduino LilyPad

The Arduino LilyPad was made for projects in which technology is combined with textiles to aid in the development of e-textiles or wearable electronics projects. The LilyPad and its accompanying breakout boards (printed circuit board that make it easy to integrate various components without the need to build your own boards) can be sewn together using conductive thread instead of conventional wire. This board was designed and developed by Leah Buechley of MIT (`http://web.media.mit.edu/~leah/`) and SparkFun Electronics. If you're interested in e-textiles or wearable electronics, check out the excellent tutorial on Sparkfun's site to introduce the latest version of the board and the ProtoSnap kit here: `http://www.sparkfun.com/tutorials/308`.

Arduino Fio

The Fio (whose full name is the Arduino Funnel I/O) was designed by Shigeru Kobayashi with wireless applications in mind. It is based on the design of the LilyPad but includes a mini USB port, a lithium battery connector, and space for an XBee wireless module.

Arduino Pro

The Arduino Pro is a minimal and super skinny Arduino, by SparkFun Electronics, based on the same microcontroller as those used in the Uno R3. It comes without any of the normal headers or sockets but has all the same capabilities of an Uno. It's ideal when height is at a short supply and also has a battery socket which allows you to easily make your project portable.

Arduino Pro Mini

The Pro mini is another SparkFun product that pushes the minimalism of the Arduino Pro to new limits. In the scale of Arduinos, this sits neatly between the Nano and the Mini. It has none of the header pins or the Mini-USB port of the Nano, and is slightly more spread out than the Arduino Mini. This also has none of the safety features of the Uno R3, so take great care when wiring because a wrong connection can easily destroy the board.

Shopping for Arduino

Initially, Arduino was available only from a small number of hobby shops scattered across the world. Now you have lots of places to purchase an Arduino from wherever you are, as listed in the following sections. Later in this chapter, I also tell you about beginner's kits that pull the basic components together for you, which is recommended to get you started on your Arduino endeavors.

Official Arduino Store

A good place to start is the Arduino Store (`store.arduino.cc`). This location has all the latest Arduino boards, kits, and a select few components.

Distributors in the United Kingdom

There is a wealth of hobby electronics stores in the United Kingdom that have existed long before Arduino came about. Now, as well as catering for all sorts of remote control, robotic, and electronics needs, these shops also stock a lot of Arduino-specific components and equipment. Here are just a few of them:

- **Active Robots:** www.active-robots.com
- **Cool Components:** www.coolcomponents.co.uk
- **Oomlout:** www.oomlout.co.uk
- **ProtoPic:** www.proto-pic.co.uk
- **RoboSavvy:** http://robosavvy.com/store
- **SK Pang:** www.skpang.co.uk
- **Technobots:** www.technobotsonline.com

Distributors in the United States

Two of the biggest distributors and manufacturers of Arduino-compatible boards are based in the United States. They happily ship worldwide to most corners of the globe, but you can also often find their range of products in your local distributors.

- **SparkFun:** www.sparkfun.com
- **Adafruit:** www.adafruit.com

Amazon

So much has the popularity of Arduino grown that it's also now stocked in Amazon (www.amazon.com). Most Arduino boards as well as a variety of components and kits are available here, although they are harder to find than on more hobby-specific sites.

Electronics distributors

Many well-established global electronics distribution companies deliver to all corners of the world. Relatively recently, they have started stocking Arduino boards, but they are especially useful for bulk buying components once you know what you're looking for.

Be warned: Days can be lost searching through the extensive catalogues of components, so it's always a good idea to know the name of what you're looking for before you start! Here are some global distribution companies that stock Arduino boards and components:

- ✔ **RS Components:** `http://rs-online.com`
- ✔ **Farnell:** `www.farnell.com`
- ✔ **Rapid:** `www.rapidonline.com`

Kitted Out: Starting with a Beginner's Kit

By this point, you probably know a bit about the Arduino board, but no board is an island; there are lots of other bits that you need so that you can make use of it. In the same way that a computer would be no use without a mouse and keyboards, an Arduino would be no use without components. Or at least not as much fun.

There are a number of basic examples that are good for every new Arduin-ist to do that teach all the fundamentals of Arduino (which this book covers in Chapters 4 through 8). These are all achievable with a few basic components. To save you the time and effort of finding these yourself, a few enterprising individuals and companies have put together kits that let you experiment in no time!

Many of the available kits have been designed by these different individuals and companies based on their experiences, likes, and dislikes. You can also find a lot of components that do the same job but have different appearances, based on their application.

All this means that a "beginner's kit" can often be different things to different people and, especially for beginners, this can greatly add to the confusion when building your project.

The following short list describes a few core components that should be included in all good Arduino beginners' kits:

- **Arduino Uno:** The board you know and love.

- **USB A-B cable:** This is essential to make use of your Arduino. It can also be found on printers and scanners.

- **LEDs:** Light-emitting diodes in various colors are great for providing visual feedback for your project as well as for testing lighting projects on a small scale.

- **Resistors:** Also referred to as fixed resistors, these are fundamental electrical components used to resist the flow of current through a circuit. These are essential for the smooth running of most circuits. They have a fixed value that is indicated by colored bands that are on the side of the resistor.

- **Variable resistors:** Also known as potentiometers or pots, variable resistors resist current in the same way as fixed-value resistors, but they are able to change their resistance. They are most commonly used in radios and hi-fi equipment for tuning and volume control dials, although they are also available in other housings to detect other inputs such as force or flex on a surface.

- **Diodes:** Also known as rectifier diodes, diodes are similar to LEDs, but without the light. They have an extremely high resistance to the flow of current in one direction and an extremely low (ideally zero) resistance in the other. This is the same reason that an LED works in only one direction, but instead of emitting light, diodes are used to control the flow of current throughout your circuit.

- **Pushbuttons:** These are found behind the scenes in many bits of consumer electronics such as game console controllers and stereos. They're used to either connect or disconnect parts of a circuit so that your Arduino can monitor human inputs.

- **Photo diodes:** Also known as photo resistors or light-dependant resistors (LDRs), photo diodes change their resistance when light falls on them. They can have a variety of different uses depending on how they're placed relative to the light source.

- **Temperature sensors:** These sensors tell you what the ambient temperature is wherever they are placed. These are great for observing changes in your environment.

- **Piezo buzzer:** These are technically described as discrete sounding devices. These simple components can be supplied with a voltage to produce simple notes or music. They can also be attached to surfaces to measure vibrations.

- **Relays:** These electrically operated switches are used to switch higher power circuits using your low-voltage Arduino. Half of a relay is an electromagnet, and the other half is a magnetic switch. The electromagnet can be activated by the 5V of the Arduino, which moves the contact of the switch. Relays are essential for bigger lighting and motor-based projects.

- **Transistors:** These are the basis for all modern computers. They are electrically operated switches, similar to relays, but the switch happens on a chemical rather than physical level. This means that the switching can be super fast, making transistors perfect for high-frequency operations such as animating LED lighting or controlling the speed of motors.

- **DC motors:** These are simple electric motors. When electric current is passed through a motor, it spins in one direction and when that is reversed, it spins in the other. Electric motors come in great variety, from those in your phone that vibrate to those in electric drills.

- **Servo motors:** These motors have on-board circuitry that monitors their rotation. Servo motors are commonly used for precision operations such as controlled opening of valves or moving the joints of robots.

Here are a few of the better-known kits, ascending in price. They include all the components in the preceding list, and any will be an excellent companion for the examples in this book:

- Starter Kit for Arduino (ARDX) by Oomlout, available from `http://www.adafruit.com/products/170` (United States) and costing $85.00/£59.00 or `http://oomlout.co.uk/starter-kit-for-arduino-ardx-p-183.html` (United Kingdom)

- Sparkfun Inventor's Kit by Sparkfun (shown in Figure 2-5), available from `https://www.sparkfun.com/products/11227` and costing $94.95/£60.93/

- Proto-PIC Boffin Kit for Arduino Uno by Proto-Pic, available from `http://proto-pic.co.uk/proto-pic-boffin-kit-for-arduino-uno/` and costing $101.07/£64.20/

- Arduino Starter Kit from Arduino, available from `http://uk.rs-online.com/web/p/processor-microcontroller-development-kits/7617355/` and costs $102.89/£65.35/

All the basic examples in this book are possible with any of the kits in the preceding list, although there a slight variation may occur in the number and type of components. Sometimes the same component can take many different forms, so be sure to carefully read the parts list to make sure that you can identify each of the components before you start. Cheaper kits are available, but these will likely not include some components, such as motors or the variation of sensors.

Figure 2-5:
The SparkFun Inventor's Kit has a good range of components including flex sensitive and linear potentiometers.

Preparing a Workspace

When working on an Arduino project, you could sit on your sofa and work on your circuit or be at the top of a ladder, setting up an installation. I've been there before! But just because it's possible to work this way doesn't mean that it's sensible or advisable. You're far better off to have a good workspace before you dive into your experiment, and this is doubly important when you are just starting out with Arduino.

Working with electronics is a fiddly business. You're dealing with lots of tiny, delicate, very sensitive components, so you need great precision and patience when assembling your circuit. If you're in a dimly lit room trying to balance things on your lap, you will very quickly go through your supply of components by either losing or destroying them.

Anything you can do to make things easier for yourself is a good thing. The ideal workspace is

- A large, uncluttered desk or table
- A good work lamp
- A comfortable chair
- A cup of tea or coffee (recommended)

Chapter 3

Downloading and Installing Arduino

In This Chapter

▶ Obtaining and installing the Arduino software

▶ Getting a feel for the Arduino environment

*B*efore you can start working with the Arduino board, you need to install the software for it. This is similar to the software on your home computer, laptop, tablet, or phone: It's required to make use of your hardware.

The Arduino software is a type of an Integrated Development Environment (IDE). This is a tool that is common in software development and allows you to write, test, and upload programs. Versions of Arduino software are available for Windows, Macintosh OS X, and Linux.

In this chapter, you find out where to obtain the software for the platform you're using, and I walk you through the steps for downloading and installing it. Also in this chapter is a brief tour of the environment in which you develop your Arduino programs.

Installing Arduino

This section talks you through installing the Arduino environment on your platform of choice. These instructions are specifically for installation using an Arduino Uno R3, but work just as well for previous boards, such as the Mega2560, Duemilanove, Mega, or Diecimila. The only difference may be the drivers needed for the Windows installations.

Installing Arduino for Windows

The instructions and screenshots in this section describe the installation of the Arduino software and Arduino Uno drivers on Windows 7, but the same instructions work just as well for Windows Vista and Windows XP.

The only hurdle to jump is in Windows 8, which for the time being, at least, requires a few tricks to install the drivers. You can find a discussion on the Arduino forum titled "Missing digital signature for driver on Windows 8" that details a workaround (go to `http://arduino.cc/forum/index.php?topic=94651.15`).

With your Arduino Uno and a USB A-B cable (shown in Figure 3-1) at hand, follow these steps to obtain and install the latest version of Arduino on your version of Windows:

1. **Open the Arduino downloads page at** `http://arduino.cc/en/Main/Software`, **and click the Windows link to download the .zip file containing a copy of the Arduino application for Windows.**

   At the time of writing, the zipped file was 90.7MB. That's quite a large file, so it may take a while to download. When downloading is complete, unzip the file and place the Arduino folder in an appropriate location, such as

   ```
   C:/Program Files/Arduino/
   ```

2. **Plug the square end of the USB cable into the Arduino and the flat end into an available port on your PC to connect the Arduino to your computer.**

Figure 3-1:
An A-B
USB cable
and Arduino
Uno.

As soon as the board is connected, the green LED labeled ON indicates that your Arduino is receiving power. Windows then makes a valiant effort to find drivers, but it will likely fail, as indicated in Figure 3-2. It's best to close the wizard and install the driver yourself, as described in the following steps.

Figure 3-2:
New
hardware
found —
or not, as
the case
may be.

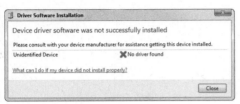

3. **Open the Start Menu and type** devmgmt.msc **in the Search Programs and Files box; then press Enter.**

   The Device Manager window opens. Device Manager shows you all the different hardware and connected peripherals in your computer, such as your Arduino board.

   If you look down the list, you should see Arduino Uno with an exclamation mark next to it. The exclamation mark indicates that it is not yet recognized.

4. **Right-click Arduino Uno and select Update Driver Software in the list that appears; then click the Browse My Computer for Driver Software option (see Figure 3-3).**

   The window advances to the next page.

5. **Click Browse to find your Arduino folder.**

   You should find this folder in the location you saved it to in Step 1 of these steps.

6. **Within your Arduino folder, click the Drivers folder and then click the Arduino UNO file.**

   Note that if you're in the FTDI USB Drivers subfolder, you have gone too far.

7. **Click Next, and Windows completes the installation.**

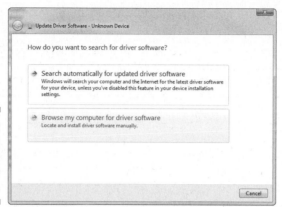

Figure 3-3:
Installing
drivers in
Device
Manager.

After you've taken care of the software installation, an easy way to launch the program is to place a shortcut on your desktop or your computer's Start menu, whichever you prefer. Just go to your main Arduino folder, find the Arduino.exe file, right-click and click Create Shortcut to make a shortcut. Double-click the shortcut icon whenever you want to launch the Arduino application. This opens a new sketch window, as shown in Figure 3-4.

Figure 3-4:
A beautiful
turquoise
Arduino
window in
Windows 7.

Installing Arduino for Mac OS X

The instructions in this section describe an installation of the Arduino Software and drivers for an Arduino Uno on Mac OS X Lion, but will work the same for Leopard, Snow Leopard and Mountain Lion. Previous operating systems may require you to search the web for your specific situation.

Follow these steps to install the Arduino software on your Mac:

1. **Go to the Arduino downloads page at** `http://arduino.cc/en/Main/Software` **and click the Mac OS X link to download a .zip file containing a copy of the Arduino application for Mac OS X.**

   At the time of writing, the file was 71.1MB. That's quite a large file, so it may take a while to download. After you've finished downloading, double-click the file to the Arduino application and place it in your Applications folder, shown in Figure 3-5.

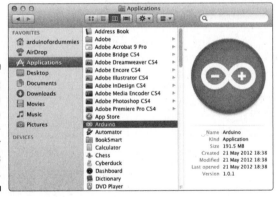

Figure 3-5: Place the Arduino application in your applications folder.

2. **Plug the square end of the USB cable into the Arduino and the flat end into an available port on your Mac to connect the Arduino to your computer.**

   As soon as the board is connected, a dialog box appears, showing the message `A new network interface has been detected` (see Figure 3-6).

Figure 3-6:
Your Mac
will think
the Arduino
board is
a new
network
interface.

A new network interface has been detected.

The "USB Modem" network interface has not been set up. To set up this interface, use Network Preferences.

Cancel   Network Preferences...

3. **Click Network Preferences, and in the window that appears, click Apply.**

   Note that your Arduino is displayed in the list on the left side of this window as Not Configured, but trust me, the software is installed and your Arduino board will work.

4. **Close the Network Preferences window.**

To launch the Arduino application, go to your Applications folder, locate the Arduino application, drag it to the Dock, and then click the Arduino icon to open the Arduino application (Figure 3-7 shows the window that appears). If you prefer, you can also drag the application to the desktop to create an alias there instead.

sketch_aug22a | Arduino 1.0.1

sketch_aug22a

Arduino Uno on /dev/tty.usbmodem411

Figure 3-7:
A beautiful
turquoise
Arduino
window in
OS X.

Installing Arduino for Linux

Installation on Linux is more involved and varies depending on the distribution you use, so it is not covered in this book. If you use Linux, you are probably already more than competent at installing the software and will relish the challenge. All the details on installing Arduino for Linux can be found in the Arduino Playground:

```
http://arduino.cc/playground/Learning/Linux
```

Surveying the Arduino Environment

Programs written for Arduino are known as *sketches*. This is a naming convention that was passed down from Processing, which allowed users to create programs quickly, in the same way that you would scribble out an idea in your sketchbook.

Before you look at your first sketch, I encourage you to stop and take a look around the Arduino software, and to that end, this section offers a brief tour. The Arduino software is an integrated development environment, or IDE, and this environment is presented to you as a graphical user interface, or GUI (pronounced *goo-ey*).

A GUI provides a visual way of interacting with a computer. Without it, you would need to read and write lines of text, similar to what you may have seen in the DOS prompt in Windows, Terminal in Mac OS X, or that bit about the white rabbit at the start of the Matrix.

The turquoise window is Arduino's GUI. It's divided into the following four main areas (labeled in Figure 3-8):

✔ **Menu bar:** Similar to the menu bar in other programs you're familiar with, the Arduino menu bar contains drop-down menus to all the tools, settings, and information that are relevant to the program. In Mac OS, the menu bar is at the top of your screen; in Windows and Linux, the menu bar is at the top of the active Arduino window.

✔ **Toolbar:** The toolbar contains several buttons that are commonly needed when writing sketches for Arduino. These buttons, which are also available on the menu bar, perform the following functions:

- *Verify:* Checks that your code makes sense to the Arduino software. Known as *compiling*, this process is a bit like a spelling and grammar checker. Be aware, however, that although the compiler checks that your code has no obvious mistakes, it does not guarantee that your sketch works correctly.

- *Upload:* Sends your sketch to a connected Arduino board. It automatically compiles your sketch before uploading it.

- *New:* Creates a new sketch.

- *Open:* Opens an existing sketch.

- *Save:* Saves the current sketch.

- *Serial monitor:* Allows you to view data that is being sent to or received by your Arduino board.

✔ **Text editor:** This area displays your sketch is displayed as text. It is almost identical to a regular text editor but has a couple of added features. Some text is color coded if it is recognized by the Arduino software. You also have the option to auto format the text so that it is easier to read.

✔ **Message area:** Even after years of using Arduino, you'll still make mistakes (everybody does), and this message area is one of the first ways for you to find out that something is wrong. (***Note:*** The second way is the smell of burning plastic.)

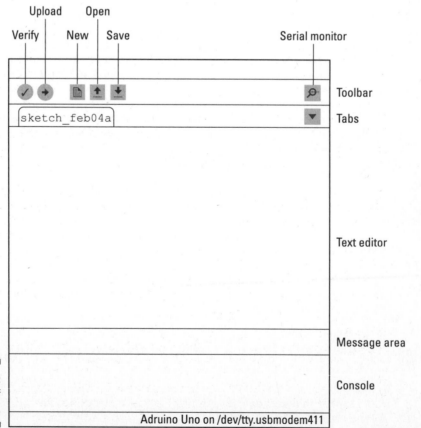

Figure 3-8:
The areas of
the GUI.

Chapter 4

Blinking an LED

. . . .

. . . .

Brace yourself. You are about to take your first real step into the world of Arduino! You've bought a board, maybe an Arduino starter kit (possibly from one of the suppliers I recommended), and you're ready to go.

It's always a good idea to have a clear work surface or desk to use when you're tinkering. It's not uncommon to drop or misplace some of the many tiny components you work with, so make sure your workspace is clear, well lit, and accompanied by a comfortable chair.

By its nature, Arduino is a device intended for performing practical tasks. The best way to learn about Arduino, then, is in practice — by working with the device and *doing* something. That is exactly the way I write about it throughout this book. In this chapter, I take you through some simple steps to get you on your way to making something.

I also walk you through uploading your first Arduino sketch. After that, you examine how it works and see how to change it to do your bidding.

Working with Your First Arduino Sketch

In front of you now should be an Arduino Uno R3, a USB cable, and a computer running your choice of operating system (Windows, Mac OS, or Linux). The next section shows what you can do with this little device.

Finding the Blink Sketch

To make sure that the Arduino software is talking to the hardware, you upload a *sketch*. What is a sketch, you ask? Arduino was created as a device that allows people to quickly prototype and test ideas using little bits of code that demonstrate the idea — kind of like how you might sketch out an idea on paper. For this reason, programs written for Arduino are referred to as sketches. Although a device for quick prototyping was its starting point, Arduino devices are being used for increasingly complex operations. So don't infer from the name *sketch* that an Arduino program is trivial in any way.

The specific sketch you want to use here is called Blink. It's about the most basic sketch you can write, a sort of "Hello, world!" for Arduino. Click in the Arduino window. From the menu bar, choose File⇨Examples⇨ 01.Basics⇨Blink (see Figure 4-1).

A new window opens in front of your blank sketch and looks similar to Figure 4-2.

Figure 4-1: Find your way to the Blink sketch.

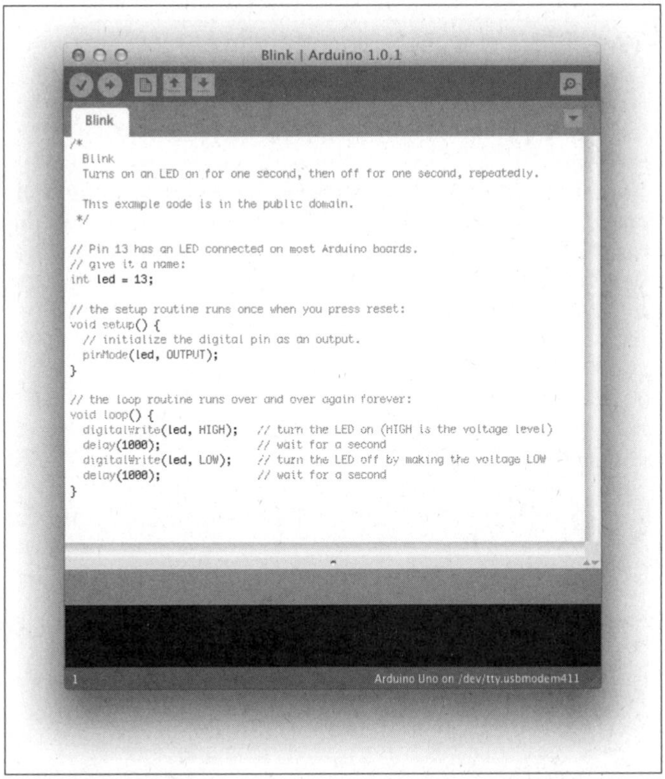

Figure 4-2:
The Arduino
Blink
sketch.

Identifying your board

Before you can upload the sketch, you need to check a few things. First you should confirm which board you have. As I mention in Chapter 2, you can choose from a variety of Arduino devices and several variations on the USB board. The latest generation of USB boards is the Uno R3. If you bought your device new, you can be fairly certain that this is the type of board you have. To make doubly sure, check the back of the board. You should see details about the board's model, and it should look something like Figure 4-3.

Also worth checking is the ATMEL chip on the Arduino. As I mention in Chapter 2, the ATMEL chip is the brains of the Arduino and is similar to the processor in your computer. Because the Uno and earlier boards allow you to replace the chip, there is always a chance, especially with a used board, that the chip has been replaced with a different one.

Although the ATMEL chip looks quite distinctive on an individual board, if you compare it to an older Arduino, telling them apart at first glance would be difficult. The important distinguishing feature is written on the surface of the chip. In this case, you are looking for ATmega328P-PU. Figure 4-4 shows a close-up of the chip.

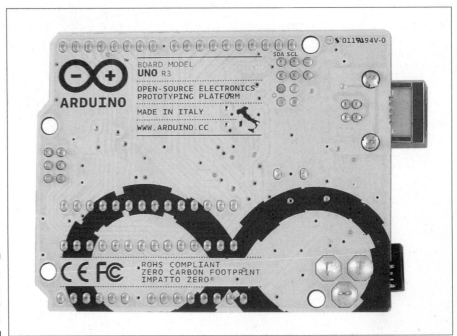

Figure 4-3:
Back side
of Arduino
Uno.

Figure 4-4:
Close-up
of the
ATmega-
328P-PU
chip.

Configuring the software

After you confirm the type of board you are using, you have to provide that information to the software. From the Arduino main menu bar (at the top of the Arduino window on Windows and at the top of the screen on Mac OS X), choose Tools⇨Board. You should see a list of the different kinds of boards supported by the Arduino software. Select your board from the list, as shown in Figure 4-5.

Next, you we need to select the serial port. The serial port is the connection that enables your computer and the Arduino device to communicate. *Serial* describes the way that data is sent, one bit of data (0 or 1) at a time. The *port* the physical interface, in this case a USB socket. I talk more about serial communication in Chapter 7.

To determine the serial port, choose Tools⇨Serial Port. A list displays of devices connected to your computer (see Figure 4-6). This list contains any device that can talk in serial, but for the moment, you're only interested in finding the Arduino. If you've just installed Arduino and plugged it in, it should be at the top of the list. For OS X users, this is shown as `/dev/tty.usbmodemXXXXXX` (where XXXXXX is a randomly signed number). On Windows, the same is true, but the serial ports are named `COM1`, `COM2`, `COM3`, and so on. The highest number is usually the most recent device.

Figure 4-5:
Select
Arduino
Uno from
the Board
menu.

Figure 4-6:
A list of
serial con-
nections
available to
the Arduino
environment.

After you find your serial port, select it. It should appear in the bottom right of the Arduino GUI, along with the board you selected (see Figure 4-7).

Figure 4-7: Arduino GUI board and port.

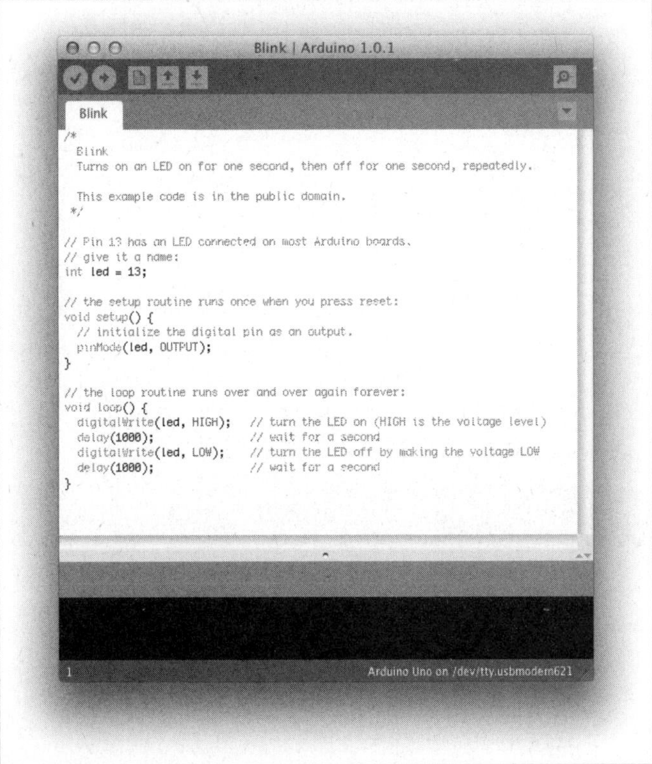

Uploading the sketch

Now that you have told the Arduino software what kind of board you are communicating with and which serial port connection it is using, you can upload the Blink sketch you found earlier in this chapter.

First click the Verify button. Verify checks the code to make sure it makes sense. This doesn't necessarily mean your code will do what you are anticipating, but it verifies that the syntax is written in a way Arduino can understand (see Chapter 2). You should see a progress bar and the text `Compiling Sketch` (see Figure 4-8) for a few seconds, followed by the text `Done compiling` after the process has finished.

Figure 4-8:
The prog-
ress bar
shows that
the sketch is
compiling.

If the sketch compiled successfully, you can now click the Upload button next to the verify button. A progress bar appears, and you see a flurry of activity on your board from the two LEDs marked RX and TX (that I mentioned in Chapter 2). These show that the Arduino is sending and receiving data. After a few seconds, the RX and TX LEDs stop blinking, and a Done Uploading (see Figure 4-9) message appears at the bottom of the Arduino window.

Figure 4-9:
The Arduino
GUI is done
uploading.

Congratulate yourself!

You should see the LED marked L blinking away reassuringly: on for a second, off for a second. If that is the case, give yourself a pat on the back. You've just uploaded your first piece of Arduino code and entered the world of physical computing!

If you don't see the blinking L, go back through all the preceding sections. Make sure you have installed Arduino properly and then give it one more go. If you still don't see the blinking L, check out the excellent troubleshooting page on the official Arduino site: `http://arduino.cc/en/Guide/ troubleshooting`.

What just happened?

Without breaking a sweat you've just uploaded your first sketch to an Arduino. Well done (or good job, if you're from the States)!

Just to recap, you have now

- ✔ Plugged your Arduino into your computer
- ✔ Opened the Arduino software
- ✔ Set the board and serial port
- ✔ Opened the Blink sketch from the Examples folder and uploaded it to the board

In the following section, I walk you through the various sections of the first sketch you just uploaded.

Looking Closer at the Sketch

In this section, I show you the Blink sketch in a bit more detail so that you can see what's actually going on. When the Arduino software reads a sketch, it very quickly works through it one line at a time, in order. So the best way to understand the code is to work through it the same way, very slowly.

Arduino uses the programming language C, which is one of the most widely used languages of all time. It is an extremely powerful and versatile language, but it takes some getting used to.

If you followed the previous section, you should already have the Blink sketch on your screen. If not, you can find it by choosing File➪ Examples➪01.Basics➪Blink (refer to Figure 4-1).

When the sketch is open, you should see something like this:

```
/*
  Blink
  Turns on an LED on for one second,
  then off for one second, repeatedly.

  This example code is in the public domain.
*/

// Pin 13 has an LED connected on most Arduino boards.
// give it a name:
```

```
int led = 13;

// the setup routine runs once when you press reset:
void setup() {
  // initialize the digital pin as an output.
  pinMode(led, OUTPUT);
}


// the loop routine runs over and over again forever:
void loop() {
  digitalWrite(led, HIGH);    // turn the LED on (HIGH is the voltage level)
  delay(1000);                // wait for a second
  digitalWrite(led, LOW);     // turn the LED off by making the voltage LOW
  delay(1000);                // wait for a second
}
```

The sketch is made up of lines of code. When looking at the code as a whole, you can identify four distinct sections:

✔ Comments

✔ Declarations

✔ void loop

✔ void setup

Read on for more details about each of these sections.

Comments

Here's what you see in the first section of the code:

```
/*
  Blink
  Turns on an LED on for one second, then off for one second, repeatedly.

  This example code is in the public domain.
*/
```

Multiline comment

Notice that the code lines are enclosed within the symbols /* and */. These symbols mark the beginning and end of a *multi-line* or *block comment*. Comments are written in plain English and, as the name suggests, provide an explanation or comment on the code. Comments are completely ignored by the software when the sketch is compiled and uploaded. Consequently, comments can contain useful information about the code without interfering with how the code runs.

In this example, the comment simply tells you the name of the sketch, and what it does, and provides a note explaining that this example code is in the public domain. Comments often include other details such as the name of the author or editor, the date the code was written or edited, a short description of what the code does, a project URL, and sometimes even contact information for the author.

Single-line comment

Further down the sketch, inside the setup and loop functions, text on your screen appears with the same shade of gray as the comments above. This text is also a comment. The symbols // signify a single-line comment as opposed to a multiline comment. Any code written after these lines will be ignored for that line. In this case, the comment is describing the piece of code that comes after it:

```
// Pin 13 has an LED connected on most Arduino boards.
// give it a name:
int led = 13;
```

This single line of code is in the declarations section of the sketch, but "what is a declaration?" I hear you ask. Read on to find out.

Declarations

Declarations (which aren't something you put up at Christmas, ho ho ho) are values that are stored for later use by the program. In this case, a single variable is being declared, but you could declare many other variables or even include libraries of code in your sketch. For now, all that is important to remember is that variables can be declared before the setup function.

Variables

Variables are values that can change depending on what the program does with them. In C, you can declare the type, name, and value of the variable before the main body of code, much as ingredients are listed at the start of a recipe.

```
int led = 13;
```

The first part sets the type of the variable, creating an integer (int). An integer is any whole number, positive or negative, so no decimal places are required. It's worth noting that for Arduino, there are lower and upper limits for the int type of variable: -32,768 to 32,767. Beyond those limits, a different type of variable must be used, known as a `long` (you learn more about these in Chapter 11). But for now, an `int` will do just fine. The name of the variable is `led` and is purely for reference; it can be any single word that's useful for figuring out what the variable applies to. Finally, the value of the variable is set to 13. In this case, that is the number of the pin that is being used.

Variables are especially useful when you refer to a value repeatedly. In this case, the variable is called `led` because it refers to the pin that the physical LED is attached to. Now, every time you want to refer to pin 13, you can write `led` instead. Although this approach may seem like extra work initially, it means that if you decided to change the pin to pin 11, you would need only to change the variable at the start; every subsequent mention of `led` would automatically be updated. That's a big timesaver over having to trawl through the code to update every occurrence of 13.

With the declaration made, the code enters the `setup` function.

Functions

The next two sections are functions and begin with the word `void`: `void setup` and `void loop`. A *function* is a bit of code that performs a specific task, and that task is often repetitive. Rather than writing the same code out again and again, you can use a function to tell the code to perform this task again.

Consider the general process you follow to assemble IKEA furniture. If you were to write these general instructions in code, using a function, they would look something like this:

```
void buildFlatpackFurniture() {
        buy a flatpack;
        open the box;
        read the instructions;
        put the pieces together;
        admire your handiwork;
        vow never to do it again;
}
```

The next time you want to use these same instructions, rather than writing out the individual steps, you can simply call the procedure named `build-FlatpackFurniture()`.

Although not compulsory, there is a naming convention for function or variable names containing multiple words. Because these names cannot have spaces, you need a way to distinguish where all the words start and end; otherwise, it takes a lot longer to scan over them. The convention is to capitalize the first letter of each word after the first. This greatly improves the readability of your code when scanning through it, so I highly recommend that you adhere to this rule in all your sketches for your benefit and the benefit of those reading your code!

The word *void* is used when the function returns no value, and the word that follows is the name of that function. In some circumstances, you might either put a value(s) into a function or expect a value(s) back from it, the same way you might put numbers into a calculation and expect a total back, for example.

void setup and void loop must be included in every Arduino sketch; they are the bare minimum required to upload. But it is also possible to write your own custom functions for whatever task you need to do. For now, you just need to remember that you have to include void setup and void loop in every Arduino sketch you create. Without these functions, the sketch will not compile.

Setup

Setup is the first function an Arduino program reads, and it runs only once. Its purpose, as hinted in the name, is to set up the Arduino device, assigning values and properties to the board that do not change during its operation. The setup function looks like this:

```
// the setup routine runs once when you press reset:
void setup() {
  // initialize the digital pin as an output.
  pinMode(led, OUTPUT);
}
```

Notice on your screen that the text void setup is orange. This color indicates that the Arduino software recognizes it as a *core* function, as opposed to a function you have written yourself. If you change the case of the words to Void Setup, you see that they turn black, which illustrates that the Arduino code is *case sensitive*. This is an important point to remember, especially when it's late at night and the code doesn't seem to be working.

The contents of the setup function are contained within the curly brackets, { and }. Each function needs a matching set of curly brackets. If you have too many of either bracket, the code does not compile, and you are presented with an error message that looks like the one shown in Figure 4-10.

Figure 4-10:
The Arduino software is telling you that a bracket is missing.

PinMode

The pinMode function configures a specified pin either for input or output: to either receive or send data. The function includes two parameters:

- pin: The number of the pin whose mode you want to set

- mode: Either INPUT or OUTPUT

In the Blink sketch, after the two lines of comments, you see this line of code:

```
pinMode(led, OUTPUT);
```

The word pinMode is highlighted in orange. As I mentioned earlier in this chapter, orange indicates that Arduino recognizes the word as a core function. OUTPUT is also coloured blue so that it can be identified as a constant, which is a predefined variable in the Arduino language. In this case, that constant sets the mode of this pin. You can find more about constants in Chapter 7.

That's all you need for setup. The next section moves on to the loop section.

Loop

The next section you see in the Blink sketch is the `void loop` function. This is also highlighted in orange so the Arduino software recognizes it as a core function. `loop` is a function, but instead of running one time, it runs continuously until you until you press the reset button on the Arduino board or you remove the power. Here is the `loop` code:

```
void loop() {
  digitalWrite(led, HIGH);   // set the LED on
  delay(1000);               // wait for a second
  digitalWrite(led, LOW);    // set the LED off
  delay(1000);               // wait for a second
}
```

DigitalWrite

Within the `loop` function, you again see curly brackets and two different orange functions: `digitalWrite` and `delay`.

First is digitalWrite:

```
  digitalWrite(led, HIGH);    // set the LED on
```

The comment says `set LED on`, but what exactly does that mean? The function `digitalWrite` sends a digital value to a pin. As mentioned in Chapter 2, digital pins have only two states: on or off. In electrical terms, these can be referred to as either a `HIGH` or `LOW` value, which is relative to the voltage of the board.

An Arduino Uno requires 5V to run, which is provided by either a USB or a higher external power supply, which the Arduino board reduces to 5V. This means that a `HIGH` value is equal to 5V and `LOW` is equal to 0V.

The function includes two parameters:

- pin: The number of the pin whose mode you want to set
- value: Either `HIGH` or `LOW`

So `digitalWrite(led, HIGH);` in plain English would be "send 5V to pin 13 on the Arduino," which is enough voltage to turn on an LED.

Delay

In the middle of the `loop` code, you see this line:

```
  delay(1000);               // wait for a second
```

This function does just what it says: It stops the program for an amount of time in milliseconds. In this case, the value is 1000 milliseconds, which is equal to one second. During this time, nothing happens. Your Arduino is chilling out, waiting for the delay to finish.

The next line of the sketch provides another `digitalWrite` function, to the same pin, but this time writing it low:

```
digitalWrite(led, LOW);    // set the LED off
```

This tells Arduino to send 0V (ground) to pin 13, which turns the LED off. This is followed by another delay that pauses the program for one second:

```
delay(1000);               // wait for a second
```

At this point, the program returns to the start of the loop and repeats itself, ad infinitum.

So the loop is doing this:

✔ Sending 5v to pin 13, turning on the LED

✔ Waiting a second

✔ Sending 0v to pin 13, turning off the LED

✔ Waiting a second

As you can see, this gives you the blink!

Blinking Brighter

I have mentioned pin 13 a few times in this chapter. Why does that pin blink the LED on the Arduino board? The LED marked L is actually connected just before it reaches pin 13.On early boards, it was necessary to provide your own LED. Because the LED proved so useful for debugging and signaling, there is now one in permanent residence to help you out.

For this next bit, you need a loose LED from your kit. LEDs come in a variety of shapes, colors, and sizes but should look something like the one shown in Figure 4-11.

Take a look at your LED and notice that one leg is longer than the other. Place the long leg (anode or +) of the LED in pin 13 and the short leg (cathode or -) in GND (ground). You see the same blink, but it is (hopefully) bigger and brighter depending on the LED you use. Insert the LED as shown in Figure 4-12.

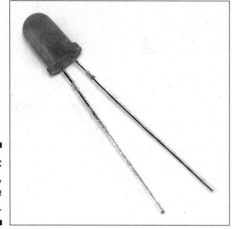

Figure 4-11:
A lone LED,
ready to be
put to work.

Figure 4-12:
Arduino LED
Pin 13.

From the description of the `digitalWrite` function in the preceding section, you know that your Arduino is sending 5V to pin 13 when it is HIGH. This can be too much voltage for most LEDs. Fortunately, another feature of pin 13 is a built-in pull-down resistor. This resistor keeps your LED at a comfortable voltage and ensures it has a long and happy life.

Tweaking the Sketch

I've gone over this sketch in great detail, and I hope everything is making sense. The best way to understand what is going on, however, is to experiment! Try changing the delay times to see what results you get. Here are a couple of things you can try:

✔ Make the LED blink the SOS signal.

✔ See how fast you can make the LED blink before it appears to be on all the time.

Part II
Getting Physical with Arduino

The 5th Wave   By Rich Tennant

"I think I've fixed the intercom. Just remember to speak into the ceiling fan when the doorbell rings."

In this part . . .

Ready to get down to business? Part I of this book gives you an introduction, but in this part, you learn more about the prototyping tools you need to build your projects. You briefly dip into a bit of electronics theory before getting back to the physical side of Arduino. From this point on, it's all downhill as you learn new and interesting things that your Arduino can do by building a few basic examples. All that's left is to think of your own projects to apply your Arduino to.

Chapter 5

Tools of the Trade

In This Chapter

▶ Introducing the breadboard, a blank canvas for circuits

▶ Assembling a tool kit

▶ Becoming an electronics super-sleuth, with a multimeter

*I*n Chapter 4, I cover one of the most basic Arduino applications: blinking an LED. This application requires only an Arduino and a few lines of code. Although blinking an LED is fun, you can use an Arduino for an almost unlimited number of other things — making interactive installations, controlling your home appliances, and talking with the Internet, to name a few.

In this chapter, you branch out by gaining an understanding of prototyping and how to use some basic prototyping tools to do more with your Arduino. Prototyping tools allow you to make temporary circuits to try new components, test circuits, and build simple prototypes. In this chapter, you find out about all the equipment and techniques you'll need to build your own circuits and prototype your ideas.

Finding the Right Tools for the Job

Prototyping is all about exploring ideas, which also happens to be the core of what Arduino is all about. Although theory is important, you often learn better and faster from doing an experiment.

This section introduces you to some prototyping tools and components that you can use to start building circuits. You can then use these circuits to form the basis for your own projects.

There are a great number of tools at your disposal to help you experiment. This is a short list of the recommended ones. Breadboards and jumper wires are included in most kits and are essential for building circuits for your Arduino project. Needle-nose pliers are not essential but are highly recommended.

Breadboard

Breadboards are the most essential part of your prototyping kit. They are the base on which you can prototype your circuits. Breadboards allow you to temporarily use components rather than committing them to a circuit and soldering them in place. (Soldering is covered in Chapter 10.).

Breadboards get their name from a practice used in the early 1900s. At that time, components were a lot bigger, and people would prototype circuits by fixing them to an actual breadboard — that is, a board intended for cutting bread on. The components were joined together by wrapping lengths of wire around nails that came in contact with the components. By unwrapping the wire from one nail and wrapping it around another, you could quickly change the circuit.

Modern breadboards are much more refined. The outside consists of a plastic case with rows and columns of holes, underneath which are tracks of copper. These tracks allow you to quickly and easily connect components electrically.

Breadboards come in many different shapes and sizes, and many have connectors to allow you to lay them out in an arrangement suitable for what you're doing.

Figure 5-1 shows a fairly standard breadboard. If you were to remove the cream-colored plastic coating, copper tracks would run down each of the long sides of the board, broken in the middle. These copper lengths are generally used to provide a source of power (PWR) and ground (GND) and are sometimes marked with a positive (+) or negative (-) symbol or a red and black or red and blue line. Red is always positive (+) in this and black or blue is negative (-).

A power or ground "rail" is basically a source of voltage or ground. Circuits often need power or ground for a variety of different functions, and often, one source isn't enough. You may have multiple wires that all need to get to the same place, so you use a rail. From this rail, jump wires can source whatever is needed, without your having to fear running out of space.

Although these tracks are marked, you can use them for anything. However, keeping to convention ensures that other people can easily understand your circuit, so I advise that you do so.

Down the center of the breadboard are lots of short tracks running parallel to the short edge, separated with a trench down the middle. The primary reason for this middle trench is to mount integrated circuits (such as the 74HC595 Shift Register, described in Chapter 15) because the trench means that the legs on one side aren't connected to the legs on the other, and also provides space for jump wires to connect them to the places they need to get to. Lots of other components are also able to make use of this gap, including pushbuttons (discussed in Chapter 5) and optocouplers (see bonus chapter at www.dummies.com/go/arduinofd), making it easier to lay out your circuit.

When you place a jump wire or component into one of these sockets, you should feel a bit of friction. This is a pincer-like device that holds the wire or component in place. It provides enough grip to hold things in place for a project while working at a desk, but it's loose enough for you to easily remove it with your fingers.

I have seen people taping breadboards into boxes for their final projects, but this isn't advisable. Smaller components or loose wires can easily come loose, and it can be a real pain to figure out why something isn't working. If you have a project working and want to get it out into the real world, you should jump ahead to soldering (explained in Chapter 10) because soldering makes your project last longer, and it's a lot of fun, too!

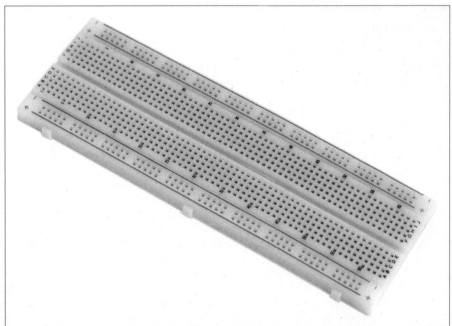

Figure 5-1:
A
breadboard.

Jump wires

Jump wires (shown in Figure 5-2) are essential to make use of your breadboard. They're short lengths of insulated equipment wire used to connect your components to the rows of your breadboard, other components and your Arduino. A jump wire is no different from other wire in a material sense, but it's usually cut to a short length that is useful for breadboards.

You can find insulated wire everywhere. It can be the thick mains cable used to plug in any of your household appliances, or it can be much thinner, like wire used for an earphone. Insulated wire is basically a conductive metal wire surrounded by an insulator that protects you from the electricity and protects the electrical signal from any outside interference.

The wire used most often in this book (and that's most useful for your Arduino projects) could be subcategorised as insulated equipment wire. This type of wire is generally used on a small scale for low-voltage electrical applications.

The equipment wire you use is one of two varieties: single core and multicore. Single core is a single piece of wire, just as a coat hanger is a single piece. Single-core wire is extremely good for holding its shape, but if you bend it too much, it shears. Therefore, this type of wire is useful for laying out wires on your breadboard neatly as long as you won't need to move them much.

Multicore wire can have the same diameter as single core, but instead of just one wire, it consists of lots of little ones. The little wires are twisted together, giving the multicore wire more strength and resistance to bending than a single core wire has. This twisted design is the same technique used on suspension bridges. Multicore wires are especially suited to connections that will change often, and they last a long time.

You can cut jump wires yourself, but they also come in handy packs of assorted colors and lengths. Each alternative has its pros and cons.

Cutting them yourself is significantly cheaper because you can buy a large reel of wire. On the other hand, if you want a variety of colors, you have to buy a reel for each color, which can amount to a fairly big investment for your first circuit. The packs save you this initial cost and give you the variety you need. You can buy the large reels when you know you'll need them.

Also, when considering cutting your own, bear in mind the difference in finishing for homemade jump wires. Single-core wires are much the same whether you cut them yourself or someone else does, but they deteriorate quicker as they bend. Multicore wires last longer, but if they are cut from a reel, you are left with a few small wires on the ends that can easily fray in the same way as the end of a piece of string or thread does. You have to fiddle with them often, twisting with your thumb and forefinger between uses to ensure that the small wires stay as straight and ridged as possible.

The pre-made multicore jump wire packets have the benefit of being usually either soldered to a point or have a connecting pin soldered to the end of the wire. This design ensures that the connecting end is as reliable as single core while giving you the flexibility of multicore.

Ideally, you should have a pack of pre-made multicore jump wires to get you going. These are the most versatile and long-lasting choice for your prototyping kit. Eventually, you'll want to have a variety so that you can be prepared for any situation when building a circuit.

Figure 5-2:
A selection
of jump
wires.

Needle-nose pliers

Needle-nosed pliers, shown in Figure 5-3, are the same as your regular pliers but with a very fine point, ideal for picking up tiny components. Electronics can be an extremely fiddly business, and it's extremely easy to mangle the delicate legs of components when pushing them into a breadboard. These specialist pliers are not essential but add a little bit of finesse to building circuits.

Figure 5-3:
Needle
nose pliers:
the con-
noisseur's
choice.

Multimeter

A multimeter is a meter that measures volts, amps, and resistance. It can tell you the values of different components and what's going on with different parts of your circuit. Because you can't see what's going on in a circuit or component, a multimeter is essential for understanding its inner workings. Without it, you have to rely on guesswork, which is always a bad idea with electronics.

Figure 5-4 shows a good mid-range digital multimeter. As does this one, most multimeters include:

✔ **A digital display:** This is the same as on your digital alarm clock and displays the values that you're reading. Because of the limited number of digits, the decimal place moves to accommodate larger or smaller numbers. The number is found automatically by a multimeter with an auto-ranging function, or, if your multimeter doesn't have that feature, you have to change the mode manually to the range that you require.

✔ **A mode-selection dial:** This dial allows you to choose among the different functions on the multimeter. These functions can be for volts, amperes, and ohms as well as for the range within each of those, such as ohms on hundred, thousand, tens of thousands, hundreds of thousands, and millions. The best multimeters also include a continuity tester that tells you whether your connections are actually connected by sounding a tone. Having a tone has saved me hours of work of having to retrace my steps on projects, so I definitely recommend investing in a good mid-range multimeter with this feature.

✔ **A set of probes:** These are the implements that you use to test parts of
your circuit. Most multimeters come with two skewer-like probes that
are designed to be poked into contact with the wires. You can also find
probes, or test leads as they are sometimes known, that have crocodile
clips on the end, or you can simply buy crocodile clips that you can
attach yourself. These are especially useful for grabbing onto wires.

✔ **A set of sockets:** The probes can be repositioned into different sockets
depending on the use. In this case, the sockets are labeled A, mA, COM,
and VΩHz. The socket marked A is for measuring large currents in amps
(A), up to 20A. There is also a warning that it can read that current for
only 10 seconds. These limits are indicated on a line between this socket
and the COM socket, which also indicates that the two probes should
be placed in A (red probe) and COM (black probe). The mA socket (red
probe) is for smaller currents that are less than 500mA. The COM socket
(black probe) is short for Common and is a point of reference for your
measurements. In most cases, this is the ground of your circuit and uses
the black probe. The socket marked VΩ Hz (red probe) is used for measuring voltage (V or volts), resistance (Ω or ohms) and frequency (Hz or
hertz) between this socket and the COM port (black probe).

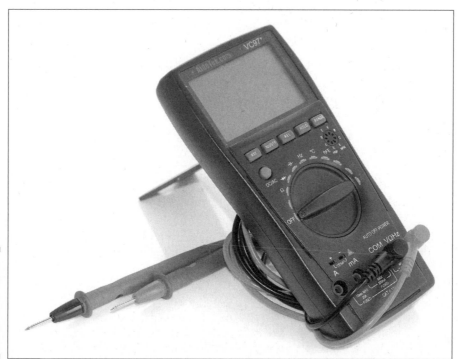

Figure 5-4:
A good
digital multi-
meter can
often save
your project.

Using the Multimeter to Measure Voltage, Current, and Resistance

There are a few basic techniques that all Arduin-ists should know to check their circuit. Volts, amps, and current can all be calculated in advance (as you learn in Chapter 6), but in the real world, many other factors can arise that you can't account for. If you have a broken component or a faulty connection, you can lose hours of time guessing at what could be wrong, so a multimeter becomes essential for solving problems on your circuit. In this section, you learn about measuring voltage, current, and resistance and checking the continuity of your connections.

Measuring voltage (in volts) in a circuit

Measuring the voltage is essential. It could be checking the voltage of a battery or checking the voltage that is passing through a component. If things aren't lighting up or whirring, you might just have a loose connection or you've sent too much power and burnt out what you were trying to power. This is the perfect occasion to check the voltage in your circuit and make sure it is correct.

First you need to check that the probes of your multimeter are in the correct sockets. These sockets should be marked V for volts using the red probe and COM (common) for ground using the black one. Next, you set your multimeter to Volts in DC, which can be signified by a V followed by a square-shaped digital wave, as opposed to an AC voltage, which is indicated by a smooth, analog wave. In this case, my multimeter has a button to toggle between DC and AC.

Voltage is measured in parallel, which means that you must bridge the part of the circuit that you want to measure without interfering in it. Figure 5-5 shows how you do this. The positive probe should always be on the positive side of the component and the negative on the other side. Getting the probes the wrong way won't cause any damage to your circuit but will give you a negative reading rather than a positive one.

Figure 5-5:
A multimeter is used in parallel to find the voltage.

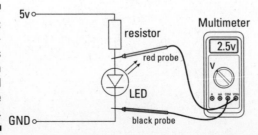

A good way to test your multimeter is to measure the voltage between the 5V pin and GND on your Arduino. Make sure that your Arduino is plugged in, and connect a jump wire to each pin to make them easier to access with your probes. Place the red voltage probe on the 5V wire and the black common probe on the GND wire. This should return a value of 5V on the screen of your multimeter and prove that your Arduino is supplying 5 volts as expected.

Measuring current (in amps) in a circuit

You may have the right voltage, but sometimes there just won't be enough current to power the light or motor that you're driving. The best way to find out is to check the circuit to see how much current is being drawn and compare that to the power supply you're using.

Check that your probes are connected to the correct sockets of the multimeter. Some meters have two possible sockets, one for very high currents measured in amps (or A) and another for low currents measures in milliamps (mA). In most cases, basic Arduino circuits require only a reading in milliamps, but if you are using large lights, motors, or other devices, you should set it to amps. Then turn the dial on your meter to select the correct level of amps, A or mA or even µA (microamps).

Current is measured in series, which means that the multimeter must be placed in line with the other components the circuit so that the current flows through the multimeter as if it were another component. Figure 5-6 shows this series measurement in action.

If you built a circuit similar to this on your breadboard, you can use two jump wires to break the circuit, allowing your multimeter to fill the gap. This should display the current in the circuit.

Note: If you are blinking or fading the output, your current changes, so you may want to set it to always be on to be sure of the maximum continuous current.

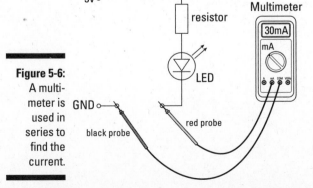

Figure 5-6: A multimeter is used in series to find the current.

Measuring resistance (in ohms) of a resistor

Sometimes it can be difficult to read the value of a resistor, and it is necessary, or just easier, to confirm it with a multimeter. Simply set the multimeter to Ohms or Ω and place one probe on each leg of the resistor, as shown in Figure 5-7.

Multimeter

Figure 5-7:
Finding the
resistance
of a resistor.

brown, black, orange

Measuring resistance (in ohms) of a variable resistor

With variable resistors, it can be good to know that you're getting the full range of resistances promised on the label. Variable resistors are similar to passive resistors but have three legs. If you connect the probes across the legs on either side, you should be reading the maximum resistance of the variable resistor, and the reading does not change when you move the dial. If you place the probes between the center and one side of the resistor, you should read the actual value of variable resistance, which changes as you turn the dial, as shown in Figure 5-8. If you switch to the center and the opposite side, doing so should change the direction of the dial.

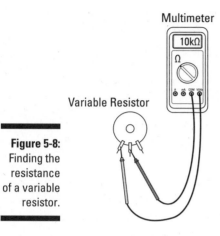

Figure 5-8:
Finding the
resistance
of a variable
resistor.

Checking the continuity (in bleeps) of your circuit

If you have a quality multimeter, it should have a speaker or sound symbol on the dial. This speaker or symbol is a continuity tester. You use it to verify that parts of your circuit are connected, and the multimeter communicates the connection to you by bleeping, ideally producing a continuous tone when the connection is good. Turn your dial to the continuity test symbol and touch the ends together to test that it is working. If you hear an unbroken tone, the connection is working correctly. Place the probes along any length of wire or connection, as shown in Figure 5-9, to test the connection.

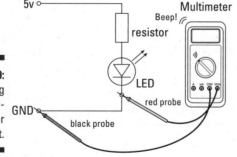

Figure 5-9:
Checking
the continu-
ity of your
circuit.

Chapter 6

A Primer on Electricity and Circuitry

*I*n this chapter, you look at the fundamentals of electricity. In later chapters, you delve deeper into electronics, so it's important that you have a basic understanding of how electricity behaves in your circuit.

The great thing about Arduino is that you don't need to study electronics for years to use it. That being said, it's a good idea to know a bit of the theory to back up the practical side of your project. In this chapter, you look at a few equations to help you build a balanced and efficient circuit; you look at circuit diagrams, which provide you with a roadmap of your circuit; and you learn a bit about color coding, which can make your life easier when building circuits.

Understanding Electricity

Electricity is one of those things that most people take for granted but find difficult to define. Simply put, electricity is a form of energy resulting from the existence of charged particles (such as electrons or protons), either statically as an accumulation of charge or dynamically as a current.

This definition of electricity is describing electricity on an atomic level, which is more complex than you need to know for dealing with the circuitry of your Arduino projects. Your main concern is simply to understand that electricity is energy and that it has a current. For those of you who want to understand electricity at this level, you can check out *Electronics For Dummies*, by Dickon Ross, Cathleen Shamieh, and Gordon McComb.

To illustrate the idea of the flow of a current, take a look at a simple light switch circuit (see Figure 6-1). The circuit is similar to those you may have made in physics or electronics classes at school with no Arduino involved, using only a battery, a switch, a resistor, and an LED.

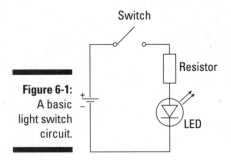

Figure 6-1:
A basic
light switch
circuit.

In this circuit, you have a source of electrical power in the form of a battery. Power is supplied in watts and is made up of voltage (in volts) and current (in amps). Voltage and current are supplied to the circuit through the positive (+) end of the battery.

You use a switch to control the power to the circuit. The switch can either be open, which breaks the circuit and stops the flow of current, or closed, which completes the circuit and allows it to function.

The power can be used for various applications. In this case, the circuit is powering an LED. The battery is supplying the LED with 4.5V, which is more than the LED needs to light. If the LED were supplied with this much voltage, you would risk damaging it, so you need a resistor before it to resist the voltage. Also, if the voltage is too low, the LED will not reach full brightness.

To complete the circuit, the power must return to ground at the negative (-) end of the battery. The LED draws as much current as necessary to light to full brightness.

By drawing current, the LED is also resisting the flow, ensuring that only the required current is drawn. If the current is not used or resisted by components (that is, if the positive is connected directly to the negative) it draws all the available current as quickly as possible. This is known as a *short circuit*.

The basic principles that you need to understand are

- An electrical circuit is, as the name suggests, a circular system.
- The circuit needs to use the power inside it before it returns to the source.

✔ If the circuit does not use the power, that power has nowhere to go and can damage the circuit.

✔ The easiest way to interact with a circuit is to break it. By controlling when and where the power is, you have instant control over the outputs.

Using Equations to Build Your Circuits

You are now aware of a few characteristics of electricity.

✔ Power in watts (P), such as 60W

✔ Voltage in volts (V or E), such as 12V

✔ Current in amps or amperes (I), such as 3A

✔ Resistance in ohms (R), such as 150Ω

These characteristics can be quantified and put into equations, which allow you to carefully balance your circuit to ensure that everything works in perfect harmony. A variety of equations exist for determining all manner of attributes, but in this section I cover two of the most basic ones that will be of most use to you when working with Arduino: Ohm's Law and Joule's Law.

Ohm's Law

Perhaps the most important relationship to understand is that among voltage, current, and resistance. In 1827, Georg Simon Ohm discovered that the voltage and current were directly proportional if applied to a simple equation (recall from the preceding list that "I" stands for "amps," or "amperes"):

$$V = I \times R$$

This equation became known as Ohm's Law. Using algebra, the equation can be rearranged to give you any one value from the remaining two:

$$I = V / R$$

or

$$R = V / I$$

You can take a look at this equation at work in an actual circuit. Figure 6-2 shows a simple circuit with a power source and a resistor.

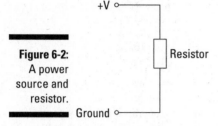

Figure 6-2:
A power
source and
resistor.

In many situations, you will know the voltage of your power supply and the value of the resistor, so you can first calculate the current of the circuit as follows:

$I = V / R = 4.5V / 150\Omega = 0.03A$

This equation works in any order you want to put the values:

$R = V / I = 4.5V / 0.03A = 150\Omega$

$V = I \times R = 0.03A \times 150\ \Omega = 4.5V$

The easiest way to remember Ohm's Law is as a pyramid (see Figure 6-3). By eliminating any one element from the pyramid, you are left with the equation.

Figure 6-3:
Ohm's Law
pyramid.

"But how is this calculation useful to me in the context of Arduino?" I hear you cry. Here's a practical example that you might run into in a basic Arduino circuit.

The digital pins on an Arduino can supply up to 5V, so this is the most common supply of power that you use. An LED is one of the most basic outputs you want to control, and a fairly standard LED requires a voltage of 2V and about 30 milliamps or 30mA (0.03A) of current.

If you plug in the LED directly to the power supply, you promptly witness a bright light followed by a plume of smoke and a burning smell. You're not likely to want that! To make sure that you can use the LED again and again safely, you should add a resistor.

Ohm's Law tells you that

R = V / I

But you also have to include two different voltage values, the voltage of the power supply (supply voltage) and the voltage required to power the LED (forward voltage). *Forward voltage* is a term that is often found in datasheets, especially when referring to diodes, indicating the recommended amount of voltage that the component can take in the direction that the current is intended to flow. For LEDs, this direction is from anode to cathode, with the anode connected to positive and the cathode to negative. When referring to a nonlight-emitting diodes (covered in Chapter 8), you are using them to resist the flow of current on the opposite direction, from cathode to anode. In this case, the term you will be looking for is *reverse voltage*, which indicates the value in volts that the circuit must exceed for current to flow through the diode.

In this case, the voltages are labelled V_{SUPPLY} and $V_{FORWARD,}$ respectively. The Ohm's Law equation requires the voltage across the resistor (voltage that passes through the resistor), which is equal to the supply voltage minus the LED forward voltage, or

$V_{SUPPLY} - V_{FORWARD}$

The new equation looks like this:

$R = (V_{SUPPLY} - V_{FORWARD}) / I = (5V - 2V) / 0.03A = 100\Omega$

This tells you that you need a 100 ohm resistor to power an LED safely; the example circuit is shown in Figure 6-4.

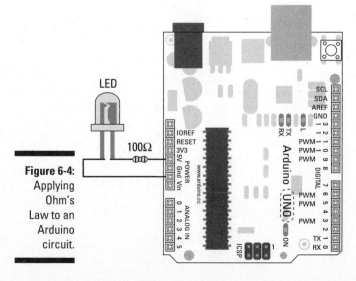

Figure 6-4: Applying Ohm's Law to an Arduino circuit.

Calculating power

To calculate the power consumption of your circuit in watts, you multiply the voltage and current of the circuit. The equation is

$P = V \times I$

If you apply this equation to the same circuit as the example used in "Ohm's Law," earlier in this chapter, you can calculate its power.

$P = (V_{SUPPLY} - V_{FORWARD}) \times I = (5V - 2V) \times 0.03A = 0.09W$

This algebra works in the same way as Ohm's Law and can be reconfigured to find the missing value:

$V = P / I$

$I = P / V$

This calculation is useful because some hardware, such as light bulbs, shows only the power and voltage rating, leaving you to figure out the current draw. This is especially useful if you are trying (or failing) to run power hungry devices, such as lighting or motors, off your Arduino pins. A USB-powered Arduino is capable of supplying 500mA of current, but an Arudino Uno can supply only a maximum of 40mA per pin *and* 200mA in total from all the pins being used, which is not much at all. (You can find more details at `http://playground.arduino.cc/Main/ArduinoPinCurrentLimitations`.).

This is a very simple calculation, but you can combine it with your knowledge of Ohm's Law to help you fill in the blanks in a number of different circuits.

Joule's Law

Another man who gave his name to an equation was James Prescott Joule. Although not as well known as ohm, he discovered a similar and perhaps complementary mathematical relationship between power, current, and resistance in a circuit.

Joule's Law is written like so:

$P = I^2R$

The best way to understand it is to look at how you arrive at it.

If, $V = I \times R$ (Ohm's Law) and $P = I \times R$ (Power Calculation)

Then, $P = I \times (I \times R)$

Which can also be written as

$P = I^2 \times R$

If this is applied to the same circuit as before we can discover the power consumption of the circuit

$P = I^2 \times R = (0.03A \times 0.03A) \times 100\Omega = 0.09W$

As you can see, this tallies with our previous power calculation. This allows us to calculate the power with only the knowing the current and resistance or any value with any combination of other values.

$I = P / (I \times R)$

$R = P / I^2$

We can also do the same calculation for situations where we only know the voltage and resistance

If, $I = V / R$ (Ohm's Law) and $P = I / V$ (Power Calculation)

Then, $P = (V / R) * V$

Which can also be written as

$P = V^2 / R$

Try the same circuit again to check the results.

$P = V^2 / R = ((5V-2V) * (5V-2V)) / 100\Omega = 0.09W$

This can also be rearranged into any combination, depending on which values you know.

$V = P / (V * R)$

$R = V^2 / P$

Many Arduin-ists, myself included, are more practical than theoretical, attempting to build the circuit based on examples and documentation before doing the sums ourselves. This is perfectly all right and in the spirit of Arduino! In most cases, your circuit will have the desired outcome, but it's always good to know what equations you need, when you need them. With these few equations, it's possible to fill in the blanks to most circuits and ensure that everything is in order, so you can always refer back to them as needed.

Working with Circuit Diagrams

Recreating circuits from photos or illustrations can be difficult, and for that reason, standardized symbols are used to represent the variety of components and connections that you may want to use in your circuit. These circuit diagrams are like maps of the underground: They show you everything connection clearly but have very little resemblance to the way things look or connect in the physical world. The following sections delve a bit more into circuit diagrams.

A simple circuit diagram

This section takes a look at a basic light switch circuit (shown in Figure 6-5) made up of four components: a battery, a pushbutton, a resistor, and an LED.

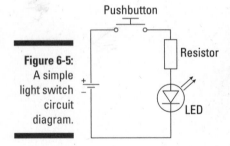

Figure 6-5:
A simple light switch circuit diagram.

Table 6-1 shows the individual symbols for each component.

Table 6-1	Basic Symbols
Name	*Symbol*
Battery	
Pushbutton	
Resistor	
LED	

Figure 6-6 shows the same circuit laid out on a breadboard. The first thing you may notice is that this example has no battery. Because your Arduino has a 5V pin and a GND pin, these take the place of the positive (+) and negative (-) of the battery and allow you make the same circuit. The second thing you may notice is that the physical circuit uses a pushbutton and, therefore, is not technically a light *switch*. This is more convenient, given that the components in most Arduino kits and the pushbutton can easily be swapped out for a switch later if you desire.

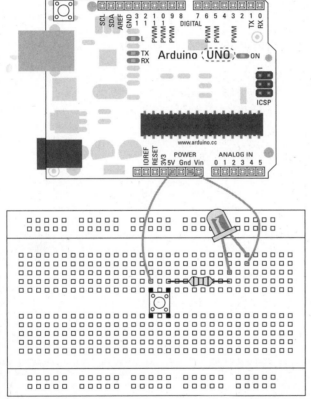

Figure 6-6:
A simple light switch circuit laid out on a breadboard.

I find that the best way is to compare a circuit diagram to the actual circuit is to follow the connections from positive to negative.

If you start at the positive (+) 5V pin on the Arduino, it leads on to the pushbutton. The physical pushbutton has four legs, whereas the symbol has only two. The legs of the physical pushbutton are actually mirrored so that two are connected on one side and two on the other. For this reason, it's very important to get the orientation of the pushbutton right. The legs of the physical switch are this way to make it more versatile, but as far as the circuit diagram is concerned, there is only one switch with one line in and one line out.

The other side of the pushbutton is connected to a resistor. The resistor symbol on the diagram is not as bulbous as the physical resistor, but apart from that the diagram and physical resistor match up well; there is one wire into the resistor and another out. The value of the resistor is written alongside the component, as opposed to having color-coded stripes on the physical one. There is no polarity for resistors (no positive or negative), so there is nothing else to show.

An LED, by contrast, does have a polarity. If you connect it the wrong way around, it won't illuminate. On the circuit diagram, the symbol marks the polarity with an arrow pointing in the direction of the current flow from + (anode) to - (cathode) and uses a horizontal line as a barrier in the other direction. On the physical LED, a long leg marks the anode and the flat section on the side of the lens marks the cathode (in case the legs are chopped off; see Figure 6-7).

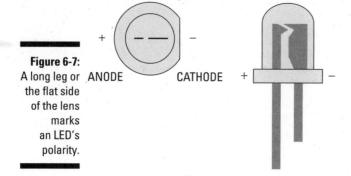

Figure 6-7:
A long leg or the flat side of the lens marks an LED's polarity.

ANODE   CATHODE

The - (cathode) of the LED is then connected to the negative (-) GND pin on the Arduino to the negative terminal of the battery to complete the circuit.

Using a circuit diagram with an Arduino

Although it's useful to understand this simple circuit, you will most likely be using an Arduino in your circuit somewhere, so take a look again at the same circuit powered from an Arduino (see Figure 6-8).

This circuit has more components than the circuit described in the previous section.

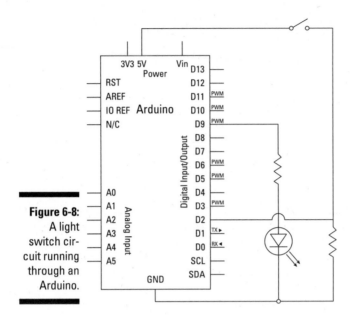

Figure 6-8:
A light switch circuit running through an Arduino.

The large, caterpillar-shaped item on the diagram is the Arduino. This is the standard symbol for an integrated circuit and is similar to the physical representation — a rectangle with lots of legs poking out. All the legs or pins are labeled so that you can tell them apart.

Also, rather than have one circuit, the diagram shows two, each running back to the Arduino. This is good to illustrate how the Arduino fits in with conventional circuits. Instead of switching the power on and off, you're sending a signal to the Arduino, which interprets it and outputs it to the LED.

This is a great practice to adopt when you have a complicated circuit: Rather than tackle it as a whole, break it up into its components. This circuit has one input circuit and one output. I describe this circuit in more depth in Chapter 7.

Color Coding

An important technique in electronics is color coding, and it becomes even more important as you progress to more complex circuits. Wiring circuits correctly can be hard enough, but staring at a sea of same-colored wires makes the task infinitely harder.

You're probably aware of this even if you're new to electronics. Traffic lights, for example, are color coded to give a clear message to drivers of what to do.

✔ Green means proceed.

✔ Amber means prepare to stop.

✔ Red means stop.

Color coding is a quick and easy way to visually get a message across without lots of words.

All sorts of electrical applications, such as the 120v or 240v plugs and sockets in your home are color coded. Because plugs and sockets are widely used and potentially dangerous, the colors need to be consistent from plug to plug and match the national standards. This makes it easy for any electrician or DIY enthusiast to make the correct connections.

Less potential for causing yourself serious harm exists with low voltage DC electronics, but you still have great potential to destroy the delicate components in your circuit. No definitive rules exist for organizing your circuit, but here are a few conventions that help you and others know what's going on:

✔ Red is positive (+).

✔ Black is negative (-).

✔ Different colors are used for different signal pins.

This is true on most breadboard circuits. Power and ground colors can change; for example, they can be white (+) and black (-) or brown (+) and blue (-), sometimes depending on the wire that is available to the person. As long as you use a color-coding system of some sort (and it's consistent), reading, copying, and fixing the circuit will be easier.

I've fixed many circuits that have broken because of the simple error of connecting the wires to the wrong places.

If the color coding of the wire is ever questionable, checking the connection (using the continuity checker on your multimeter) or the voltage running through the wire (using the voltage meter on your multimeter) is always advisable to make sure that everything is as expected.

Datasheets

Picture the scene. Your friend has heard that you know a bit of electronics and has asked you to have a look at a circuit, copied from the Internet, that isn't working. But the board has lots of non-descript integrated circuits, so what do you do? The answer: Google!

The world contains millions, if not billions, of different components. The information you need to make sense of them is normally presented in the form of a datasheet. Every component should have its own datasheet provided by the manufacturer. This datasheet should list every detail of the component and often gives more details than you need.

The easiest way to find a datasheet is to Google it. To find the right one, you need to know as much about the component as you can find out. The most important information for search purposes is the model number of the component. Figure 6-9 shows the model number of a transistor. If you Google that number plus the word *datasheet*, you should locate numerous PDF files that provide the details about the component. If you can't find a model or part number, try to find it out from the place you purchased the component.

Figure 6-9:
The small print on this transistor tells you exactly what it is.

Resistor Color Charts

Resistors are extremely important to Arduino projects, and you can find a great variety of them to allow you to finely tune your circuit. Resistors can also be extremely small, meaning that, unlike the transistor shown in Figure 6-9, it's impossible to fit the resistance value on the resistor in writing. For this reason, a color chart system exists to tell you what you need to know about these tiny components. If you take a close look at a resistor, you can see a number of colored bands that run all the way around it (see Figure 6-10), which indicate the value in ohms of the resistor.

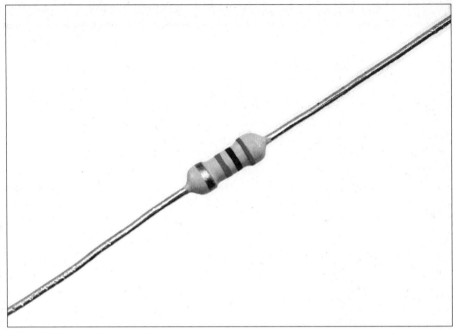

Figure 6-10:
A close look
at the color
bands on
a resistor.

Table 6-2 lists the value in ohms of the colors and what they mean depending on the band.

Table 6-2	Resistor Color Chart		
Color	*Value*	*Multiplier*	*Tolerance*
Black	0	$\times 10^0$	-
Brown	1	$\times 10^1$	±1%
Red	2	$\times 10^2$	±2%
Orange	3	$\times 10^3$	-
Yellow	4	$\times 10^4$	±5%
Green	5	$\times 10^5$	±0.5%
Blue	6	$\times 10^6$	±0.25%
Violet	7	$\times 10^7$	±0.1%
Gray	8	$\times 10^8$	±0.05%
White	9	$\times 10^9$	-
Gold	-	$\times 10^{-1}$	±5%
Silver	-	$\times 10^{-2}$	±10%
None	-	-	±20%

Now that you know each band's meaning and value, you need to know what order to read them in. There will normally be an equal-sized gap between the first three bands and a larger one separating out the fourth tolerance band.

For example, a few values you might find in your kit are

Orange, Orange, Brown, Gold = 33*10 = 330 ohms with ±5% tolerance

Red, Red, Red, Gold = 22*10*10 = 2.2K ohms ±5% tolerance

Brown, Black, Orange, Gold = 10*10*10*10 = 10K ohms ±5% tolerance

It can be difficult to see the colors and sometimes even to be able to tell which end to start reading from. So, in most situations it's advisable to use a multimeter to check the value of your resistor in ohms. You should find an ohm symbol (Ω) on the dial of your multimeter that will allow you to get an accurate reading for your resistor.

Resistors of the same value will also often be supplied on a reel of paper tape, holding the resistors together in a kind of ladder. The reason for this arrangement is to allow machines to easily feed in a reel of resistors in an orderly fashion before placing them on a PCB. This paper tape is also a handy place for writing the value of that reel of resistors, which will save you the time reading or measuring resistors each time you use them.

Chapter 7

Basic Sketches: Inputs, Outputs, and Communication

*I*n this chapter, I discuss some of the basic sketches that you need to get you on your Arduino feet. This chapter covers a broad range of inputs and outputs using the sensors in your kit. If you don't yet have a kit, I suggest reading through Chapter 2 to find one of the recommended ones.

The Blink sketch (described in Chapter 4) gives you the basis of an Arduino sketch, but in this chapter, you expand on it by adding circuits to your Arduino. This chapter walks you through building circuits using a breadboard, as mentioned in Chapter 5, and additional components from your kit to build a variety of circuits.

I detail uploading the appropriate code to your Arduino, walk you through each sketch line by line, and suggest tweaking the code yourself to gain a better understanding of it.

Uploading a Sketch

Throughout this chapter and much of the book, you learn about a variety of circuits, each with their respective sketches. The content of the circuits and sketches can vary greatly and are detailed in each of the examples in this book. Before you get started, there is one simple process for uploading a sketch to an Arduino board that you can refer back to.

Follow these steps to upload your sketch:

1. **Connect your Arduino using the USB cable.**

   The square end of the USB cable connects to your Arduino and the flat end connects to a USB port on your computer.

2. **Choose Tools⇨Board⇨Arduino Uno to find your board in the Arduino menu.**

   In most of the examples in this book, the board is Arduino Uno, but you can also find many other boards through this menu as well, such as the Arduino MEGA 2560 and Arduino Leonardo.

3. **Choose the correct serial port for your board.**

   You find a list of all the available serial ports by choosing Tools⇨Serial Port⇨ comX or /dev/tty.usbmodemXXXXX. X marks a sequentially or randomly assigned number. In Windows, if you have just connected your Arduino, the COM port will normally be the highest number, such as com 3 or com 15. Many devices can be listed on the COM port list, and if you plug in multiple Arduinos, each one will be assigned a new number. On Mac OS X, the /dev/tty.usbmodem number will be randomly assigned and can vary in length, such as /dev/tty.usbmodem1421 or /dev/tty.usb modem262471. Unless you have another Arduino connected, it should be the only one visible.

4. **Click the Upload button.**

   This is the button that points to the right in the Arduino environment, as detailed in Chapter 3. You can also use the keyboard shortcut Ctrl+U for Windows or Cmd+U for Mac OS X.

Now that you know how to upload a sketch, you should be suitably hungry for some more Arduino sketches. To help you understand the first sketch in this chapter, I first tell you about a technique called Pulse Width Modulation (PWM). The next section briefly describes PWM and prepares you for fading an LED.

Using Pulse Width Modulation (PWM)

When I tell you about the board in Chapter 2, I mention that sending an analog value uses something called Pulse Width Modulation (PWM). This is a technique that allows your Arduino, a digital device, to act like an analog device. In the following example, this allows you to fade an LED rather than just turn it on or off.

Here's how it works: A digital output is either on or off. But it can be turned on and off extremely quickly thanks in part to the miracle of silicon chips. If the output is on half the time and off half the time, it is described as having a 50 percent duty cycle. The *duty cycle* is the period of time during which the output is active, so that could be any percentage — 20 percent, 30 percent, 40 percent, and so on.

When you're using LEDs as an output, the duty cycle has a special effect. Because it is blinking faster than the human eye can perceive, an LED with a 50 percent duty cycle looks as though it is at half brightness. This is the same effect that allows you to perceive still images shown at 24 frames per second (or above) as a moving image.

With a DC motor as an output, a 50 percent duty cycle has the effect of moving the motor at half speed. So in this case PWM allows you to control the speed of a motor by pulsing it at an extremely fast rate.

So despite PWM's being a digital function, it is referred to as an `analogWrite` because of the perceived effect it has on components.

The LED Fade Sketch

In this sketch, you make an LED fade on and off. In contrast to the sketch that resulted in a blinking LED in Chapter 4, you need some extra hardware to make the LED fade on and off.

For this project you need:

- ✔ An Arduino Uno
- ✔ A breadboard
- ✔ An LED
- ✔ A resistor (greater than 120 ohm)
- ✔ Jump wires

It's always important to make sure that your circuit is not powered while you're making changes to it. You can easily make incorrect connections, potentially damaging the components. So before you begin, make sure that the Arduino is unplugged from your computer or any external power supply.

Lay out the circuit as shown in Figure 7-1. This makes a simple circuit like the one used for the Blink sketch in Chapter 4, using pin 9 instead of pin 13. The reason for using pin 9 instead of 13 is that 9 is capable of Pulse Width Modulation (PWM), which is necessary to fade the LED. However, note that pin 9 requires a resistor to limit the amount of current supplied to the LED. On pin 13, this resistor is already included on the Arduino board itself, so you didn't need to worry about this.

Putting up resistance

As you learn from Chapter 6, calculating the correct resistance is important for a safe and long lasting circuit. In this case you are potentially supplying your LED with a source 5V (volts), the maximum that a digital pin can supply. A typical LED such as those in your kit has an approximate maximum forward voltage of 2.1V (volts), so a resistor is needed to protect it. It draws a maximum voltage of approximately 25mA (milliamps). Using these figures, you can calculate the resistance (ohms):

$R = (V_S - V_L) / I$

$R = (5-2.1) / 0.025 = 116$ ohms

The nearest fixed resistor above this calculation that you can buy is 120 ohms (brown, red, brown), so if you have one of those you are in luck. If not you can apply the rule of using the nearest resistor above this value. This resists more voltage than the optimum, but your LED is safe and you can always switch out the resistor later when you are looking to make your project more permanent. Suitable values from various kits would include 220Ω, 330Ω, and 560Ω.

You can always refer to Chapter 6 to find your resistor value on the color chart or use a multimeter to measure the value of your resistors. There are even apps for your smartphone that have resistor color charts (although this may be a source of great embarrassment and ridicule among friends).

Figure 7-2 shows the schematic of the circuit. This schematic shows you the simple circuit connection. Your digital pin, pin 9, is connected to the long leg of the LED; the short leg connects to the resistor and that goes on to ground, GND. In this circuit, the resistor can be either before or after the LED, as long as it is in the circuit.

It's always a good idea to color code your circuits — that is, use various colors to distinguish one type of circuit from another. Doing so greatly helps keep things clear and can make problem solving much easier. There are a few good standards to keep to. The most important areas to color code are power and ground. These are nearly always colored red and black, respectively, but you might occasionally see them as white and black as well, as mentioned in Chapter 6.

The other type of connection is usually referred to as a signal wire, which is a wire that sends or receives an electrical signal between the Arduino and a component. Signal wires can be any color that is not the same as the power or ground color.

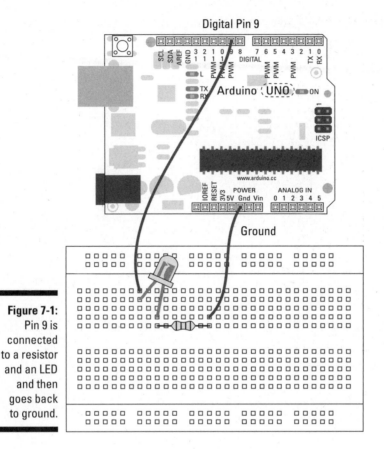

Figure 7-1:
Pin 9 is connected to a resistor and an LED and then goes back to ground.

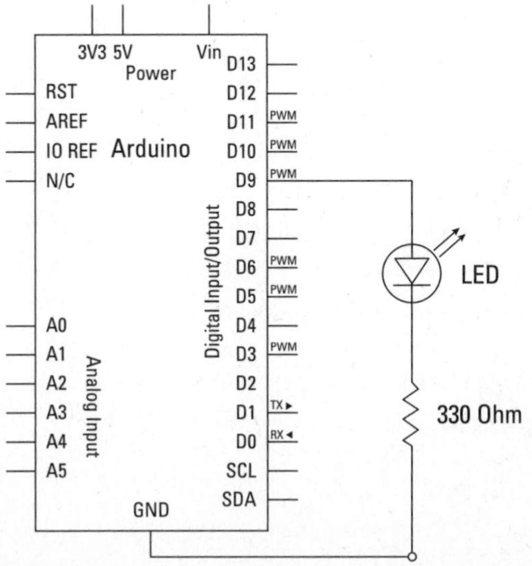

Figure 7-2:
A schematic of the circuit to fade an LED.

After you assemble your circuit, you need the appropriate software to use it. From the Arduino menu, choose File⇨Examples⇨01.Basics⇨Fade to call up the Fade sketch. The complete code for the Fade sketch is as follows:

```
/*
 Fade

 This example shows how to fade an LED on pin 9
 using the analogWrite() function.

 This example code is in the public domain.
*/

int led = 9;            // the pin that the LED is attached to
int brightness = 0;     // how bright the LED is
int fadeAmount = 5;     // how many points to fade the LED by

// the setup routine runs once when you press reset:
void setup()  {
  // declare pin 9 to be an output:
  pinMode(led, OUTPUT);
}

// the loop routine runs over and over again forever:
void loop()  {
  // set the brightness of pin 9:
  analogWrite(led, brightness);

  // change the brightness for next time through the loop:
  brightness = brightness + fadeAmount;

  // reverse the direction of the fading at the ends of the fade:
  if (brightness == 0 || brightness == 255) {
    fadeAmount = -fadeAmount ;
  }
  // wait for 30 milliseconds to see the dimming effect
  delay(30);
}
```

Upload this sketch to your board following the instructions at the start of the chapter. If everything has uploaded successfully, the LED fades from off to full brightness and then back off again.

If you don't see any fading, double-check your wiring:

- ✔ Make sure that you're using the correct pin number.

- ✔ Check that your LED is correctly situated, with the long leg connected by a wire to pin 9 and the short leg connected via the resistor and a wire to GND (ground).

- ✔ Check the connections on the breadboard. If the jump wires or components are not connected using the correct rows in the breadboard, they will not work.

Understanding the fade sketch

By the light of your fading LED, take a look at how this sketch works.

The comments at the top of the sketch reveal exactly what's happening in this sketch: Using pin 9, a new function called `analogWrite()` causes the LED to fade off and on. After the comments, three declarations appear:

```
int led = 9;           // the pin that the LED is attached to
int brightness = 0;    // how bright the LED is
int fadeAmount = 5;    // how many points to fade the LED by
```

Declarations, as mentioned in Chapter 4, are declared before the `setup` or `loop` functions. The Fade sketch has three variables: `led`, `brightness` and `fadeAmount`. These are integer variables and are capable of the same range of values, but are all used for different parts of the process of fading an LED.

With declarations made, the code enters the setup function. The comments are reminders that setup runs only once and that just one pin is set as an output. Here you can see the first variable at work. Instead of writing `pinMode(9, OUTPUT)`, you have `pinMode(led, OUTPUT)`. Both work exactly the same, but the latter uses the `led` variable.

```
// the setup routine runs once when you press reset:
void setup()  {
  // declare pin 9 to be an output:
  pinMode(led, OUTPUT);
}
```

The loop starts to get a bit more complicated:

```
// the loop routine runs over and over again forever:
void loop()  {
  // set the brightness of pin 9:
  analogWrite(led, brightness);

  // change the brightness for next time through the loop:
  brightness = brightness + fadeAmount;

  // reverse the direction of the fading at the ends of the fade:
  if (brightness == 0 || brightness == 255) {
    fadeAmount = -fadeAmount ;
  }
  // wait for 30 milliseconds to see the dimming effect
  delay(30);
}
```

Instead of just on and off values, a fade needs a range of values. `analogWrite` allows you to send a value of 0 to 255 to a PWM pin on the Arduino. 0 is equal to 0v and 255 is equal to 5v, and any value in between gives a proportional voltage, thus fading the LED.

The loop begins by writing the brightness value to pin 9. A `brightness` value of `0` means that the LED is currently off.

```
// set the brightness of pin 9:
  analogWrite(led, brightness);
```

Next you add the fade amount to the `brightness` variable, making it equal to 5. This won't be written to pin 9 until the next loop.

```
// change the brightness for next time through the loop:
  brightness = brightness + fadeAmount;
```

The brightness must stay within the range that the LED can understand. This is done using an `if` statement, which essentially tests variables to determine what to do next.

The word `if` starts the statement. The conditions are in the brackets that follow, so in this case you have two: the first being, is brightness equal to 0? The second is, is brightness equal to 255? In this case `==` is used rather than `=`. The double equal sign indicates that the code is comparing two values (if a is equal to b) rather than assigning a value (a equals b). In between the two conditional statements is the symbol `||`, which is the symbol for `OR`.

```
if (brightness == 0 || brightness == 255) {
    fadeAmount = -fadeAmount ;
  }
```

So the complete statement is, "If the variable named brightness is equal to 0 or equal to 255, then do whatever is inside the curly brackets." When this eventually becomes true, the line of code inside the curly brackets is read. This is a basic mathematical statement that inverts the variable named `fadeAmount`. During the fade up to full brightness, 5 is added to the brightness with every loop. When 255 is reached, the `if` statement becomes true and `fadeAmount` changes from 5 to -5. Then every loop updates to "add minus 5" to the brightness until 0 is reached, when the `if` statement becomes true again. This inverts the `fadeAmount` of -5 back to 5 to bring everything back to where it started.

```
    fadeAmount = -fadeAmount ;
```

These conditions give us a number that is continually counting up and then down that an Arduino can use to continually fade your LED on and then off again.

Tweaking the fade sketch

There are many ways to get something done, but I don't cover them all in this book; I can, however, show you one different way to fade an LED using the circuit that you created in the previous section. The following code is the Fading code from a previous release of Arduino, and in some ways I prefer it to the current example. Upload it and you will see that no visible difference exists between this and the previous example.

Some areas of the code appear colored on your screen, most often either orange or blue. This marks a function or a statement that is recognized by the Arduino environment (can be extremely handy for spotting typos). Color can be difficult to recreate in a black-and-white book, so any colored code appears in **bold.**

```
/*
 Fading

 This example shows how to fade an LED using the analogWrite() function.

 The circuit:
 * LED attached from digital pin 9 to ground.

 Created 1 Nov 2008
 By David A. Mellis
 modified 30 Aug 2011
 By Tom Igoe

 http://arduino.cc/en/Tutorial/Fading

 This example code is in the public domain.

 */


int ledPin = 9;    // LED connected to digital pin 9

void setup()  {
  // nothing happens in setup
}

void loop()  {
  // fade in from min to max in increments of 5 points:
  for(int fadeValue = 0;fadeValue <= 255;fadeValue +=5) {
    // sets the value (range from 0 to 255):
    analogWrite(ledPin, fadeValue);
    // wait for 30 milliseconds to see the dimming effect
    delay(30);
  }

  // fade out from max to min in increments of 5 points:
  for(int fadeValue = 255 ; fadeValue >= 0; fadeValue -=5) {
    // sets the value (range from 0 to 255):
    analogWrite(ledPin, fadeValue);
    // wait for 30 milliseconds to see the dimming effect
    delay(30);
  }
}
```

The default example is very efficient and does a simple fade very well, but it relies on the `loop` function to update the LED value. This version uses `for` loops, which operate within the main Arduino `loop` function.

Using for loops

After a sketch enters a `for` loop, it sets up the criteria for exiting the loop and cannot move out of it until the criteria are met. `for` loops are often used for repetitive operations; in this case, `for` loops are used for increasing or decreasing a number at a set rate to create the repeating fade.

The first line of the `for` loop defines the initialization, the test, and the amount of increment or decrement:

```
for(int fadeValue = 0;fadeValue <= 255;fadeValue +=5)
```

In plain English, this would read: "Make a variable called `fadeValue` (that is local to this `for` loop) equal to a value of 0; check to see whether it is less than or equal to 255; if it is, set `fadeValue` to be equal to `fadeValue` plus 5." `fadeValue` is equal to 0 only when it is created; after that, it is increased by 5 every time the `for` loop cycles.

Within the loop, the code updates the `analogWrite` value of the LED and waits 30 milliseconds (ms) before attempting the loop one more time.

```
for(int fadeValue = 0 ; fadeValue <= 255; fadeValue +=5) {
    // sets the value (range from 0 to 255):
    analogWrite(ledPin, fadeValue);
    // wait for 30 milliseconds to see the dimming effect
    delay(30);
  }
```

This `for` loop behaves the same as the main `loop` in the default Fade example, but because the `fadeValue` is contained in its own loop, and broken into fade up and fade down loops, it is a lot easier for to start experimenting with fading patterns in a more controlled way. For example, try changing +=5 and −=5 to different values (that divide into 255 neatly) and you can have some interesting asymmetrical fading.

You could also copy and paste the same `for` loops to create further fading animations. Bear in mind, however, that while it's in a `for` loop, your Arduino can do nothing else.

The Button Sketch

This is the first and perhaps most basic of inputs that you can and should learn for your Arduino projects: the modest pushbutton.

For this project, you need:

- An Arduino Uno
- A breadboard
- A 10k ohm resistor
- A pushbutton
- An LED
- Jump wires

Figure 7-3 shows the breadboard layout for the Button circuit. It's important to note which legs of the pushbutton are connected. In most cases, these small pushbuttons are made to bridge the gap over the center of your breadboard exactly. If they do bridge the gap, the legs are usually split at 90 degrees to the gap (left to right on this diagram).

You can test the legs of a pushbutton with a continuity tester if your multimeter has that function (as detailed in Chapter 5).

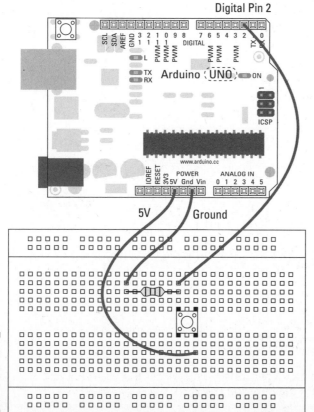

Figure 7-3: Pin 2 is reading the pushbutton.

From the schematic in Figure 7-4, you can see that the resistor leading to ground should be connected to the same side as pin 2, and that when the button is pressed, it connects those to the 5V pin. This setup is used to compare ground (0V) to a voltage (5V) so that you can tell whether the switch is open or closed.

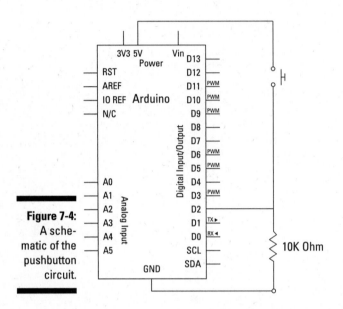

Figure 7-4:
A schematic of the pushbutton circuit.

Build the circuit and upload the code from File⇨Examples⇨02.Digital⇨Button.

```
/*
  Button

  Turns on and off a light emitting diode(LED) connected to digital
  pin 13, when pressing a pushbutton attached to pin 2.


  The circuit:
  * LED attached from pin 13 to ground
  * pushbutton attached to pin 2 from +5V
  * 10K resistor attached to pin 2 from ground

  * Note: on most Arduinos there is already an LED on the board
  attached to pin 13.


  created 2005
  by DojoDave <http://www.0j0.org>
  modified 30 Aug 2011
```

```
by Tom Igoe

This example code is in the public domain.

http://www.arduino.cc/en/Tutorial/Button
*/

// constants won't change. They're used here to
// set pin numbers:
const int buttonPin = 2;      // the number of the pushbutton pin
const int ledPin =  13;       // the number of the LED pin

// variables will change:
int buttonState = 0;          // variable for reading the pushbutton status

void setup() {
  // initialize the LED pin as an output:
  pinMode(ledPin, OUTPUT);
  // initialize the pushbutton pin as an input:
  pinMode(buttonPin, INPUT);
}

void loop(){
  // read the state of the pushbutton value:
  buttonState = digitalRead(buttonPin);

  // check if the pushbutton is pressed.
  // if it is, the buttonState is HIGH:
  if (buttonState == HIGH) {
    // turn LED on:
    digitalWrite(ledPin, HIGH);
  }
  else {
    // turn LED off:
    digitalWrite(ledPin, LOW);
  }
}
```

After you upload the sketch, give your button a press and you should see
the pin 13 LED light up. You can add a bigger LED to your Arduino board
between pin 13 and GND to make it easier to see.

If you don't see anything lighting up, you should double-check your wiring:

- Make sure that your button is connected to the correct pin number.

- If you are using an additional LED, check that it is correctly situated,
  with the long leg in pin 13 and the short leg in GND. You can also remove
  it and monitor the LED mounted on the board (marked L) instead.

- Check the connections on the breadboard. If the jump wires or components are not connected using the correct rows in the breadboard, they
  will not work.

Understanding the Button sketch

This is your first interactive Arduino project. The previous sketches were all about outputs, but now you are able to affect those outputs by providing your own real-world, human input!

While pressed, your button turns on a light. When released, the light turns off. Take a look at the sketch from the top to see how this happens.

As before, the first step is to declare variables. In this case, there are a couple of differences. The word const is short for constant, so instead of changing these two values, they are fixed for the duration of the program. This approach is best used for values that aren't supposed to change; this way, you can make doubly sure that they won't. In this case, pin numbers are being assigned because you won't change the pin number physically.

The variable buttonState is set to 0. This is used to monitor changes to the button.

```
const int buttonPin = 2;       // the number of the pushbutton pin
const int ledPin =  13;        // the number of the LED pin

// variables will change:
int buttonState = 0;           // variable for reading the pushbutton status
```

Setup establishes pinMode, with ledPin (pin 13) as the output and buttonPin,(pin 2) as the input.

```
void setup() {
  // initialize the LED pin as an output:
  pinMode(ledPin, OUTPUT);
  // initialize the pushbutton pin as an input:
  pinMode(buttonPin, INPUT);
}
```

In the main loop, you can see the order of things quite clearly. First, the digitalRead function is used on pin 2. Just as digitalWrite can write a HIGH or LOW (1 or 0) value to a pin, digitalRead can read a value from a pin. That value is then stored in the variable buttonState.

```
void loop(){
  // read the state of the pushbutton value:
  buttonState = digitalRead(buttonPin);
```

With the button state established, a test is used to determine what happens next using an `if` statement. The statement reads: "If there is a HIGH value (voltage connected to the circuit), then send a HIGH value to `ledPin` (pin 13) to turn the LED on; if there is a LOW value (the pin is grounded), then send a LOW value to `ledPin` to turn the LED off; repeat."

```
// check if the pushbutton is pressed.
// if it is, the buttonState is HIGH:
if (buttonState == HIGH) {
  // turn LED on:
  digitalWrite(ledPin, HIGH);
}
else {
  // turn LED off:
  digitalWrite(ledPin, LOW);
}
}
```

Tweaking the Button sketch

It's often necessary to invert the output of a switch or sensor, and you have two ways to do this. The easiest is to change one word in the code.

By changing the line of code in the above sketch from

```
if (buttonState == HIGH)
```

to

```
if (buttonState == LOW)
```

the output is reversed.

This means that the LED is on until the button is pressed. If you have a computer, this is the easiest option. Simply upload the code.

However, there are often occasions (such as when your laptop battery is dead) when you don't have the means to upload the edited code. Often, the easiest way to flip the logic is to flip the polarity of the circuit.

Instead of connecting pin 2 to a resistor and then GND, connect that resistor to 5V and move the GND wire to the other side of the button, as shown in Figure 7-5.

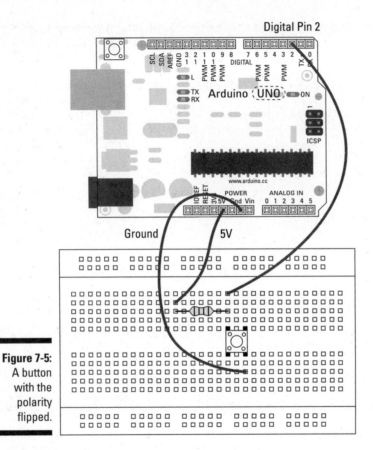

Figure 7-5:
A button
with the
polarity
flipped.

The AnalogInput Sketch

The previous sketch showed you how to use a `digitalRead` to read either on or off, but what if you want to handle an analog value such as a dimmer switch or volume control knob?

For this project, you need

- ✔ An Arduino Uno
- ✔ A breadboard
- ✔ A 10k ohm variable resistor
- ✔ An LED
- ✔ Jump wires

Variable resistors

As do your standard passive resistors, variable resistors (also known as potentiometers or pots) resist the flow of current in a circuit. The difference is that rather than having a fixed value, they have a range. Normally, the upper limit of this range is printed on the resistor. For example, a variable resistor with a value of 10K Ω gives you a range of 0 ohms to 10,000 ohms. This change is something that can be monitored electrically to give a variable analog input.

Variable resistors come in a variety of different shapes and sizes, as shown in the following figure. Think of anything with this analog movement in your house, such as a thermostat, the dial on your washing machine, or the dial on your toaster to set the time, and it most likely has a potentiometer underneath.

In Figure 7-7 you see the layout for this circuit. You need an LED and a resistor for your output, and a variable resistor for your input. If you're not quite sure what a variable resistor is, check out the "Variable resistors" sidebar.

In Figures 7-6 and 7-7, the variable resistor has power and ground connected across opposite pins, with the central pin providing the reading. To read the analog input, you need to use the special set of analog input pins on the Arduino board.

It's also worth noting that if you were to swap the polarity (swap the positive and negative wires) of the resistor, you would invert the direction of the potentiometer. This can be a quick fix if you find that you're going in the wrong direction.

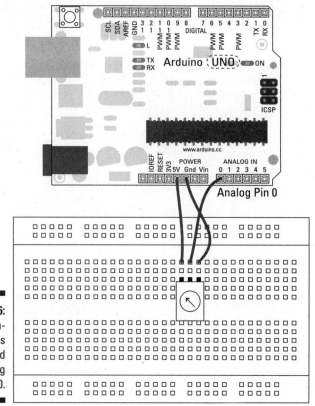

Figure 7-6:
The poten-
tiometer is
connected
to Analog
Pin 0.

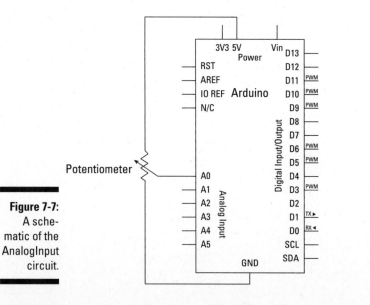

Figure 7-7:
A sche-
matic of the
AnalogInput
circuit.

Build the circuit and upload the code from File➪Examples➪03.Analog➪ AnalogInput.

```
/*
  Analog Input
Demonstrates analog input by reading an analog sensor on analog pin 0 and
turning on and off a light emitting diode(LED)  connected to digital pin 13.
The amount of time the LED will be on and off depends on
the value obtained by analogRead().

The circuit:
* Potentiometer attached to analog input 0
* center pin of the potentiometer to the analog pin
* one side pin (either one) to ground
* the other side pin to +5V
* LED anode (long leg) attached to digital output 13
* LED cathode (short leg) attached to ground

* Note: because most Arduinos have a built-in LED attached
to pin 13 on the board, the LED is optional.


Created by David Cuartielles
modified 30 Aug 2011
By Tom Igoe

This example code is in the public domain.

http://arduino.cc/en/Tutorial/AnalogInput

*/

int sensorPin = A0;    // select the input pin for the potentiometer
int ledPin = 13;       // select the pin for the LED
int sensorValue = 0;   // variable to store the value coming from the sensor

void setup() {
  // declare the ledPin as an OUTPUT:
  pinMode(ledPin, OUTPUT);
}

void loop() {
  // read the value from the sensor:
  sensorValue = analogRead(sensorPin);
  // turn the ledPin on
  digitalWrite(ledPin, HIGH);
  // stop the program for <sensorValue> milliseconds:
  delay(sensorValue);
  // turn the ledPin off:
  digitalWrite(ledPin, LOW);
  // stop the program for for <sensorValue> milliseconds:
  delay(sensorValue);
}
```

After the sketch is uploaded, turn the potentiometer. The result is an LED that blinks slower or faster depending on the value of the potentiometer. You can add another LED between pin 13 and GND to improve the effect of this spectacle.

If you don't see anything lighting up, double-check your wiring:

✔ Make sure that you're using the correct pin number for your variable resistor.

✔ Check that your LED is the correct way around, with the long leg in pin 13 and the short leg in GND.

✔ Check the connections on the breadboard. If the jump wires or components are not connected using the correct rows in the breadboard, they will not work.

Understanding the AnalogInput sketch

Analog sensors come in a variety of forms, but the principle is generally the same for each of them. In this section you examine the sketch to get a better understanding of how Arduino interprets these sensors.

The declarations state the pins that this sketch uses. The pin for the analog reading is written as A0. This is short for analog input pin 0 to mark it as the first analog input pin in the row of 6 (numbered 0 to 5). Both `ledPin` and `sensorValue` are declared as standard variables. It's worth noting that `ledPin` and `sensorPin` could both be declared as constant integers (const) because they don't change. The variable `sensorValue` stores the analog value so it *does* change and must remain as a variable.

```
int sensorPin = A0;    // select the input pin for the potentiometer
int ledPin = 13;       // select the pin for the LED
int sensorValue = 0;   // variable to store the value coming from the sensor
```

During setup, you need only declare the `pinMode` of the digital `ledPin`. The analog input pins are, as their name implies, for input only.

You can also use the analog input pins as more basic digital input or output pins. Instead of referring to them as analog pins A0 – A5, you could number them as digital pins 14 – 19, as an extension of the existing digital pins. Each must then be declared as either an input or output using the `pinMode` function, as with any digital pin:

```
void setup() {
  // declare the ledPin as an OUTPUT:
  pinMode(ledPin, OUTPUT);
}
```

Similarly to the button sketch, the AnalogInput sketch reads the sensor first. When using the function `analogRead` it interprets the voltage value of an analog pin. As the resistance changes so does the voltage. The accuracy of this depends on the quality of the variable resistor. The Arduino uses the analog-to-digital converter on the ATmega328 chip to read this analog voltage. Instead of 0V, 0.1V, 0.2V, and so on, the Arduino returns a value as an integer in the range of 0–1023. For example a voltage of 2.5V would be interpreted as 511.

It's generally a good idea to read the sensor data first. Although the loop happens extremely quickly, it's better for the sensor to be read first to prevent any delays when reading values. Otherwise, this can give the effect of a lag in the response of the sensor.

After the `sensorValue` is read, the sketch is essentially the same as the Blink sketch, but with a variable delay. The `ledPin` is written HIGH, waits, is written LOW, waits for the same amount of time, and then updates the sensor value and repeats.

Using the raw sensor value (0–1023) will make the delay be between 0 seconds and 1.023 seconds.

```
void loop() {
  // read the value from the sensor:
  sensorValue = analogRead(sensorPin);
  // turn the ledPin on
  digitalWrite(ledPin, HIGH);
  // stop the program for <sensorValue> milliseconds:
  delay(sensorValue);
  // turn the ledPin off:
  digitalWrite(ledPin, LOW);
  // stop the program for for <sensorValue> milliseconds:
  delay(sensorValue);
}
```

This sketch blinks your LED at various rates, but bear in mind that as the blinks become slower, the delays in the loop are becoming longer and, therefore, the readings from the sensor are less frequent. This can make your sensor less responsive when it's at the higher values, giving you less consistent readings. For another look at sensors, as well as how to smooth and calibrate them, head over to Chapter 11.

Tweaking the AnalogInput sketch

The `analogRead` function has supplied an integer value, and you can apply all sorts of conditions or calculations to that number in your sketch. In this example I show you how to measure whether a sensor value is above a certain number or threshold.

By putting an `if` statement around the `digitalWrite` part of the loop, you are able to set a threshold. In this example, the LED blinks only if it is over the sensors halfway value of 511.

```
void loop() {
  // read the value from the sensor:
  sensorValue = analogRead(sensorPin);
if (sensorValue > 511){
  // turn the ledPin on
  digitalWrite(ledPin, HIGH);
  // stop the program for <sensorValue> milliseconds:
  delay(sensorValue);
  // turn the ledPin off:
  digitalWrite(ledPin, LOW);
  // stop the program for for <sensorValue> milliseconds:
  delay(sensorValue);
  }
}
```

Try adding dome conditions yourself, but be aware that if there are too many delays, the sensor doesn't update as frequently. For other sketches that remedy this problem, check out the BlinkWithoutDelay sketch in Chapter 11.

Talking Serial

It's good to see the effects of your circuit through an LED, but unless you can see the actual values, you might find it difficult to know whether a circuit is behaving as expected. The project in this section and the one following are designed to display the value of inputs using the *serial monitor*

Serial is a method of communication between a peripheral and a computer. In this case, it is serial communication over Universal Serial Bus (USB). Data is sent one byte at a time in the order that it is written. When reading sensors with an Arduino, the values are sent over this connection and can be monitored or interpreted on your computer.

The DigitalReadSerial Sketch

In the DigitalReadSerial project you monitor the HIGH and LOW values of a button over the serial monitor.

For this project, you need:

- ✔ An Arduino Uno
- ✔ A breadboard
- ✔ A 10k ohm resistor
- ✔ A pushbutton
- ✔ Jump wires

Figures 7-8 and 7-9 use the same circuit as you use for the Button sketch described earlier in this chapter, but note that there are some slight changes to the code for this project.

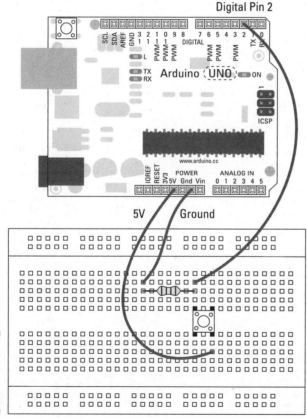

Figure 7-8: Pin 2 is reading the pushbutton.

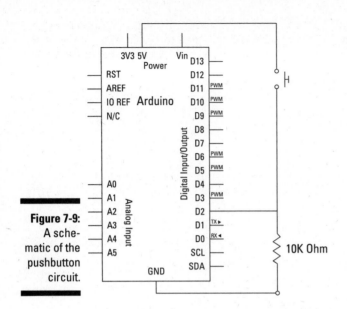

Figure 7-9:
A schematic of the pushbutton circuit.

Complete the circuit and upload the code from File➪Examples➪01.Basics➪ DigitalReadSerial.

```
/*
  DigitalReadSerial
  Reads a digital input on pin 2, prints the result to the serial monitor

  This example code is in the public domain.
 */

// digital pin 2 has a pushbutton attached to it. Give it a name:
int pushButton = 2;

// the setup routine runs once when you press reset:
void setup() {
  // initialize serial communication at 9600 bits per second:
  Serial.begin(9600);
  // make the pushbutton's pin an input:
  pinMode(pushButton, INPUT);
}

// the loop routine runs over and over again forever:
void loop() {
  // read the input pin:
  int buttonState = digitalRead(pushButton);
  // print out the state of the button:
  Serial.println(buttonState);
  delay(1);        // delay in between reads for stability
}
```

After you upload the sketch, click the serial monitor button on the top right of the Arduino window. Clicking this button opens the serial monitor window (shown in Figure 7-10) and displays any values being sent to the currently selected serial port (which is the same as the one you have just uploaded to unless you selected otherwise).

In the window, you should see a cascade of 0 values. Press the button a few times, and you should see some 1 values appear.

Figure 7-10:
The serial monitor window is great for keeping an eye on whatever your Arduino is up to.

If you don't see anything, or you see incorrect values, double-check your wiring:

- ✔ Make sure that you're using the correct pin number for your button.

- ✔ Check the connections on the breadboard. If the jump wires or components are not connected using the correct rows in the breadboard, they will not work.

- ✔ If you are receiving strange characters instead of 0s and 1s, check the baud rate in the serial monitor; if it is not set to 9600, use the drop-down menu to select that rate.

Understanding the DigitalReadSerial sketch

The only variable to declare in this sketch is the pin number for the pushbutton:

```
int pushButton = 2;
```

In the setup, there is a new function called `Serial.begin`. This function initializes serial communication. The number in parentheses represents the speed of the communication. This is referred to as the baud rate and is the number of bits sent per second; in this case, it is sending 9600 bits per second. When viewing the communication in the serial monitor, it is important to read the data at the same rate it is being written. If you don't, the data is scrambled and you are presented with what looks like gibberish. In the bottom right of the window, you can set the baud rate, but by default it should be set to 9600.

```
void setup() {
  // initialize serial communication at 9600 bits per second:
  Serial.begin(9600);
  // make the pushbutton's pin an input:
  pinMode(pushButton, INPUT);
}
```

In the loop, `pushButton` is read and its value stored in the variable `buttonState`.

```
void loop() {
  // read the input pin:
  int buttonState = digitalRead(pushButton);
```

The value of `buttonState` is then written to the serial port using the function `Serial.println`. When `println` is used, it signifies that a carriage return (new line) should be added after the value is printed. The carriage return is especially useful when you're reading the values because they appear much clearer than they do in one line of values.

```
  // print out the state of the button:
  Serial.println(buttonState);
```

A delay of 1ms is added to the end of the loop to slow down the speed at which the button is read. Having values written faster than they can be displayed can cause unstable results, so it's advisable to keep this delay.

```
  delay(1);        // delay in between reads for stability
}
```

The AnalogInOutSerial Sketch

In this project, you monitor an analog value sent by a variable resistor over the serial monitor. These variable resistors are the same as the volume control knobs on your stereo, but people often have no idea how they work. In this example, you monitor the value as detected by your Arduino and display it on your screen in the serial monitor, giving you a greater understanding of the range of values and performance of this analog sensor.

You need:

- ✔ An Arduino Uno
- ✔ A breadboard
- ✔ A 10k ohm variable resistor
- ✔ A resistor (greater than 120 ohm)
- ✔ An LED
- ✔ Jump wires

The circuit, as shown in Figures 7-11 and 7-12, is similar to the previous example for the `AnalogInput` circuit, but with the addition of an LED connected to pin 9 as in the Fade circuit. The code fades the LED on and off according to the turn of the potentiometer. Because the input and the output have a different range of values, the sketch needs to include a conversion to use the potentiometer to fade the LED. This is a great example of using the serial monitor for debugging and displays both the input and output values for maximum clarity.

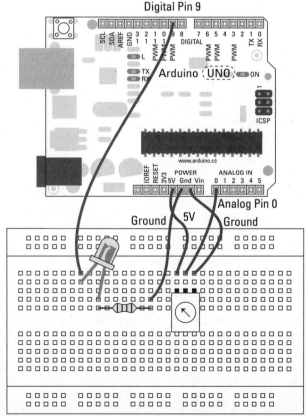

Figure 7-11: Dimmer circuit to be read over serial.

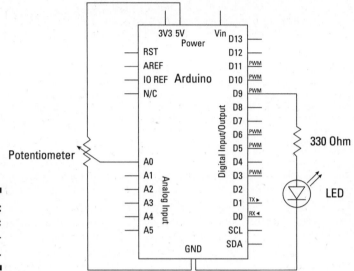

Figure 7-12:
A schematic
of the dim-
mer circuit.

Complete the circuit and upload the code from File➪Examples➪03.Analog➪
AnalogInOutSerial.

```
/*
   Analog input, analog output, serial output

 Reads an analog input pin, maps the result to a range from 0 to 255,
 and uses the result to set the pulsewidth modulation (PWM) of an output pin.
 Also prints the results to the serial monitor.

 The circuit:
 * potentiometer connected to analog pin 0.
   Center pin of the potentiometer goes to the analog pin.
   side pins of the potentiometer go to +5V and ground
 * LED connected from digital pin 9 to ground

 created 29 Dec. 2008
 modified 9 Apr 2012
 by Tom Igoe

 This example code is in the public domain.

 */

// These constants won't change.  They're used to give names
// to the pins used:
const int analogInPin = A0;  // Analog input pin that the potentiometer is
                             // attached to
```

```
const int analogOutPin = 9; // Analog output pin that the LED is attached to

int sensorValue = 0;        // value read from the pot
int outputValue = 0;        // value output to the PWM (analog out)

void setup() {
  // initialize serial communications at 9600 bps:
  Serial.begin(9600);
}

void loop() {
  // read the analog in value:
  sensorValue = analogRead(analogInPin);
  // map it to the range of the analog out:
  outputValue = map(sensorValue, 0, 1023, 0, 255);
  // change the analog out value:
  analogWrite(analogOutPin, outputValue);

  // print the results to the serial monitor:
  Serial.print("sensor = " );
  Serial.print(sensorValue);
  Serial.print("\t output = ");
  Serial.println(outputValue);

  // wait 2 milliseconds before the next loop
  // for the analog-to-digital converter to settle
  // after the last reading:
  delay(2);
}
```

After you upload the sketch, turn the potentiometer with your fingers. The result should be an LED that fades on and off depending on the value of the potentiometer. Now click the serial monitor button on the top right of the Arduino window to monitor the same values that you are receiving and sending to the LED.

If you don't see anything happening, double-check your wiring:

✔ Make sure that you're using the correct pin number for your variable resistor.

✔ Check that your LED is the correct way round, with the long leg connected to Pin 9 and the short leg in GND, via a resistor.

✔ Check the connections on the breadboard. If the jump wires or components are not connected using the correct rows in the breadboard, they will not work.

✔ If you are receiving strange characters instead of words and numbers, check the baud rate in the serial monitor. If it is not set to 9600, use the drop-down menu to select that rate.

Understanding the AnalogInOutSerial sketch

The start of the sketch is fairly straightforward. It declares both of the pins in use for the analog input and the PWM output. There are also two variables for the raw data from the sensor (sensorValue) and the value that is sent to the LED (outputValue).

```
const int analogInPin = A0;  // Analog input pin that the potentiometer is
                attached to
const int analogOutPin = 9; // Analog output pin that the LED is attached to

int sensorValue = 0;        // value read from the pot
int outputValue = 0;        // value output to the PWM (analog out)
```

In setup, you have very little to do beyond opening the serial communication line:

```
void setup() {
  // initialize serial communications at 9600 bps:
  Serial.begin(9600);
}
```

The loop is where the real action is. As in the Fade sketch, the best place to start is with reading the input. The variable sensorValue stores the reading from analogInPin, which will be in the range of 0–1024.

```
void loop() {
  // read the analog in value:
  sensorValue = analogRead(analogInPin);
```

Because fading an LED using PWM requires a range of 0–255, you need to scale the sensorValue down to make it fit the lower range of outputValue. To do so, you use the map function. The map function takes a variable, the variable's minimum and maximum, and a new minimum and maximum and and handles all the scaling for you. Using the map function creates an outputValue directly proportional to the sensorValue, but on a smaller scale.

```
  // map it to the range of the analog out:
  outputValue = map(sensorValue, 0, 1023, 0, 255);
```

Sometimes functions like this are useful, but other times they can be overkill. In this case, it's also possible to do some simple math and divide the sensor value by 4 to achieve the same result.

```
outputValue = sensorValue/4;
```

The `outputValue` is then written to the LED using the `analogWrite` function.

```
// change the analog out value:
analogWrite(analogOutPin, outputValue);
```

This is enough for the circuit to function, but if you want to know what's going on, you need to write some values to the serial port. The code has three lines of `Serial.print`, before the `Serial.println`, which means that each of those parts is written on one line of the serial monitor every time the program completes a loop.

Text inside the quotation marks is for labeling or adding characters. You can also use special characters such as `\t`, which adds a tab for spacing.

```
// print the results to the serial monitor:
Serial.print("sensor = " );
Serial.print(sensorValue);
Serial.print("\t output = ");
Serial.println(outputValue);
```

An example of this line in the serial monitor would read:

```
sensor = 1023    output = 511
```

The loop is finished with a short delay to stabilize the results and then repeats the loop, updating the input, output, and readings on the serial monitor.

```
// wait 2 milliseconds before the next loop
// for the analog-to-digital converter to settle
// after the last reading:
delay(2);
}
```

This delay time is largely arbitrary and instead of 2 ms could just as well be 1 ms, as in the previous example. These small delays are something that you may have to experiment with. If a sensor is particularly jumpy, you may want to go up to 10 ms, or you may find that the reading is perfectly smooth and can be removed completely. There is no magic value.

Chapter 8

More Basic Sketches: Motion and Sound

Chapter 7 shows you how to use some simple LEDs as outputs for various circuits. Although in Arduino land nothing is more beautiful than a blinking LED, you have a variety of other outputs as options. In this chapter, I explore two other areas: motion provided by motors, and sound from a buzzer.

Working with Electric Motors

Electric motors allow you to move things with electricity using the power of electromagnetism. When an electrical current is passed through a coil of wire, it creates an electromagnetic field. This process works similarly to a normal permanent bar magnet but gives you control over the presence of the field, meaning that you can turn it on and off at will and even change the direction of the magnetism. As you may remember from school, magnets have two possible states: attraction or repulsion. In an electromagnetic field, you can switch between these by changing the polarity, which in practical terms means switching the positive and negative wires.

Electromagnets have a variety of uses, such as for electrically operated locks, automated plumbing valves, and read-write heads on hard disks. They're also used for lifting scrap metal. Even the CERN Larger Hadron Collider uses an electromagnet.

In this chapter, I focus on another important use: electric motors.

An electric motor is made up of a coil of wire (electromagnet) between two regular, permanent magnets. By alternating the polarity of the coil, it is possible to rotate it because it is pulled by one magnet and then pushed toward the next. If this is done fast enough, the coil gathers momentum to spin.

The first part to understand is how the coil can spin if it is attached to wires. This is achieved by mounting two copper brushes on the axel. These brushes stay in contact with two semicircles of copper, as shown in Figure 8-1. This means that a connection can be maintained without any fixed wires. The semicircles also mean that the two points are never in contact, which would cause a short circuit.

Figure 8-1: How a motor's axle can be connected but still be free to spin.

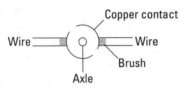

With a freely spinning coil in place on an axle, you can affect the coil by placing two permanent bar magnets near it. As shown in Figure 8-2, the magnets are placed on either side of the coil, with different poles on each side. If you put electrical current across the coil, you give it a polarity — either north or south, as with conventional bar magnets. If the coil is north, it is repelled by the north bar magnet and attracted by the south bar magnet.

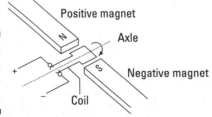

Figure 8-2: A diagram of an electric motor.

If you look at the brush again, you realize that something else happens when the coil does a half rotation: the polarity flips. When this happens, the cycle starts again and the north coil becomes south and is pushed away by the south magnet back to north again. Because of the momentum produced when the coil is repelled, this movement continues in the same direction while sufficient power exists.

This is the most basic form of electric motor, and modern ones are highly refined, having more coils and magnets to produce a smoother movement. Other motors are also based on this principle but have more advanced control to move, for example by a precise number of degrees or to a specific location. In your kit, you should have two varieties of electric motor: a DC motor and a servo motor.

Discovering Diodes

An essential component for motor control circuits is the diode. As explained earlier in this chapter, you can spin an electric motor by putting voltage through it. But if a motor is spinning or is turned without having a voltage put through it, it generates a voltage in the opposite direction; this is how electric generators and dynamos produce electricity from movement.

If this reversal of voltage happens in your circuit, the effects can be disastrous, including damaged or destroyed components. So to control this reverse current, you use a diode. Diodes block current in one direction and allow it in the other. Current can flow from the anode to the cathode. Figure 8-3 shows how this is marked for both the physical diode and the circuit diagram, with a band on the physical one and a solid line on the schematic, both indicating the cathode.

Figure 8-3:
A physical diode and its schematic symbol.

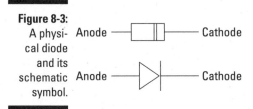

Spinning a DC Motor

The DC motor in your kit (also known as a hobby motor or brushed DC motor) is the most basic of electric motors and is used in all types of hobby electronics such as model planes and trains. When current is passed through a DC motor, it spins continuously in one direction until the current stops. Unless specifically marked with a + or -, DC motors have no polarity, meaning that you can swap the two wires over to reverse the direction of the motor. There are many other, bigger motors, but in this example I stick to the small hobby motors.

The Motor sketch

In this section, I show you how to set up a simple control circuit to turn your motor on and off.

You need:

- An Arduino Uno
- A breadboard
- A transistor
- A DC motor
- A diode
- A 2.2k ohm resistor
- Jump wires

Figure 8-4 shows the layout for this circuit, and the circuit diagram in Figure 8-5 should clarify exactly what is going on. To power the motor, you need to send 5V through it and then on to ground. This voltage spins the motor, but you have control of it. To give your Arduino control of the motor's power, and therefore its rotation, you place a transistor just after the motor. The transistor, as described in the sidebar "Understanding Transistors," is an electrically operated switch that can be activated by your Arduino's digital pins. In this example it is controlled by pin 9 on your Arduino, in the same way as an LED except that the transistor allows you the turn the motor circuit on and off.

This circuit works, but it still allows the chance of creating a reverse current because of the momentum of the motor as it slows down, or because the motor could be turned. If reverse current is generated, it travels from the negative side of the motor and tries to find the easiest route to ground. This route may be through the transistor or through the Arduino. You can't know for sure what will happen, so you need to provide a way to control this excess current.

To be safe, you place a diode across the motor. The diode faces toward the source of the voltage, meaning that the voltage is forced through the motor, which is what you want. If current is generated in the opposite direction, it is now be blocked from flowing into the Arduino.

Understanding transistors

Sometimes it's not possible or advisable to power an output directly from your Arduino pins. By using a transistor, you can control a bigger circuit from your modestly powerful Arduino.

Motors and other larger outputs (such as lots of LED lighting) often require more voltage and current than your Arduino pins can supply, so they need their own circuits to supply this power. To allow you to control these bigger circuits, you can use a component called a transistor. In the same way that a physical switch is used to turn a circuit on and off, a transistor is an electronic switch that can be turned on and off by using a very small voltage.

Types of transistors abound, and each has its own product number that you can Google to find out more about it. The one I use in this section's example is a P2N2222A, which is an NPN-type type transistor. There are two types of transistor — NPN and PNP.

A transistor has three legs: base, collector, and emitter. The base is where the Arduino digital signal is sent; the collector is the power source; and the emitter is the ground. These can sometimes go by the other names Gate (Base), Drain (Collector), and Source (Emitter). These are all numbered and, you hope, named in the datasheet to tell you which leg is which. In a circuit diagram, it is drawn as in the following figure, with the collector at the top, the base to the left, and the emitter at the bottom.

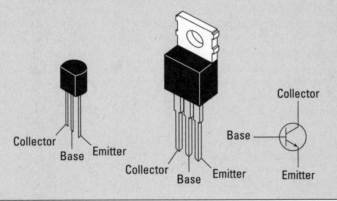

If you place the diode the wrong way, the current bypasses the motor and you create a short circuit. The short circuit tries to ground all the available current and could break your USB port or at the very least, show a warning message, informing you that your USB port is drawing too much power.

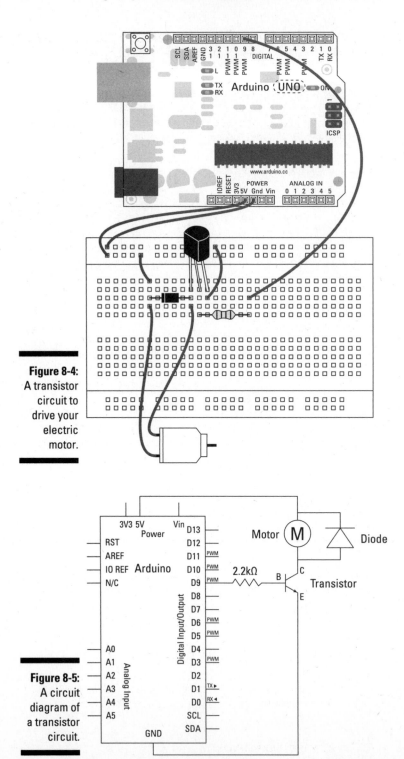

Figure 8-4:
A transistor circuit to drive your electric motor.

Figure 8-5:
A circuit diagram of a transistor circuit.

Build the circuit as shown, and open a new Arduino sketch. Choose the Save button and save the sketch with a memorable name, such as myMotor, and then type the following code:

```
int motorPin = 9;

void setup() {

  pinMode(motorPin, OUTPUT);

}

void loop() {

  digitalWrite(motorPin, HIGH);
  delay(1000);

  digitalWrite(motorPin, LOW);
  delay(1000);

}
```

After you've typed the sketch, save it and press the Compile button to check your code. The Arduino Environment checks your code for any syntax errors (grammar for your code) and highlights them in the message area (as covered in Chapter 3). The most common mistakes include typos, missing semicolons, and case sensitivity.

If the sketch compiles correctly, click Upload to upload the sketch to your board. You should see your motor spinning for one second and stopping for one second repeatedly.

If that's not what happens, you should double-check your wiring:

✔ Make sure that you're using pin number 9.

✔ Check that your diode is facing the correct way, with the band facing the 5v connection.

✔ Check the connections on the breadboard. If the jump wires or components are not connected using the correct rows in the breadboard, they will not work.

Understanding the Motor sketch

This is a very basic sketch, and you may notice that it's a variation on the Blink sketch. This example changes the hardware but uses the same code to control an LED.

First, the pin is declared using digital pin 9.

```
int motorPin = 9;
```

In setup, pin 9 is defined as an output.

```
void setup() {

  pinMode(motorPin, OUTPUT);

}
```

The loop tells the output signal to go to HIGH, wait for 1000mS (1 second), go to LOW, wait for another 1000mS, and then repeat. This scenario gives you the most basic of motor control, telling the motor when to go on and off.

```
void loop() {

  digitalWrite(motorPin, HIGH);
  delay(1000);

  digitalWrite(motorPin, LOW);
  delay(1000);

}
```

Changing the Speed of Your Motor

On and off is all well and good, but sometimes you need to have greater control over the speed of your motor. The following sketch shows you how to control the speed of your motor with the same circuit.

The MotorSpeed sketch

Using the same circuit as in the preceding section, open a new Arduino sketch, save it with another memorable name, such as myMotorSpeed, and then type the following code.

```
int motorPin = 9;

void setup(){

  pinMode(motorPin, OUTPUT);

}
```

```
void loop()  {

  for(int motorValue = 0 ; motorValue <= 255; motorValue +=5){
    analogWrite(motorPin, motorValue);
    delay(30);
  }

  for(int motorValue = 255 ; motorValue >= 0; motorValue -=5){
    analogWrite(motorPin, motorValue);
    delay(30);
  }

}
```

After you've typed the sketch, save it and press the Compile button to check your code. The Arduino Environment should highlight any grammatical errors in the Message Area if they are discovered.

If the sketch compiles correctly, click Upload to upload the sketch to your board. When uploading is done, you should have a motor that spins very slowly to start with, speeds up to its fastest spin, spins back down to a stop, and then repeats. It can be difficult to see this, so you should fix something more visible, such as a piece of tape or adhesive putty (such as Blu-Tack), to show you what's going on.

You may find that at its slowest point, the motor just hums. If so, this is not a problem; it just means that the electromagnet doesn't have enough voltage to spin the motor; it needs more voltage to generate the magnetism and gain momentum.

Understanding the MotorSpeed sketch

This sketch is a slight variation on the Fade sketch described in Chapter 7, but works in exactly the same way.

The pin you are using to control the motor circuit, digital pin 9, is declared.

```
int motorPin = 9;
```

Because it's an output, you define it in setup.

```
void setup()  {
  pinMode(motorPin, OUTPUT);
}
```

In the main loop, you use `analogWrite` to send a PWM value to pin 9. This is the same principle as in the Fade sketch, used to fade an LED. The first `for` loop sends a gradually increasing value to pin 9 until it reaches the maximum PWM value of 255. The second `for` loop gradually returns this value to 0; then the cycle repeats itself

```
void loop() {

  for(int motorValue = 0 ; motorValue <= 255; motorValue +=5){
    analogWrite(motorPin, motorValue);
    delay(30);
  }

  for(int motorValue = 255 ; motorValue >= 0; motorValue -=5){
    analogWrite(motorPin, motorValue);
    delay(30);
  }

}
```

This process could be likened to revving a car engine. If you push the pedal down, you accelerate to full speed. If you tap the gas pedal, the engine accelerates and then slows down. If you tap it at a constant rate before it slows, you will maintain some of the momentum of the spinning motor and achieve an average (if somewhat jerky) speed. This is what the transistor is doing, but very quickly. The intervals between on and off and the momentum of the motor allow you to achieve analog behavior from a digital signal.

Controlling the Speed of Your Motor

The sketch in the preceding section gave you control of the motor. In this section, you find out how to put some input into it to give you full control of the motor on the fly.

The MotorControl sketch

To gain control of the speed of your motor whenever you need it, you need to add a potentiometer to your circuit.

You need:

✔ An Arduino Uno

✔ A breadboard

✔ A transistor

✔ A DC motor

✔ A diode

✔ A 10k ohm variable resistor

✔ A 2.2k ohm resistor

✔ Jump wires

Follow the diagram in Figure 8-6 and the circuit diagram in Figure 8-7 to add a potentiometer alongside your motor control circuit.

Find a space on your breadboard to place your potentiometer. The central pin of the potentiometer is connected back to pin 9 using a jump wire, and the remaining two pins are connected to 5V on one side and GND on the other. The 5V and GND can be on either side, but switching them will invert the value that the potentiometer sends to the Arduino. Although the potentiometer uses the same power and ground as the motor, note that they are separate circuits that both communicate through the Arduino.

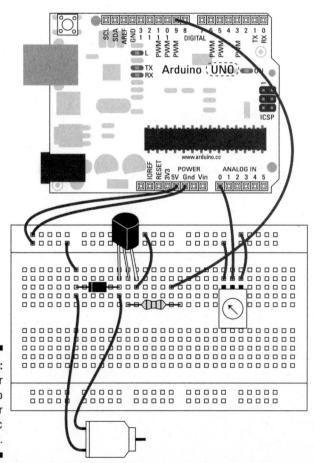

Figure 8-6:
A transistor circuit to drive your electric motor.

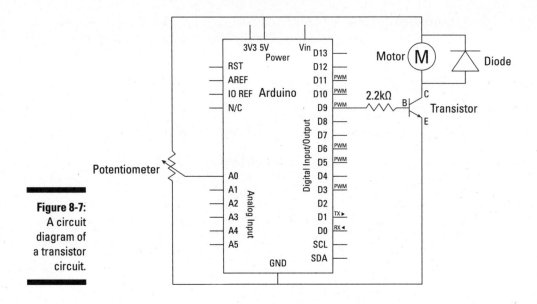

Figure 8-7:
A circuit
diagram of
a transistor
circuit.

After you have built the circuit, open a new Arduino sketch and save it
with another memorable name, such as myMotorControl. Then type the
following code.

```
int potPin = A0;
int motorPin = 9;

int potValue = 0;
int motorValue = 0;

void setup() {
  Serial.begin(9600);
}

void loop() {
  potValue = analogRead(potPin);
  motorValue = map(potValue, 0, 1023, 0, 255);

  analogWrite(motorPin, motorValue);

  Serial.print("potentiometer = " );
  Serial.print(potValue);                    ("potValue = ");
  Serial.print("\t motor = ");
  Serial.println(motorValue);                ("motorValue = ");

  delay(2);
}
```

After you've typed the sketch, save it and click the Compile button to highlight any syntax errors. .

If the sketch compiles correctly, click Upload to upload the sketch to your board. When it is done uploading, you should be able to control your motor using the potentiometer. Turning the potentiometer in one direction causes the motor to speed up; turning it the other way causes it to slow down. The next section explains how the code allows the potentiometer to change the speed.

Understanding the MotorControl Sketch

This sketch is a variation on the AnalogInOutSerial sketch and works in exactly the same way with a few name changes to better indicate what you are controlling and monitoring on the circuit.

As always, you declare the different variables used in the sketch. You use the potPin to assign the potentiometer pin and motorPin to send a signal to the motor. The potValue variable is used to store the raw value of the potentiometer and the motorValue variable stores the converted value that you want to output to the transistor to switch the motor.

```
int potPin = A0;
int motorPin = 9;

int potValue = 0;
int motorValue = 0;
```

For more details on the workings of this sketch, see the AnalogInOutSerial example in Chapter 7.

Tweaking the MotorControl sketch

You may find that there is a minimum speed after which the motor will just hum. It does so because it doesn't have enough power to spin. By monitoring the values sent to the motor using the MotorControl sketch, you can find the motor's minimum value to turn and optimize the motorValue to turn the motor within its true range.

To find the range of motorValue, follow these steps:

1. **With the MotorControl sketch uploaded, click the serial monitor button at the top right of your Arduino window.**

   The serial monitor window will show you the potentiometer value followed by the output value that is being sent to the motor, in this fashion:

   potentiometer = 1023 motor = 255

   These values are displayed in a long list and update as you turn the potentiometer. If you don't see the list scrolling down, make sure that the Autoscroll option is selected.

2. **Starting with your potentiometer reading a value of 0, turn your potentiometer very slowly until the humming stops and the motor starts spinning.**

3. **Make a note of the value displayed at this point.**

4. **Use an** `if` **statement to tell the motor to change speed only if the value is greater than the minimum speed needed to spin the motor, as follows:**

   (a). Find the part of your code that writes the `motorValue` to the motor:

   ```
   analogWrite(motorPin, motorValue);
   ```

   (b). Replace it with the following piece of code:

   ```
   if(motorValue > yourValue) {
     analogWrite(motorPin, motorValue);
   } else {
     digitalWrite(motorPin, LOW);
   }
   ```

5. **Now replace** `yourValue` **with the number that you made a note of.**

   If the value `motorValue` is greater than that, the motor speeds up. If it is lower than that, the pin is written `LOW` so that it is fully off. You could also type `analogWrite(motorPin, 0)` to accomplish the same thing. Tiny optimizations like this can help your project function smoothly, with no wasted movement or values.

Getting to Know Servo Motors

A servo motor is made up of a motor and a device called an encoder that can track the rotation of the motor. Servo motors are used for precision movements, moving by a number of degrees to an exact location. Using your Arduino, you can tell the servo motor what degree you want it to move to, and it will go there from its current position. Most servo motors can move only 180 degrees, but you can use gearing to extend this.

The servo in your kit will most likely be a hobby servo, similar to those shown in Figure 8-8. A hobby servo motor has plastic gears and can manage only relatively light loads. After you experiment with small servos, you have plenty of larger ones to choose from for heavy lifting. Servos are widely used in the robotics community for walkers that need precise movement in each of their feet.

The examples in the following section walk you through the basic operations of how to send signals to a servo and how to control one directly with a potentiometer.

Figure 8-8:
A servo
motor.

Creating Sweeping Movements

This first servo motor example requires only a servo motor and will allow you to turn the motor through its full range of movement. The servo sweeps from 0° to 179° and then back again, in a similar way to the movement of an old rotary clock.

The Sweep sketch

You need:

- ✔ An Arduino Uno
- ✔ A servo
- ✔ Jump wires

The wiring for a servo is extremely simple because it comes with a neat, three-pin socket. To connect it to your Arduino, simply use jump wires between the Arduino pins and the servo sockets directly or use a set of header pins to connect the socket to your breadboard. As shown in Figures 8-9 and 8-10, the servo has a set of three sockets with wires connected to them, usually red, black, and white. All the calculations and readings to move the motor are done on the circuitry inside the servo itself, so all that is needed is power and a signal from the Arduino. Red is connected to 5V on the Arduino to power the motor and the circuitry inside it; black is connected to GND to ground the servo; and white is connected to pin 9 to control the servos movement. The colors of these wires can vary, so always check the datasheet or any available documentation for your specific motor. Other common colors are red (5V), brown (GND), and yellow (signal).

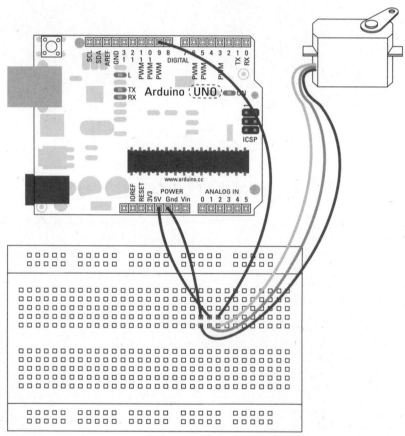

Figure 8-9:
A servo
motor wired
to your
Arduino.

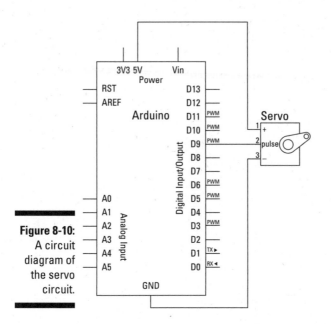

Figure 8-10:
A circuit diagram of the servo circuit.

Complete the circuit as described and open the Sweep sketch by choosing File⇨Examples⇨Servo⇨Sweep. The Sweep sketch is as follows:

```
// Sweep
// by BARRAGAN <http://barraganstudio.com>
// This example code is in the public domain.


#include <Servo.h>

Servo myservo;  // create servo object to control a servo
                // a maximum of eight servo objects can be created

int pos = 0;    // variable to store the servo position

void setup()
{
  myservo.attach(9);  // attaches the servo on pin 9 to the servo object
}
```

```
void loop()
{
  for(pos = 0; pos < 180; pos += 1)   // goes from 0 degrees to 180 degrees
  {                                    // in steps of 1 degree
    myservo.write(pos);                // tell servo to go to position in variable
                                       // 'pos'
    delay(15);                         // waits 15ms for the servo to reach the
                                       // position
  }
  for(pos = 180; pos>=1; pos-=1)       // goes from 180 degrees to 0 degrees
  {
    myservo.write(pos);                // tell servo to go to position in variable
                                       // 'pos'
    delay(15);                         // waits 15ms for the servo to reach the
                                       // position
  }
}
```

After you have found the sketch, press the Compile button to check the code. The compiler should, as always, highlight any grammatical errors in red in the Message Area when they are discovered.

If the sketch compiles correctly, click Upload to upload the sketch to your board. When the sketch has finished uploading, your motor should start turning backward and forward through 180 degress, doing a dance on the table.

If nothing happens, you should double-check your wiring:

✔ Make sure that you're using pin 9 for the data (white/yellow) line.

✔ Check that you have the other servo wires connected to the correct pins.

Understanding the Sweep sketch

At the start of this sketch, a library is included. This is the servo library and will help you to get a lot out of your servo with very little complex code.

```
#include <Servo.h>
```

The next line makes a servo object. The library knows how to use servos but needs you to give each one a name so that it can talk to each servo. In this case, the new Servo object is called `myservo`. Using a name is similar to naming your variables; that is, they can be any name as long as they are consistent throughout your code and you don't use any names that are reserved by the Arduino language, such as `int` or `delay`.

```
Servo myservo;   // create servo object to control a servo
                 // a maximum of eight servo objects can be created
```

The final line in the declarations is a variable to store the position of the servo.

```
int pos = 0;     // variable to store the servo position
```

In setup, the only item to set is the pin number of the Arduino pin that is communicating with the servo. In this case, you are using pin 9, but it could be any PWM pin.

```
void setup()
{
  myservo.attach(9);  // attaches the servo on pin 9 to the servo object
}
```

The loop performs two simple actions, and both are `for` loops. The first `for` loop gradually increases the `pos` variable from 0 to 180. Because of the library, you can write values in degrees rather than the normal 0 to 255 used for PWM control. With every loop, the value is increased by 1 and sent to the servo using a function specific to the servo library, `<servoName>.write(<value>)`. After the loop updates the value, a short delay of 15 milliseconds occurs while the servo reaches its new location. In contrast to other outputs, after a servo is updated it starts moving to its new position instead of needing to be constantly told.

```
void loop()
{
  for(pos = 0; pos < 180; pos += 1)  // goes from 0 degrees to 180 degrees
  {                                  // in steps of 1 degree
    myservo.write(pos);              // tell servo to go to position in variable
                                     // 'pos'
    delay(15);                       // waits 15ms for the servo to reach the
                                     // position
  }
```

The second `for` loop does the same in the opposite direction, returning the servo to its start position.

```
for(pos = 180; pos>=1; pos-=1)      // goes from 180 degrees to 0 degrees
{
   myservo.write(pos);              // tell servo to go to position in variable
                                    // 'pos'
   delay(15);                       // waits 15ms for the servo to reach the
                                    // position
}
}
```

This is the most simple servo example, and it's a good idea to test whether the servo is working correctly.

Controlling Your Servo

Now that you have mastered control of the servo, you can try something with a bit more interaction. By using a potentiometer (or any analog sensor), it's possible to directly control your servo in the same way that you'd control a mechanical claw at the arcades.

The Knob sketch

This example shows you how you can easily use a potentiometer to move your servo to a specific degree.

You need:

- An Arduino Uno
- A breadboard
- A servo
- A 10k ohm variable resistor
- Jump wires

The servo is wired exactly as in the Sweep example, but this time you need extra connections to 5V and GND for the potentiometer, so you must use a breadboard to provide the extra pins. Connect the 5V and GND pins on the Arduino to the positive (+) and negative (-) rows on the breadboard. Connect the servo to the breadboard using either a row of three header pins or three jump wires. Connect the red socket to the 5V row, the black/brown socket to the GND row, and the white/yellow socket to pin 9 on the Arduino. Find a space on the breadboard for the potentiometer. Connect the center pin to pin A0 on the Arduino and the remaining pins to 5V on one side and GND on the other. Refer to the circuit diagram in Figure 8-11 and the schematic in Figure 8-12.

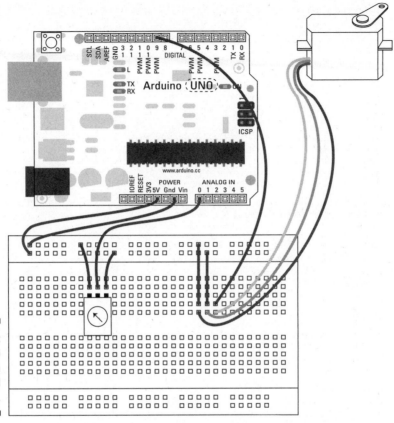

Figure 8-11:
A servo
motor with
control
knob.

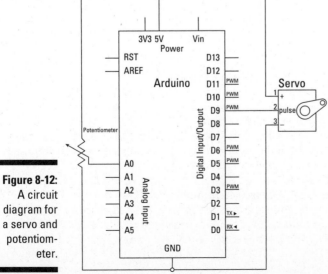

Figure 8-12:
A circuit
diagram for
a servo and
potentiom-
eter.

After you have built the circuit, open the sketch by choosing File➪Examples➪ Servo➪Knob. The code for the sketch is as follows:

```
// Controlling a servo position using a potentiometer (variable resistor)
// by Michal Rinott <http://people.interaction-ivrea.it/m.rinott>

#include <Servo.h>

Servo myservo;  // create servo object to control a servo

int potpin = 0;  // analog pin used to connect the potentiometer
int val;    // variable to read the value from the analog pin

void setup()
{
  myservo.attach(9);  // attaches the servo on pin 9 to the servo object
}

void loop()
{
  val = analogRead(potpin);          // reads the value of the potentiometer
                                     // (value between 0 and 1023)
  val = map(val, 0, 1023, 0, 179);   // scale it to use it with the servo
                                     // (value between 0 and 180)
  myservo.write(val);                // sets the servo position according to
                                     // the scaled value
  delay(15);                         // waits for the servo to get there
}
```

You may notice that there are a few discrepancies between the comments and the code. When referring to the range of degrees to move the servo, the sketch mentions both 0 to 179 and 0 to 180. With all Arduino tutorials, it's best to assume that they're works in progress and may not always be accurate.

The correct range is 0 to 179, which gives you 180 values. Counting from zero is referred to as *zero indexing* and is a common occurrence in Arduino, as you may have noticed by this point.

After you have found the sketch, press the Compile button to check the code. The compiler should highlight any syntax errors in the message box, which lights up red when they are discovered.

If the sketch compiles correctly, click Upload to upload the sketch to your board. When it is done uploading, your servo should turn as you turn your potentiometer.

If that isn't what happens, you should double check your wiring:

- ✔ Make sure that you're using pin 9 to connect the data (white/yellow) line to the servo.
- ✔ Check your connections to the potentiometer and make sure that the center pin is connected to Analog pin 0.
- ✔ Check the connections on the breadboard. If the jump wires or components are not connected using the correct rows in the breadboard, they will not work.

Understanding the Knob sketch

In the declarations, the servo library, Servo.h, and a new servo object are named. The analog input pin is declared with a value of 0, showing that you are using Analog 0.

You may have noticed that the pin is numbered as 0, not A0 as in other examples. Either is fine, because A0 is just an alias of 0, as A1 is of 1, and so on. Using A0 is good for clarity, but optional.

There is one last variable to store the value of the reading, which will become the output.

```
#include <Servo.h>

Servo myservo;  // create servo object to control a servo

int potpin = 0;  // analog pin used to connect the potentiometer
int val;     // variable to read the value from the analog pin
```

In setup, the only item to define is myservo, which is using pin 9.

```
void setup()
{
  myservo.attach(9);  // attaches the servo on pin 9 to the servo object
}
```

Rather than use two separate variables for input and output, this sketch simply uses one. First, val is used to store the raw sensor data, a value from 0 to 1023. This value is then processed using the map function to scale its range to that of the servo: 0 to 179. This value is then written to the servo using myservo.write. There is also a 15 millisecond delay to reach that location. Then the loop repeats and updates its position as necessary.

```
void loop()
{
  val = analogRead(potpin);        // reads the value of the potentiometer
                                   // (value between 0 and 1023)
  val = map(val, 0, 1023, 0, 179); // scale it to use it with the servo
                                   // (value between 0 and 180)
```

```
    myservo.write(val);                    // sets the servo position according to
                                           // the scaled value
    delay(15);                             // waits for the servo to get there
}
```

With this simple addition to the circuit, it's possible to control a servo with any sort of input. In this example, the code uses an analog input, but with a few changes it could just as easily use a digital input.

Making Noises

If you've just finished the motor sketches, you have mastered movement and must be ready for a new challenge. In this section, I look at a project that's a bit more tuneful than the previous ones: making music (or noise at least) with your Arduino. Yes, you can make electronic music — albeit simple — using a piezo buzzer.

Piezo buzzer

A piezo or piezoelectric buzzer is found in hundreds of thousands of devices. If you hear a tick, buzz, or beep, it's likely caused by a piezo. The piezo is composed of two layers, a ceramic and a metal plate joined together. When electricity passes from one layer to the other, the piezo bends on a micro-scopic level and makes a sound, as shown in Figure 8-13.

Figure 8-13: An exaggeration of the miniature movements of a piezo.

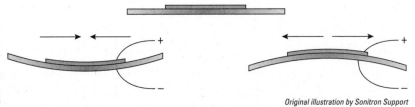

Original illustration by Sonitron Support

If you switch between a voltage and ground, the piezo bends and generates a tick sound; if this happens fast enough, these ticks turn into a tone. This tone can be quite a harsh sound, similar to the old mobile phone ringtone or computer game sounds from the 1980s, and is known as a square wave. Every time the piezo changes polarity fully, it produces a square wave with abrupt, hard edges, like a square. Other types of waves include triangle waves and sine waves, which are progressively less harsh. Figure 8-14 shows an illustration of these waves to show the differences between them.

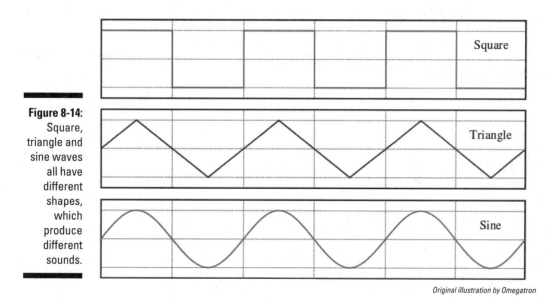

Figure 8-14: Square, triangle and sine waves all have different shapes, which produce different sounds.

Original illustration by Omegatron

Digital devices like this as well as other electronic instruments generate square waves, resulting in a buzzing sound. The buzzer isn't restricted to just one pitch. By changing the frequency that the buzzer is switched at (the width between the square waves), you can generate different frequencies and therefore different notes.

The toneMelody sketch

With this sketch, you see how to change the frequency of your piezo and play a predefined melody. This setup allows you to program your own melodies with a bit of time and consideration to figure out the notes and beats.

Piezo buzzers are supplied in most Arduino kits but can take many different forms. They can be supplied without an enclosure, as shown in Figure 8-15, or can be enclosed in plastic housing ranging from small cylinders to flat coin-like shapes. They may also have different connections, either a set of two pins protruding from the underside of the piezo or two wires protruding from its side.

You need:

- ✓ An Arduino Uno
- ✓ Breadboard
- ✓ A piezo buzzer
- ✓ Jump wires

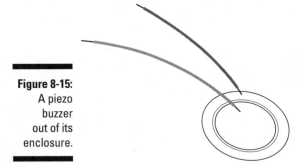

Figure 8-15:
A piezo
buzzer
out of its
enclosure.

Connect the piezo buzzer to the breadboard and use a set of jump wires to connect it to digital pin 8 on one side and ground on the other. Some piezos have a polarity, so make sure that you connect the positive (+) to pin 9 and the negative (-) to GND. Other piezos don't have a polarity, so if you see no symbols, don't worry. The piezo circuit is shown in Figure 8-16, and the circuit diagram appears in 8-17.

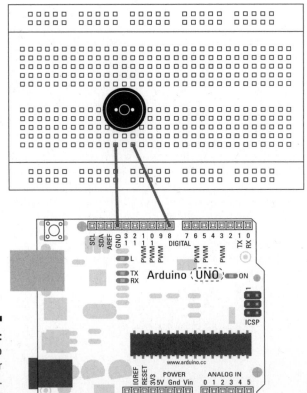

Figure 8-16:
A piezo
buzzer
circuit.

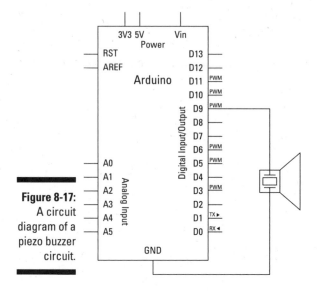

Figure 8-17:
A circuit
diagram of a
piezo buzzer
circuit.

Complete the circuit and open the sketch by choosing File➪Examples➪
02.digital➪toneMelody. You see the following code:

```
/*
  Melody

  Plays a melody

  circuit:
  * 8-ohm speaker on digital pin 8

  created 21 Jan 2010
  modified 30 Aug 2011
  by Tom Igoe

This example code is in the public domain.

  http://arduino.cc/en/Tutorial/Tone

  */
  #include "pitches.h"

// notes in the melody:
int melody[] = {
  NOTE_C4, NOTE_G3,NOTE_G3, NOTE_A3, NOTE_G3,0, NOTE_B3, NOTE_C4};

// note durations: 4 = quarter note, 8 = eighth note, etc.:
int noteDurations[] = {
  4, 8, 8, 4,4,4,4,4 };

void setup() {
```

```
    // iterate over the notes of the melody:
    for (int thisNote = 0; thisNote < 8; thisNote++) {

        // to calculate the note duration, take one second
        // divided by the note type.
        //e.g. quarter note = 1000 / 4, eighth note = 1000/8, etc.
        int noteDuration = 1000/noteDurations[thisNote];
        tone(8, melody[thisNote],noteDuration);

        // to distinguish the notes, set a minimum time between them.
        // the note's duration + 30% seems to work well:
        int pauseBetweenNotes = noteDuration * 1.30;
        delay(pauseBetweenNotes);
        // stop the tone playing:
        noTone(8);
    }
}

void loop() {
    // no need to repeat the melody.
}
```

In this sketch, you have another tab called pitches.h, which contains all the data needed to make the correct tones with your buzzer. In your Arduino sketch folder, this tab (and other, additional tabs) appears as its own individual file and must be included in the main sketch using the #include function followed by the name of the file to be included. In this case, this reads #include "pitches.h". The pitches.h file follows for your reference.

pitches.h

```
/**************************************************
 * Public Constants
 **************************************************/

#define NOTE_B0  31
#define NOTE_C1  33
#define NOTE_CS1 35
#define NOTE_D1  37
#define NOTE_DS1 39
#define NOTE_E1  41
#define NOTE_F1  44
#define NOTE_FS1 46
#define NOTE_G1  49
#define NOTE_GS1 52
#define NOTE_A1  55
#define NOTE_AS1 58
#define NOTE_B1  62
#define NOTE_C2  65
#define NOTE_CS2 69
#define NOTE_D2  73
```

```
#define NOTE_DS2  78
#define NOTE_E2   82
#define NOTE_F2   87
#define NOTE_FS2  93
#define NOTE_G2   98
#define NOTE_GS2  104
#define NOTE_A2   110
#define NOTE_AS2  117
#define NOTE_B2   123
#define NOTE_C3   131
#define NOTE_CS3  139
#define NOTE_D3   147
#define NOTE_DS3  156
#define NOTE_E3   165
#define NOTE_F3   175
#define NOTE_FS3  185
#define NOTE_G3   196
#define NOTE_GS3  208
#define NOTE_A3   220
#define NOTE_AS3  233
#define NOTE_B3   247
#define NOTE_C4   262
#define NOTE_CS4  277
#define NOTE_D4   294
#define NOTE_DS4  311
#define NOTE_E4   330
#define NOTE_F4   349
#define NOTE_FS4  370
#define NOTE_G4   392
#define NOTE_GS4  415
#define NOTE_A4   440
#define NOTE_AS4  466
#define NOTE_B4   494
#define NOTE_C5   523
#define NOTE_CS5  554
#define NOTE_D5   587
#define NOTE_DS5  622
#define NOTE_E5   659
#define NOTE_F5   698
#define NOTE_FS5  740
#define NOTE_G5   784
#define NOTE_GS5  831
#define NOTE_A5   880
#define NOTE_AS5  932
#define NOTE_B5   988
#define NOTE_C6   1047
#define NOTE_CS6  1109
#define NOTE_D6   1175
#define NOTE_DS6  1245
#define NOTE_E6   1319
#define NOTE_F6   1397
```

(continued)

pitches.h *(continued)*

```
#define NOTE_FS6 1480
#define NOTE_G6  1568
#define NOTE_GS6 1661
#define NOTE_A6  1760
#define NOTE_AS6 1865
#define NOTE_B6  1976
#define NOTE_C7  2093
#define NOTE_CS7 2217
#define NOTE_D7  2349
#define NOTE_DS7 2489
#define NOTE_E7  2637
#define NOTE_F7  2794
#define NOTE_FS7 2960
#define NOTE_G7  3136
#define NOTE_GS7 3322
#define NOTE_A7  3520
#define NOTE_AS7 3729
#define NOTE_B7  3951
#define NOTE_C8  4186
#define NOTE_CS8 4435
#define NOTE_D8  4699
#define NOTE_DS8 4978
```

After you have found the sketch, press the Compile button to check the code. The Message Area should highlight any grammatical errors in red when they are discovered.

If the sketch compiles correctly, click Upload to upload the sketch to your board. When it is done uploading, you should hear a buzzer that sings a tune to you and then stops. To hear the tune again, press the reset button on your Arduino.

If you don't hear a buzzer, you should double-check your wiring:

- Make sure you're using pin 8 as your output.

- Check that your piezo is correctly positioned. Symbols may be hidden on the underside if they are not visible on the top. If you see no markings, try the piezo in the other orientation.

- Check the connections on the breadboard. If the jump wires or components are not connected using the correct rows in the breadboard, they will not work.

Understanding the sketch

This is the first sketch in this book that uses multiple tabs. You sometimes use tabs as a convenient way of separating your sketches. In this case, the tab `pitches.h` is used as a reference or lookup table for all the possible notes in the piezo's range. Because this code won't change, it doesn't need to be in the main body of code.

At the top of the toneMelody sketch is a note to include `pitches.h`, which is treated in the same way as a library. It is an external file that can be brought into sketches if needed. In this case, it is needed to determine which frequencies are used to create the notes.

```
#include "pitches.h"
```

Now that the sketch knows the different notes, the melody can be defined. It is defined in an array so that the notes can be stepped through in order. To find out more about arrays, see the following "Introducing arrays" sidebar. The names, such as NOTE_C4, refer to the names of notes in the pitches.h tab. If you look at pitches.h, you will see that it uses a C function called `define` for each of these note references and follows them with a number, such as #define NOTE_C4 262. This means that whenever NOTE_C4 is mentioned, it is really just a variable name for the value 262.

```
// notes in the melody:
int melody[] = {
  NOTE_C4, NOTE_G3,NOTE_G3, NOTE_A3, NOTE_G3,0, NOTE_B3, NOTE_C4};
```

Introducing arrays

In its simplest form, an array is a list of data. Think of it as being like a shopping list, as shown in the following table. Each row has a number, referred to as the index, and the data contained in that part of the list. This kind of array is a one-dimensional array, containing only one item of data for each, in this case the name of a piece of fruit.

Index	Value
1	apples
2	bananas
3	oranges

How is an array relevant to Arduino? Arrays can store integers, floats, characters, or any other type of data, but I use integers here to keep things simple. Here is an array of six integer values.

```
int simpleArray[] =
       {1, 255, -51,
 0, 102, 27};
```

First, `int` defines the type of data that is being stored as integers (whole numbers). The data type could also be `float` for floating-point numbers or `char` for characters. The name of the array is `simpleArray`, but this can

(continued)

(continued)

be any relevant name that best describes your array. The square brackets (`[ ]`) store the length of the array (the number of values that can be stored in it), but in this case, the space is left blank, meaning that this array has no fixed length. The numbers inside the curly braces `{ }` are values that are defined in the array. These are optional, so if they are not defined, the array will be left empty.

There are other correct ways to declare arrays, including:

```
int simpleArray[10];
float simpleArray[5] =
    {2.7, 42.1, -9.1, 300.6};
char simpleArray[14] = "hello, world!";
```

You may notice that the last entry for a character array has one more space than there are characters. This is required for character arrays, so if you're getting errors, that's why!

Now that your array is defined, you need to know how to use it. To use values in an array, you refer to them by their index. If you wanted to send a value to the serial monitor, you would write

```
Serial.println(simpleArray[2]);
```

This would display a value of -51 because that is stored in index 2 of the array.

You can also update values in the array. An effective way to do this is with a `for` loop, to count through each index in the array (see Chapter 11 for more details) as in the following example:

```
for (int i = 0; i < 6; i++) {
    simpleArray[i] = analogRead(sensor
        Pin);
}
```

The `for` loop in this case will loop six times, increasing the variable `i` by 1 each loop. The variable `i` is also used to represent the index of the array, so with each loop, a new analog reading from `sensorPin` is stored in the current index and the index of the array is incremented for the next loop.

This is a very clever and efficient way to work through arrays, either using or updating the data stored in them. Arrays can get even more complicated, storing many strings of text, or they can even be multidimensional, like a spreadsheet, with many values associated with each index. For more information, head over to the official Arduino reference page on arrays at `http://arduino.cc/en/Reference/Array`.

Without the beat, your melody wouldn't sound right, so another array stores the duration for each note.

```
// note durations: 4 = quarter note, 8 = eighth note, etc.:
int noteDurations[] = {
  4, 8, 8, 4,4,4,4,4 };
```

In setup, a for loop is used to cycle through each of the eight notes, from 0 to 7. The thisNote value is used as an index to point to the correct items in each array.

```
void setup() {
  // iterate over the notes of the melody:
  for (int thisNote = 0; thisNote < 8; thisNote++) {
```

The duration is calculated by dividing 1,000 (or 1 second) by the required duration, 4 for a quarter note or crotchet, 8 for and eighth note or quaver, and so on. This is then written to the function tone, which sends the current note to pin 8 for the duration that is assigned.

```
    // to calculate the note duration, take one second
    // divided by the note type.
    //e.g. quarter note = 1000 / 4, eighth note = 1000/8, etc.
    int noteDuration = 1000/noteDurations[thisNote];
    tone(8, melody[thisNote],noteDuration);
```

A small pause between notes is used so that they are better defined. In this case, it is relative to the length of the note, which is set to 30 percent of the current duration.

```
    // to distinguish the notes, set a minimum time between them.
    // the note's duration + 30% seems to work well:
    int pauseBetweenNotes = noteDuration * 1.30;
    delay(pauseBetweenNotes);
```

Next, the noTone function is used to turn off pin 8, stopping the note after it has played for its duration.

```
    // stop the tone playing:
    noTone(8);
  }
}
```

In the loop, nothing happens. As it stands, the melody plays once at the start and then ends. The melody could be moved to the loop to play forever, but this may cause mild headaches.

```
void loop() {
  // no need to repeat the melody.
}
```

This is a great example of using a melody as an audio signal at the start of a sketch. If your project is out of sight, it can sometimes be more helpful to have a sound to say "I'm okay" rather than have an LED flash.

Making an Instrument

In the preceding section, you find out how to make your project play a sound rather than blink a light, as in previous sketches. In the example in this section, you see how to go beyond playing a sound — you create your own instrument, similar to the Theremin. The *Theremin*, named after its inventor Léon Theremin, was one of the first electronic instruments, developed in the 1920s. It worked by detecting the electromagnetic field of the player's hands to change signals: one hand for volume and the other for pitch.

The PitchFollower sketch

In this sketch, you find out how to make a budget Theremin using a piezo as a light sensor to control the pitch.

You need:

- An Arduino Uno
- A breadboard
- A piezo
- A light sensor
- A 4.7k ohm resistor
- Jump wires

This circuit has two separate halves, the piezo and the light sensor circuit. The piezo is wired as in the toneMelody sketch, with one wire to digital pin 8 and the other to GND. The light sensor is connected to analog 0 on one side and 5V on the other; the 4.7K resistor is connected between analog 0 and ground (as shown in Figures 8-18 and 8-19). If you do not have a 4.7K resistor, use the nearest you have to that value.

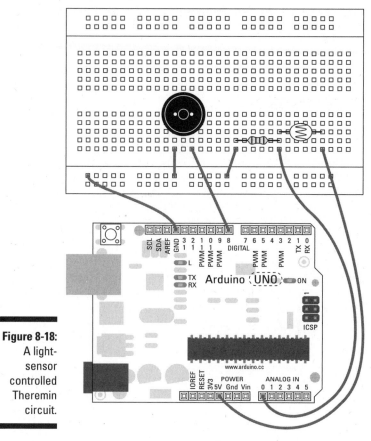

Figure 8-18:
A light-sensor controlled Theremin circuit.

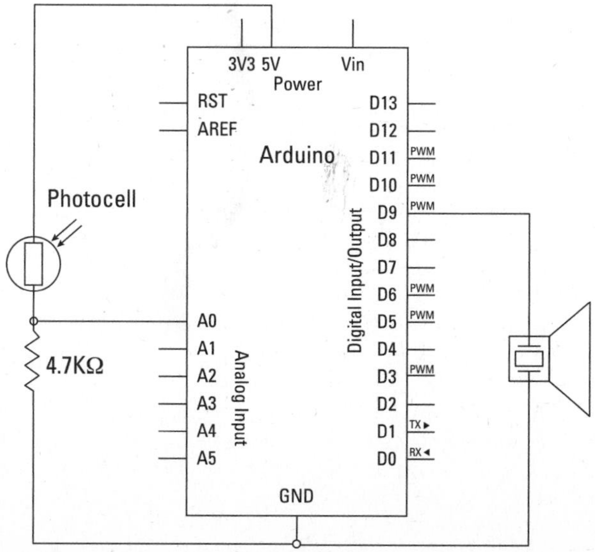

Figure 8-19:
A circuit diagram of the light-sensor controlled Theremin.

Complete the circuit, and open the sketch by choosing File⇨Examples⇨ 02.Digital⇨tonePitchFollower.

```
/*
  Pitch follower

  Plays a pitch that changes based on a changing analog input

  circuit:
  * 8-ohm speaker on digital pin 8
  * photoresistor on analog 0 to 5V
  * 4.7K resistor on analog 0 to ground

  created 21 Jan 2010
  modified 9 Apr 2012
  by Tom Igoe

 This example code is in the public domain.

  http://arduino.cc/en/Tutorial/Tone2

  */


void setup() {
  // initialize serial communications (for debugging only):
  Serial.begin(9600);
}

void loop() {
  // read the sensor:
  int sensorReading = analogRead(A0);
  // print the sensor reading so you know its range
  Serial.println(sensorReading);
  // map the pitch to the range of the analog input.
  // change the minimum and maximum input numbers below
  // depending on the range your sensor's giving:
  int thisPitch = map(sensorReading, 400, 1000, 100, 1000);

  // play the pitch:
  tone(8, thisPitch, 10);
  delay(1);          // delay in between reads for stability
}
```

After you have found the sketch, press the Compile button to check the code. Any syntax errors turn the Message box red when they are discovered, and you see an error message stating what is wrong.

If the sketch compiles correctly, click Upload to upload the sketch to your board. When it is done uploading, you should have a light sensor that will change the pitch of your buzzer. If you don't hear any change, make sure that you are in a well-lit area or turn a desk lamp on over your breadboard. This will help increase the difference when you cover the light sensor with your hand.

If nothing happens, you should double-check your wiring:

- ✔ Make sure that you're using the correct pin number for the inputs and outputs.
- ✔ Check that your piezo is turned the correct way. Symbols may be hidden on the underside if they are not visible.
- ✔ Check the connections on the breadboard. If the jump wires or components are not connected using the correct rows in the breadboard, they will not work.

Understanding the sketch

This sketch is a lot shorter than the toneMelody sketch, presented earlier in the chapter, because it is directly converting the readings from the light sensor to a frequency rather than requiring a lookup table. This means that you can slide between notes as well as choose them individually.

In setup, the serial port is opened to allow you to monitor the sensor readings as they come in.

```
void setup() {
  // initialize serial communications (for debugging only):
  Serial.begin(9600);
}
```

In the main loop, the light sensor is read from analog pin 0. This reading is also forwarded onto the serial monitor.

```
void loop() {
  // read the sensor:
  int sensorReading = analogRead(A0);
  // print the sensor reading so you know its range
  Serial.println(sensorReading);
```

To convert the sensor's range to the range of frequencies that the buzzer can cover, you use the map function.

```
  // map the pitch to the range of the analog input.
  // change the minimum and maximum input numbers below
  // depending on the range your sensor's giving:
  int thisPitch = map(sensorReading, 400, 1000, 100, 1000);
```

The tone function then outputs the note with the mapped sensor value and a very short duration of 10 milliseconds. This duration serves to make the sound audible, but the real duration will be determined by how long you hold your hand over the sensor, as described previously.

```
// play the pitch:
tone(8, thisPitch, 10);
```

Finally, a tiny delay occurs at the end of the loop to improve the stability for the readings.

```
delay(1);        // delay in between reads for stability
}
```

With this setup, you can quickly make an easy controller and maybe even form a traveling Theremin band with your friends.

Part III
Building on the Basics

The 5th Wave
By Rich Tennant

"I had a little trouble with the automatic video tracking camera, so during the video conference, before speaking, say 'Here Rollo!' and wait for Rollo to get his paws up on your knees before beginning to speak."

In this part . . .

To get your mind in gear, this part starts with showing you some of the varied uses of Arduino through a few projects that are already out in the world. After you have some food for thought, you'll be itching to make your own projects, so in this part you learn how to make your basic prototypes into something more solid by learning all about soldering. You also learn more about using code to improve the reliability of your project, as well as how to choose the right sensors for the right job.

Chapter 9

Learning by Example

*I*n previous chapters, I show you the beginnings of Arduino projects, but it can be difficult to know what to do with that knowledge. In this chapter, you read about a few Arduino projects that already exist and are functioning in the world. Read this chapter for a taste of the vast variety of uses and huge potential of Arduino. In this chapter, you discover projects that have used Arduino to create breathtaking art installations, long-lasting interactive exhibitions, and prototypes for products that have made it out into the world.

Skube

The Skube project was developed by Andrew Nip, Ruben van der Vleuten, Malthe Borch, and Andrew Spitz as part of the Tangible User Interface module at the Copenhagen Institute of Interaction Design (CIID). It is an excellent example of how to use Arduino for product prototyping and development.

Skube (shown in Figure 9-1) is a product that allows you to interact with digital music services that you would usually access on your computer. The project aims to rethink the way audio devices work and how they are used to make better use of digital music services. Each Skube has two modes, Playlist and Discovery, that you select by tapping the top of the device. Playlist plays through a predefined playlist of music, and Discovery searches for similar artists or tracks. Skubes can also be combined to shuffle between each of the predefined playlists. They will physically snap together, giving the user a tangible way of mixing different playlists and discovering new music.

Courtesy of Andrew Spitz

Figure 9-1:
A single
Skube.

How it works

Thankfully, the Skube team offers a great amount of documentation and an excellent video of both the finished prototypes as well as good look under the hood. Inside each Skube is an Arduino and an XBee Wireless Module (unfortunately,this book doesn't have enough room to cover these amazing modules, but with a quick Google search, you should find ample resources online). The Arduino's main function is to act as the middleman, hosting a number of different sensors and communication devices and relaying the correct data to the correct places. The tap sensor is the same as that described in Chapter 12 of this book and uses a simple piezo element to monitor vibrations. When Skubes snap together, the magnet is actually acting as a switch as well, activating a reed switch. The reed switch closes its metal contacts when a magnet comes near, giving the device a clear indication of when the magnet is present.

The project also has an FM radio module, which is used to output the music for each Skube. Using the XBee Wireless Modules, you can communicate with each Skube and coordinate them using custom software on a computer, which is written in Max/MSP.

Max/MSP is a visual programming language that is used for many audio and music projects. Using Max/MSP, the Skube team used data from the music services Last.fm and Spotify to make use of their playlist and find similar artist features. These companies both provide various features to their customers (such as assembling playlists based on your favorite tracks or providing a database of albums and artists), but they also provide access to these features for developers that have interesting ideas for their own projects, smartphone applications, or products. This resource is known as an Application Programming Interface (API). The API for Last.fm (`http://www.last.fm/api`) and Spotify (`https://developer.spotify.com/technologies/web-api/`) are just two examples, but many more are available for other specific web services as well; so always give it a Google!

You can see that this project has many elements, involving not just communicating wirelessly using Arduino (which can be a task in itself) but also communicating with other software, and from that software, communicating with other services on the Internet. For the more code-savvy among you, this application of Arduino may allow you to build from your existing knowledge to integrate hardware with other software. In Part V, I introduce you to the other available software and look in more depth at communicating with Processing.

Further reading

You can find out more about this project by checking out the project pages on the CIID website at `http://ciid.dk/education/portfolio/idp12/courses/tangible-user-interface/projects/skube/` and Andrew Spitz's website at `http://www.soundplusdesign.com/?p=5516`.

Chorus

Chorus is a kinetic installation by United Visual Artists (UVA), a London-based art and design practice. UVA's work crosses many disciplines, including sculpture, architecture, live performance, moving image, and installation. The group has a reputation for creating visually stunning projects that push the boundaries of all those disciplines.

Chorus (shown in Figure 9-2) uses sound, light, and motion with dramatic effect and is an excellent example of how Arduino can play a role in huge installations as well as tiny prototypes. The installation is made up of eight tall black pendulums swinging back and forth, simultaneously emitting light and sound. Spectators can walk underneath the pendulums, immersing themselves in the performance, as "the rhythm of the work moves between chaos and unison." Each pendulum has its own score, composed by Mira Calix, which can be heard when the audience gets near enough.

Figure 9-2:
Chorus in
full swing.

How it works

In this project, an Arduino is used not only for light and sound but also the motion of the pendulums. The swing of each pendulum is controlled by an electric motor mounted on a reduction gearbox. This motor can be controlled with a relay circuit, allowing the Arduino to affect this huge mechanical object. Each pendulum has two custom circuit boards, each with 50 LEDs to provide the light for the piece and one speaker mounted in the base of the pendulum, both of which are controlled by the Arduino. The Arduino itself is controlled by custom software that is constantly sending and receiving data to make sure that the pendulums are coordinated at the right moments to coincide with the score that is playing.

This project shows that you can use Arduino to great effect when combined with an understanding of other disciplines, such as art, mechanical engineering, and architecture. On their own, each of the elements of this project is relatively simple: controlling a motor; controlling an LED; playing a melody. The real challenge is when the scale of each of these increases. Controlling high-powered motors requires knowledge of loads and mechanics; controlling lots of LEDs requires an understanding of controlling higher voltage and current; and playing high-quality sound requires specific hardware. Chapter 13 introduces you to shields that can make a lot of functions, similar to those used in Chorus, a lot easier to achieve with your Arduino. Increasing the scale of your project in either size of the hardware or the number of outputs can be a challenge, but Chapters 14 and 15 walk you through some of the issues you face to make everything more manageable.

Further reading

You can find the project page at UVA's website: `http://www.uva.co.uk/work/chorus-wapping-project#/0`. There is also an excellent paper by Vince Dziekan that looks at both UVA's working practice and the Chorus project in detail: `http://fibreculturejournal.org/wp-content/pdfs/FCJ-122Vince%20Dziekan.pdf`.

Push Snowboarding

Push Snowboarding is a collaborative project between Nokia and Burton that aimed to visualize all the data about your snowboarding run that you usually wouldn't see. A company called Vitamins Design Ltd was contacted by the creative agency Hypernaked to design and build a set of wireless sensors to communicate with a mobile phone in the snowboarder's pocket. Vitamins was founded by Duncan Fitzsimons, Clara Gaggero, and Adrian Westaway, who dub themselves a "design and invention studio." They are located in London where they develop and make products, experiences, concepts, and systems for their clients. They have worked on a variety of projects, which is best described in their own words, having "worked on fashion catwalks and in operating theatres . . . with pro snowboarders and factory workers . . . for experimental theatre as well as techno-phobic pensioners."

For the snowboarding project, Vitamins designed a set of 3D printed sensor boxes (as shown in Figure 9-3) to measure galvanic skin response, heart rate, balance, 3D motion, position, geographical location, speed, and altitude. This data was then layered over a live video of the snowboarding run to show the links between different situations and the physical response of the snowboarder. This project is an excellent example of making well-finished Arduino products that are closer to bespoke products than prototypes.

Courtesy of Vitamins Design Ltd

Figure 9-3:
Snow-
boarding
sensors in
bespoke
sensor
boxes.

How it works

Each sensor is in a waterproof enclosure with a power button. When switched on, the Arduino talks wirelessly to the smartphone, communicating whatever data it finds. From there, the smartphone, with its superior processing power, crunches the numbers and compiles the data to present the snowboard run visually to the snowboarder.

The first challenge of this project is the size. Many sensors can be tiny, but the Arduino itself creates quite a big footprint, and if a snowboarder were wearing several sensor boxes, the data would be useless if the boxes were obstructing his or her movement. For this reason, each sensor box has an Arduino Pro Mini, which is wafer thin and only 18mm x 33mm. The same is true for the power source, which is provided by a rechargeable lithium battery, the same kind that is found in model aircraft and even smartphones. The project uses a variety of sensors: pressure sensors on the feet to judge balance; inertial measurement units (IMU), also referred to as degrees of freedom sensors, which are used to find the 3D orientation of the snowboarder;

galvanic skin-response sensors to monitor sweat levels of the snowboarder; and a heart rate monitor to track the snowboarder's BPM.

This data is sent back to the phone wirelessly using a Bluetooth module, located in each sensor box. The Bluetooth module is small, has a reliable, secure connection, and will reliably work over the short distance between the sensor box and the phone in the snowboarder's pocket. The gathered data can then be combined with other data, such as GPS, that can be gathered by the phone and then formatted by custom software on the phone.

Each of the sensors in this project is available from most online Arduino-related shops, along with examples and tutorials of how you can integrate them into your own project. The execution of this project is what makes it a great example for aspiring Arduin-ists. The combination of sensors provides a wealth of information to snowboarders that could be used to improve their technique or rate their performance in different ways. In addition, these products have been made to survive in extremely tough environments. The electronics are carefully packaged away so that they are accessible but located behind a tough case to protect from impact, and they're carefully padded to be protected from shock. There is even a damp course to trap any moisture that may get in.

Further reading

You can find more details about the project on the Vitamins website at `http://vitaminsdesign.com/projects/push-snowboarding-for-nokia-burton/`.

Baker Tweet

Baker Tweet is a project by Poke that tweets the latest freshly baked goods from the Albion Café as they come out of the oven. Poke is a creative company based in London and New York that specializes in all things digital. The project resulted from an assignment Poke London was given to put the newly opened Albion Café on the map. It proposed a "magical box" that allowed the café to announce its freshly baked goods using Twitter so that the locals would know when to visit to get the freshest bread, croissants, and buns. You can see a picture of the Baker Tweet device in Figure 9-4, or pop in to the café if you're in the neighborhood!

Figure 9-4:
Baker
Tweet in
the Albion
Bakery.

Courtesy of Poke London

How it works

The "magical box" that produces Twitter messages has a simple interface consisting of a dial, a button, and an LCD screen. The dial is used to select the freshly baked item to be tweeted, and the tweet is displayed on the LCD screen. After it finds the correct item, the pushbutton sends the tweet and the user is given feedback on the LCD when the tweet is successfully sent. This simple interface is ideal for a busy café, requiring very little time for the online status to be updated. To have new items added, the project uses an easy-to-use web interface that updates the list.

At the heart of this project is an Arduino that communicates with the Internet. This can be accomplished either with a wired Ethernet connection, using the Arduino Ethernet shield, or wirelessly, using a Linksys Wi-Fi adapter. The dial provides an analog input; the button, and a digital input. When they combine with the LCD screen, they create a user interface for easily moving through the list and sending tweets. The prototype is encased within a sturdy enclosure to prevent dough and floury hands from damaging the circuit.

This project shows a great application for Arduino that performs the often time-consuming activity of updating an online status quickly and easily. The prototype is also built to suit its environment, being robust enough to survive constant use with stainless steel inputs. It's also easy to clean considering the messy bakery environment. The complexity of this project lies in the communication with the Internet, which for the more web savvy of you may be an area of interest, allowing your physical project to send data to the World Wide Web and vice versa.

Further reading

You can find much more information on the Baker Tweet site at `http://www.bakertweet.com`) and the Poke London projects page at `www.pokelondon.com/portfolio/bakertweet`. Also, take a look at a few excellent prototyping photos that show the development of the project from breadboard to bakery (`http://flickr.com/photos/aszolty/sets/72157614293377430/`).

The National Maritime Museum's Compass Lounge and Compass Card

The Compass Lounge was developed as part of a new wing of the National Maritime Museum in London. London-based design studio Kin designed and developed the interactive areas of the Compass Lounge, which used a number of Arduino projects behind the scenes to allow the public to interact with the digital archive of the museum as well as the physical pieces on display.

A set of digital plan chests (plan chests are large drawers that usually store large prints, blueprints or paperwork) allow visitors to browse the museum's online archive and access the most popular items in high resolution. When the plan chest is opened, a large touch screen is activated, and the visitor can browse items on display. While the visitors are browsing, a hidden LED display lights up through the wallpaper (as shown in Figure 9-5), displaying the reference number of the current item so that it can be found in the physical archive.

Another aspect of the Arduino-powered part of this project is the Compass Card system. Each visitor is given a card to use to collect items from all over the museum. Next to certain items are collection points where the card is scanned to collect the item digitally and stamped to leave a physical mark on the card to show the visitors journey through the museum. Visitors can browse their collected items in the compass lounge or at home in a browser.

Figure 9-5:
The hidden
LED display
lights up
from under-
neath the
wallpaper.

How it works

The plan chests use a couple of simple Arduino projects to complement the digital content displayed on the large touch screens.

The first part of the Arduino is used to activate the screens when they are opened. If the screens are left on throughout the day when not in use, the image can often be burned into the screen, leaving shadows when the content is changed. Setting the background to black when the plan chest is closed reduces this "screen burn" and extends the lifetime of the monitors. This result is accomplished by a tiny microswitch on the back of each drawer — no different from the setup for the Button sketch in Chapter 7. Whenever the button is pressed, a character is sent over the serial port to tell the monitor to go black. This sort of communication is covered in Chapter 8.

Above the plan chests is a hidden LED display made up of rows of LEDs aligned in a grid. These rows consist of the same addressable LED ribbon as described in Chapter 15, with some clever coding to display the appropriate LEDs when letters need to be displayed. The letters are sent over the serial port as a string from the custom software that displays the images so that the correct number appears with the correct image. Because the LEDs are so bright, they can shine through the fabric wallpaper when on and remain hidden when not. This is an excellent example of using a premade product in a different arrangement to suit the purpose.

The compass cards are also a great example of using (relatively) old and existing technologies in a new and interesting way. The compass cards themselves use barcodes to know which card is being scanned. This returns a number to the Arduino that can be forwarded to a central server that coordinates the barcode number and the scanner number to identify where the card has been scanned and by who. All this information is sent over the Ethernet to a server using an Ethernet shield, where the information can be collated and outputted as needed. This is a great example of using Arduinos to do the relatively complicated task of relaying back data over a network without the need for computers at every collection point. This scenario not only cuts the cost of data transfer down but also makes the operation of the network easier because an Arduino requires no startup or shutdown procedures. This digital system works alongside a physical stamping system to mark the cards with an embosser, which makes an impression into the card when the lever is pushed (the inside of the compass card collection point can be seen in Figure 9-6).

Figure 9-6:
A look inside the compass card collection points.

Courtesy of Kin

This collection of projects gives a great example of how many applications you can bring together to create an experience, providing many different forms of interaction and feedback. It's also a great example of an extreme-use case for Arduino. Many projects, prototypes, or installations show that Arduino can work, but it is often regarded unreliable and seen as a temporary solution rather than a long-term one. In this case, the museum demands a reliable and robust solution, and this project shows that Arduino is more than capable of the task when used correctly.

Further reading

You can find much more information as well as illustrations on the Kin project page at http://kin-design.com/project.php?id=147 and on the National Maritime Museum website at http://www.rmg.co.uk/visit/exhibitions/compass-lounge/.

The Good Night Lamp

The Good Night Lamp is an Internet-connected family of lamps founded by Alexandra Dechamps-Sonsino. Each family is made up of a Big Lamp and numerous Little Lamps. When the Big Lamp is on, the Little Lamps that are connected turn on as well, wherever they are in the world. They allow loved ones to remain in touch with each other by simply going about their daily routine, without actively using any application. The Good Night Lamp is currently in development using Arduino as the basis for the prototypes. A set of lamps appears in Figure 9-7.

Figure 9-7:
Whenever the Big Lamp is turned on, the Little Lamp turns on as well, wherever it is in the world.

Courtesy of Good Night Lamp Ltd

How it works

The system for the preproduction prototypes of the Good Night Lamp is relatively simple. The Big Lamp is a functional light that is operated with a pushbutton, similar to the ButtonChangeState example in Chapter 11. It illuminates the light and sends the id number of the lamp and state of the light to a web server using an Arduino Wi-Fi Shield.

Somewhere else, maybe on the other side of the world, the Little Lamps download this state using the same Wi-Fi Shield and relay it to all the Little Lamps that are linked to it. If a Big Lamp is on, any Little Lamps that are paired with it are also turned on.

The lamps themselves are high-power LED bulbs running off 12V and requiring 0.15 amps for the Little Lamps and 0.4 amps for the Big Lamp. These are ideal for the high brightness needed for functional lamps and require a transistor circuit to run them, the same as the one explained in Chapter 8.

This project is a great example of using Arduino to produce a prototype of a product with relatively complex behavior. Using Arduino and other tools enable you to develop the electronics inside a product to reliably demonstrate its behaviour.

Further reading

If you would like to read more about the Good Night Lamp, go to the product home page at `http://goodnightlamp.com`.

Little Printer

Little Printer (shown in Figure 9-8) is a miniature home printer developed by Berg, a design consultancy based in London. Using your smartphone, you can manage content from the web to print all sorts of information to create your own personal newspaper. In between your phone and the web is BERG Cloud, which does all the heavy lifting. You can access BERG Cloud by smartphone to send content to your Little Printer and potentially future devices to come. Little Printer is built with custom hardware and software but was originally prototyped using Arduino.

Figure 9-8:
A Little
Printer
ready to
print
whatever
data
you'd like.

How it works

The Little Printer is made up of several parts, starting with the printer itself. This is a thermal printer, similar to those used to print shopping receipts. Thermal printers communicate over serial, so with the right code, it's possible to talk directly to a device like an Arduino. Adafruit stocks one such printer that is easy to integrate into your own Arduino projects (go to https://www.adafruit.com/products/597).

The printer itself is powered but talks wirelessly to the BERG Cloud Bridge. This is a small device that handles all data in a way similar to your home router. Data is then sent and received using a wired Internet connection, the same as that used on the Arduino Ethernet shield.

In early prototypes, XBee wireless modules — the same as those used on the Arduino Wireless Shield — handled communication between the Little Printer and the BERG Cloud Bridge.

Much of the complexity of this product is handled in the BERG Cloud, where data is gathered, sorted, and then sent to the printer as requested.

The Little Printer is a great example of a product that has used Arduino to develop and refine the idea, before being developed further into a product with its own custom hardware. It also shows that it is possible for your Arduino project to make use of the abundance of data on the Internet.

Further reading

To find out more about the Little Printer and even order one, head over to the BERG Cloud home page at `http://bergcloud.com`.

Flap to Freedom

Flap to Freedom was a game by ICO, a London-based design consultancy created as part of the V&A Village Fete, described by the V&A as a "contemporary take on the British Summer Fete." It took the form of a game where two players would race, head-to-head, to help a chicken to escape from its battery farm (as shown in Figure 9-9). If a player flaps his arms, the chicken does also, but if he flaps too quickly, the chicken tires out. Each race was timed and put on the "pecking order" leader board to determine the winner.

Figure 9-9: Chicken run!

Reproduced by permission of ICO Design Printers Ltd

How it works

For the Arduino-related project, the existing toy chickens used in this race were taken apart and given new custom circuits that communicated wirelessly with software on a computer. The circuits inside the chickens were remade to give an Arduino control of the various motors that moved the wings, beak, and feet. These were each told what to do using wireless modules, similar to the XBee modules on the Arduino wireless shield, which communicated with a piece of custom software on a computer.

The software used was openFrameworks. Using a hidden webcam, the program analysed people's movements to determine how fast the chickens should waddle and then sent the appropriate signal to each chicken.

This is an extremely fun and engaging application for Arduino. It allows people of all ages to play a game and have instant physical feedback from the toy chickens as well as elevates the toys to a new level. This example of hacking existing toys to give them a different use can also apply to other products.

Further reading

You can find much more to read on the ICO project page at `http://www.icodesign.co.uk/project/V%26A%3A+Flap+to+Freedom+Environment`. Benjamin Tomlinson and Chris O'Shea worked on technical side of the project; for more of a technical description, go to Chris O'Shea's project page at `http://www.chrisoshea.org/flap-to-freedom`.

Chapter 10

Soldering On

- -

- -

In previous chapters, I cover in great detail how to assemble circuits on a breadboard. If you read those chapters, you most likely already have a few ideas that build on or combine a few of the basic examples, so you may be asking, "What do I do next?"

This chapter takes you through the process, or art, of soldering. You find out the ins and outs of all the tools that you need to get your project ready for the real world. No more precariously balanced breadboards or flailing wires. From this point on, you can know what you need to solder circuit boards that last.

Understanding Soldering

Soldering is a technique for joining metals. By melting metal with a much lower melting point than those you're joining, you can link pieces of metal together to form your circuit. Mechanical joints are great for prototyping, allowing you to change your mind and quickly change your circuit, but after you're sure of what you're making, it's time to commit.

You use a soldering iron or solder gun to melt solder, a metal alloy (mixture of metals) with a low melting point, and apply it to the joint. When the solder has cooled around the pieces that are being connected, it forms a secure chemical bond rather than a mechanical bond. This is a far superior way to fix components in place, and bonded areas can still be melted and resoldered, if needed.

But why do you need to mess with soldering at all? Picture this: You have your circuit on a breadboard and you're ready to use it, but every time you do, the wires fall out. You could persevere and keep replacing the wires, but every time you do, you take the chance of replacing the wrong wire and damaging the Arduino or yourself.

The best solution is to make a soldered circuit board that's robust and can survive in the real world. The benefit of the solderless breadboard is that it allows you to quickly and easily build and change your circuit, but after you know that it works, you need to start soldering to keep it intact.

Creating your own circuit board is also an opportunity to refine your circuit by making circuit boards that fit the components. After you know what you want to do, the process of miniaturization can start and you're eventually left with a circuit board that takes up only the required space and no more.

Gathering What You Need for Soldering

Before you dive in to soldering, make sure that you have what you need to get the job done. Read on to find out more.

Creating a workspace

For your soldering adventures, what you need above all is a good workspace. Having a good workspace can make all the difference between a successful project and hours spent on your hands and knees, swearing at cracks in the floorboards. A large desk or workbench would be perfect, but even the kitchen table, if clear, will work. Because you're dealing with hot soldering irons and molten metal, it's a good idea to cover the surface of the table with something you don't mind damaging to prevent permanent damage to your favorite table. A cutting mat, piece of wood, or piece of cardboard will do fine for this purpose.

Your workspace should be well lit as well. Always make sure that you have ample daylight by day and a good work light at night to help find those tiny components.

For soldering, it's also good to have easy access to a power source. If your soldering iron functions at a fixed temperature and with a short lead connected directly to a plug, it can be especially important to have a plug nearby. If you overstretch your lead, you run the risk of having the iron pulled off the table and burning anything it touches. A table top power strip or multi-plug is the best solution to this problem because it will provide power for your laptop, your lamp, and your soldering iron.

A comfortable chair is always important. Also remember to stand up every half hour or so to prevent back cramp. You can easily get drawn into soldering and forget what a horrible posture you're in.

Solder fumes, although not lethal, are not good for your lungs, so make every attempt to avoid breathing them in. Always work in a well ventilated area. It's also advisable to work with lead-free solder, as mentioned later in this section.

If you're working at home and are under pressure from other people in your house to not cover every surface with bits of metal, designate a soldering surface. This could be a rigid, wooden surface that can fit all your kit on it and can be moved, neatly packed away, or covered when not in use. This arrangement saves you the chore of unboxing and packing up every time you want to solder and keeps everyone else happy as well.

Choosing a soldering iron

The most important tool for soldering is, obviously, a soldering iron or solder station. You have a huge variety to choose from, but they are generally divided into four types: fixed temperature; portable; temperature-controlled; and complete solder stations. I describe each type in the following sections and provide a rough price from my local retailers to give you an idea of the cost. When you have an idea of what you're looking for, it's always best to shop around locally to see what deals you can find. If you're lucky, you may even find some high-quality second-hand gear on eBay!

Fixed-temperature soldering iron

Fixed-temperature irons (see an example in Figure 10-1) are normally sold as just an iron on a piece of mains cable with a plug at the other end. They are usually sold with a sponge and a very flimsy piece of bent metal as a stand. Others that are slightly better have a plastic stand with a place to put your sponge and a decent spring-like holster for your iron.

Fixed-temperature irons are adequate but offer no control over the temperature of your iron. They are sold with a power rating or wattage, which is of very little help to most people. On these fixed-temperature irons, a higher wattage means a higher temperature, although that can vary wildly from manufacturer to manufacturer. This variation can cause trouble with more delicate components as you progress because a high temperature is quickly conducted and melts integrated circuits and plastic components.

A quick study of the Maplin website (a U.K. retailer for hobby electronics; U.S. equivalent is RadioShack) shows a 12W, 15W, 18W, 25W, 30W, and 40W, which could cover a range of approximately 400 degrees F to 750 degrees F. The difficulty is in finding an iron that is hot enough so that it heats the part that you want to heat quickly and allows you to melt the solder before the heat spreads. For this reason, a low-temperature iron can often do more damage than a higher temperature one. If you go too high, you encounter other problems, such as having the tips erode faster and running a higher risk of overheating parts.

If you want to go with a fixed-temperature iron, my best advice is to pick a midrange iron to start with. I recommend a 25W iron as a good starter. This costs in the region of $22.50 (£15) from Maplin.

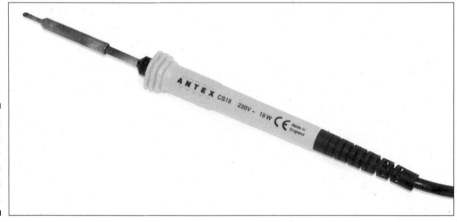

Figure 10-1:
A basic
fixed-
temperature
soldering
iron.

Portable soldering iron

Portable irons do away with cables and electricity in favor of gas power. They burn butane gas, which is more commonly known as lighter fuel, to maintain their heat. They have a wattage rating to allow comparison with other irons, but unlike the fixed-temperature ones described in the previous section, this rating indicates the maximum temperature, which can be lowered by use of a valve. The flames burn around the edge of the iron, which can make them awkward to use on precise joints, so I recommend using a portable iron only if necessary.

A portable iron (shown in Figure 10-2) is great for tight situations when an extension lead just won't reach, but it's a bit too expensive and wasteful to be used often. It's also considered a lot more dangerous than conventional irons by most airport security because of the use of gas. So if you're planning on doing any soldering abroad, take an electric iron.

Butane soldering irons vary in price, but you can usually find them in the range of $45 to $90 (£30 to £60) from Maplin. You also need to buy additional butane refill cans for $7.50 (£5) each, so bear this in mind.

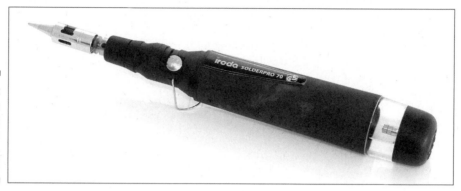

Figure 10-2:
A butane soldering iron. Watch those eyebrows!

Temperature-controlled soldering iron

A temperature-controlled soldering iron, shown in Figure 10-3, is preferable to the fixed-temperature variety because it gives you more control at a reasonable price. This increase in control can make all the difference between melting and burning. This type of soldering iron should have a wattage rating, but it will be the maximum power possible. For this type of iron, a higher wattage is preferable because it should give you a better range of higher temperatures.

Figure 10-3:
A temperature-controlled soldering iron.

A temperature control dial allows you to scale your temperature range up or down as needed. The difference between this type of temperature control and the control you have when using more accurate solder stations is that you have temperature control but no reading of the current temperature. Most temperature-controlled irons have a color wheel indicating warm to hot, so a bit of trial and error may be necessary to get just the right temperature.

You can get an affordable temperature-controlled soldering iron from Maplin for around $30 (£20). Because you have more control over the temperature of the iron, you have greater control and more longevity than a fixed-temperature iron gives you.

Solder stations

A solder station is something to aspire to. After you gain some experience (and can justify the expense), a solder station is what you'll want. It is usually made up of an iron, a stand or cage for the iron, a temperature display, a dial or buttons for temperature adjustment, and a tray for a sponge. It can also include various other accessories for de-soldering or reworking, such as a hot air gun or vacuum pickup tool, but these are generally for more professional applications and not immediately necessary.

You can find many available brands of solder stations, but one of the most reputable and widely used is Weller (see Figure 10-4). Of that company's stations, I recommend the WES51 (120V AC), the WESD51 (120V AC), or the WESD51D (240V AC). My WES51 is still performing excellently after four years of use. Note that the 120V irons need a transformer to step the voltage down in countries that use 240V AC; the transformer can often be heavier than the iron itself!

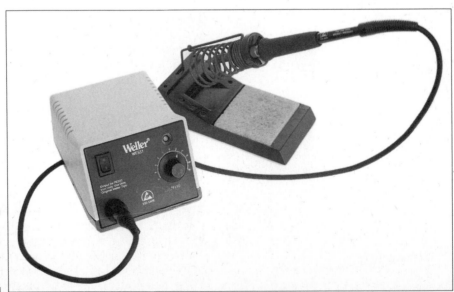

Figure 10-4:
A Weller
solder
station.

Before using a Weller solder station, I owned a cheap Maplin temperature-controlled soldering iron that did very well for a number of years. As I cover in more detail later in this chapter, the best way to maintain and get the most out of your iron is to use it correctly. Remove any melted solder from the tip using the sponge, reapply fresh solder before using it, and leave a little melted solder on the tip before replacing it.

Regardless of which iron you buy, I also recommend buying a few spare tips because tips eventually degrade. You'll find a vast variety of tips for different purposes, too, so it's good to have a selection to cover a variety of needs.

Solder

Solder is what you use to join your circuits. Although many different types of solder are used with different combinations of metals, they commonly fall into two categories: lead and leadfree. Many people I know prefer lead solder, finding it easier to work with. This might be the case because it has a lower melting point, meaning that your iron can be cooler and less likely to damage components.

Lead poisoning has been known about for a long time, but only relatively recently have attitudes about using it begun to change. Lead pipes were switched to copper as recently as the 1980s, and the use of lead solder in consumer electronics was addressed in 1996, when and the Restriction of Hazardous Substances Directive (RoHS) and the European Union Waste Electrical and Electronic Equipment Directive (WEEE) addressed use and disposal of certain materials in electronics.

You commonly find RoHS on components that comply with their guidelines, which should, therefore, be better for the environment when disposed of. Commercially, U.S. and European companies enjoy tax benefits for using lead-free solder (shown in Figure 10-5), but lead is still widely used in the rest of the world. Steven Tai, a colleague of mine, visited China to complete a project we were working on. When he asked where he could buy lead-free solder, he was laughed at outright because lead-free solder was not only was unheard of in most cases but not even available! For the more conscientious Arduin-ists, most electronics supplier and shops offer lead-free solder that contain other metals such as tin, copper, silver, and zinc. From my experience, lead-free solder works just fine for any Arduino projects, so if you want to do your bit for the environment and avoid using lead in your work, please do!

Another variety of solder is flux-cored solder. Flux is used to reduce oxidization, the reaction on the surface of a metal when it reacts with the air (oxygen), as with rust on an iron anchor. Reducing the oxidization allows a better, more reliable connection on your solder joint and allows the solder to flow more easily and fill the joint. Some solders have flux in the core of the solder, dispensing flux to the joint as the solder is melted. You sometimes see smoke as you melt your solder; in most cases, the smoke is from the flux burning off. You can be sure that you have flux core if, when you cut the solder, you see a black center surrounded by a tube of solder.

Figure 10-5:
Lead-free
solder.

Always work in a well-ventilated area and avoid breathing the solder fumes no matter which solder you are using. Solder fumes are not good for you, and neither is eating solder. Always wash your hands and face thoroughly after soldering. Sometimes the flux in solder can spit, so wear clothes that are not precious — and definitely use eye protection.

Third hand (helping hand)

Sometimes you just don't have enough hands to hold the fiddly electronics that you're trying to solder. It would be great to have someone nearby with asbestos hands to hold the tiny red-hot pieces of metal, but failing that, you can use a little device known as a third hand (a.k.a. helping hand; shown in Figure 10-6). A third hand is a set of crocodile clips on an adjustable arm. You can arrange the clips to help you get your component, circuit board, and solder into place. A third hand costs around $22.50 (£15) and can be extremely useful for holding circuit board at an angle or holding components together while you work on the soldering. The drawback is that setting it up can be extremely tricky. If you're doing lots of solder joints, you may spend a lot of time loosening, adjusting, and retightening. If you do purchase a third hand, make sure that the parts are all metal. Plastic parts, such as the grips on the vices, will not stand up to much use.

Figure 10-6:
Give the
man a hand!

Adhesive putty

A good alternative to a third hand is adhesive putty, such as Bostik's Blu-Tack, UHU's White Tack, or Locktite's Fun-Tak. Rather than use a mechanical device to grip a component or circuit board, you can use the adhesive putty to hold the objects you're soldering in place on one side of the board, leaving you free to work on the other side of the board without the components or circuit board moving. You can also use the adhesive putty to tack your work to your work surface, stopping it from moving around the surface as you solder. After the solder joints are done, you remove the adhesive putty, which you can reuse. Note that putty goes extremely soft if it is heated and takes a while to return to its usual tackiness. After it cools, you can roll the ball of putty along the circuit board to remove any remaining bits.

Wire cutters

A good pair of wire cutters or snips is invaluable. Many are available that are capable of cutting wire, but try to get the most versatile pair. Many pairs of wire cutters have a rounded, claw-like shape. These are tough but can be difficult to use when cutting in confined spaces or pinpointing a specific wire. Precision wire cutters have a more precise, pointed shape that is far more useful for the vast majority of electronics work.

Note that wire cutters are good for soft metal such as copper but do not stand up to tougher metals such as paper clips or staples. Figure 10-7 shows a pair of pointed wire cutters.

Figure 10-7: Pointed wire cutters are good for getting into and out of tight spots.

Wire strippers

To connect wires to your project, you need to strip back the plastic insulation. You can do this stripping with a knife if you're careful or don't value your finger tips, but the quickest, easiest, and safest way to strip a wire is to use a purpose-made wire stripper. There are two kinds of wire strippers: manual and mechanical (see Figure 10-8). Manual wire strippers are like clippers but have semicircular notches made to various diameters. When the wire stripper is closed on wire, it cuts just deep enough to cut through the plastic sheath but stops before it hits the wire. Mechanical wire strippers work with a trigger action to remove the insulation on the wire without any need to pull on the wire.

Mechanical wire stripers are a great time saver but can be less reliable in the long run because the mechanisms are more likely to fail than are those in the simple manual ones.

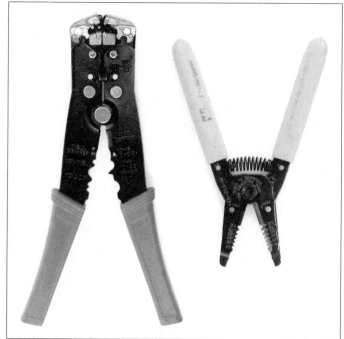

Figure 10-8:
Manual
and
mechanical
wire
strippers.

Needle-nosed pliers

Needle-nose pliers, as with a solderless breadboard, are a great help for getting to those hard to reach places. With soldering they're especially useful, because they spare your fingers from any excess heat from the soldering. I cover needle-nosed pliers in more detail in Chapter 5.

Multimeter

A multimeter is a great help for testing your circuits. When you're soldering connections, the continuity-testing function can be a great help for verifying that the solder joints are as they should be and are connected to the right places. See Chapter 5 for more about working with a multimeter.

When testing the continuity, always unplug any power supplies connected to your circuit to avoid false bleeps.

Solder sucker

Everyone makes mistakes, and they can be more difficult to undo when you're dealing with hot metal. One tool to keep handy for fixing mistakes is a solder sucker, shown in Figure 10-9, or de-soldering gun. Each of these tools is a pneumatic pump that sucks molten solder straight off the surface of a circuit board. Most have a piston that can be pressed down and will lock when all the air is pressed out. When you hit the trigger, a spring pushes the piston back out and sucks any molten solder into the piston chamber. Next time you press the piston down, it pushes out any solder that was removed. Using this type of tool takes a bit of practice because you need to heat the solder with your soldering iron in one hand and suck it away with the sucker in the other.

Figure 10-9:
A solder sucker can save your project.

Solder wick

Another method of removing solder is to use solder wick (see Figure 10-10), also known as copper braid or de-soldering wire. Solder wick is a copper wire that has been braided, and you buy it in reels. It provides lots of surface area for solder to grip into, to remove it from other surfaces. Place the braid on the joint or hole that has too much solder, and hold your soldering iron on top of it to heat the solder wick. Apply some pressure, and the solder continues to melt and fill the gaps in between the braids of the copper wire. Remove the wick and the soldering iron together, and the solder should be cleared. If it's not, repeat as necessary. After the solder is cleared, you can cut off the used solder wick and dispose of it.

Do not pull the solder wick away if the solder has cooled. If the solder has cooled, the wick is attached to the board and you risk pulling off the metal pads on your board, making it unusable.

Figure 10-10: Solder wick is great for those more stubborn mistakes.

Solder suckers and solder wick are both equally effective at removing solder, but they are each suited to different situations and require an element of dexterity and skill to use. If you're worried about overheating components, a solder sucker is more suitable; if you can't remove all the solder with the sucker or can't get close enough to the components with it, the solder wick may be a better option. I advise getting both to prepare yourself for any situation.

Equipment wire

Equipment wire is the general name given to electronics wire. It's the same as the jump wires you may have in your kit but is unfinished. You buy it in reels. Equipment wire can be either single-core or multicore. Single-core wire is made up of one solid piece of wire and is malleable, so it holds its shape if bent, but if it is bent too much, it snaps. Multicore is made up of many fine wires and can withstand a great deal more flexing than single core, but does not keep its shape if bent. To use the equipment wire, you need to cut it to length and bare the ends of the insulation to reveal the wire underneath.

Wire also comes in different diameters, indicated with numbers such as 7/0.2 or 1/0.6. In this format, the first digit is the number of wires in the bundle and the second is the diameter of those individual wires. So 7/0.2 is a bundle of 7 wires, each measuring 0.2 mm, making it multicore; 1/0.6 is one individual, single-core wire with a diameter of 0.6mm.

When you're starting out, it can be difficult to know what to invest in because wire is cheaper when bought by the reel but you don't want to be stuck with wire that isn't fit for purpose. As a general guideline, I have found that multicore wire is the most versatile and robust for most applications. The diameter 7/0.2 is a good diameter; it should fit most PCB holes. I also recommend having three colors — red, black, and a color to signify your signal wires. With three reels of this type and size, you should be able to complete most projects. Some hobby electronic shops also supply lengths in various colors, such as the ones shown in Figure 10-11, by Oomlout.

Figure 10-11:
Equipment wire in various colors.

Staying Safe while Soldering

With a few simple precautions, you can easily solder safely. Remember that soldering is not dangerous if you take proper care — but it can be if you don't. Please keep the tips in the following sections in mind whenever you're soldering.

Handling your soldering iron

A soldering iron is safe if used correctly but is still potentially dangerous. The iron has two ends, the hot end and the handle. Don't hold it by the hot end! The correct way to hold a soldering iron is like a pen, between your thumb and index finder, resting on your middle finger. When you're not using the iron, keeping it in its holster or cage is important. The cage holds the iron safely, helping to dissipate heat and preventing accidental burns.

Keeping your eyes protected

You definitely need to wear proper eye protection when soldering. Solder, especially the flux-cored kind, has a tendency to spit when it's being heated. When you use clippers to neaten up your circuit board, the small bits of metal you cut off often shoot around the room in all directions if they're not held down. Also, if you're working in a group, you need to protect yourself from the person next to you. Safety goggles are relatively inexpensive depending on what amount of comfort that you are looking for, and they're a lot cheaper than eye surgery, so make sure you keep them on.

Working in a ventilated environment

Breathing in fumes of any kind is generally bad for you, so it's important to always solder in a well ventilated environment. Also make sure that you're not working under any smoke alarms because the fumes from soldering can set them off.

Cleaning your iron

Your soldering iron should come with a sponge, which you use to wipe away excess solder. You should dampen the sponge but not use it soaking wet, so make sure to squeeze out the excess water. When you're heating solder, it oxidises on the tip of the iron. If the tip itself oxidizes, it can degrade over time. To prevent oxidizing the tip, leave a blob of solder on the end of the iron while it's in its cage. Doing so makes the blob of solder oxidize rather than the tip, and you just wipe off it off using the sponge the next time you need the iron.

Don't eat the solder!

Although the chemicals and metals in solder are not deadly, they are definitely not healthy for your body. While soldering, you should avoid touching your face and getting solder around your eyes and mouth to prevent irritation. It's also a good idea to wash your hands (and face if needed) after soldering.

Assembling a Shield

The best way to learn soldering is by doing it. Soldering requires learning a great amount of technique, and you develop good technique with practice. In this example, you find out how to assemble an Arduino shield. A *shield* is a specific printed circuit board (PCB) that sits on top of the Arduino to give it a function (you learn more about it in Chapter 13). There are many different shields for different functions that you can plug into your Arduino when you want to use them. This one is the Proto Shield Kit (as shown assembled in Figure 10-12), which is essentially a blank canvas to solder your project onto, after prototyping it on a breadboard. In this example, you see how to assemble the bare minimum of the kit to attach it to your Arduino and then how to build a simple circuit on it.

As with many Arduino kits, you need to assemble this shield yourself. The basic principles of soldering remain the same but may vary in difficulty as you encounter smaller or more sensitive components.

Figure 10-12:
A complete
Proto
Shield.

Laying out all the pieces of the circuit

When assembling a circuit, your first step should always be to lay out all the pieces to check that you have everything you're supposed to have. Your work surface should be clear and have a solid-colored cover to make things easy to find.

Figure 10-13 shows the Arduino Proto Kit laid out in an orderly fashion. It contains:

- 1 row of header pin connectors (40x1)
- 1 header pin head connector (3x2)
- 2 pushbuttons
- 1 red LED
- 1 yellow LED
- 1 green LED
- 5 10K Ohm Resistors 1/4W
- 5 220 Ohm Resistors 1/4W
- 5 1K Ohm Resistors 1/4W

Some kits may ship the PCB only and leave you to choose the headers that are connected. Remember that there is no right or wrong way as long as the assembly suits your purpose.

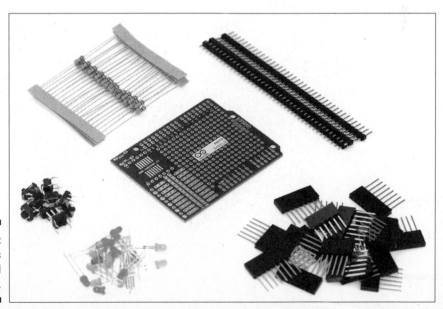

Figure 10-13:
All the parts
of the shield
laid out.

To assemble this shield, you can work from a picture to see the layout of the components, but for more difficult ones, you usually have instructions. In this example, I walk you through the construction of this shield step by step and point out various techniques for soldering along the way

Assembly

To assemble this kit, you need to solder the header pins and the pushbutton. Soldering these pieces allows the shield to sit in the header sockets on your Arduino, extending all the pin connections to the proto shield. Note that some versions of the proto board have header sockets (or stackable headers) rather than header pins. Header sockets have long legs so that they can sit on top of an Arduino in the same way as header pins but also allow sockets for another shield to be placed on top. The benefit of header pins is that your shield is shorter and needs less space for any enclosure. Header sockets are used in the assembled shield shown in Figure 10-12. They are the black sockets that run down either side on the top of the board, with pins extending underneath.

In this example, I use header pins and do not connect the ICSP (In-Circuit Serial Programming) connector, which is the 3x2 connector in the center right of the Uno. The ICSP is used as an alternative for uploading sketches with an external programmer as opposed to the Arduino and is for advanced users.

Header pins

First you will need to cut the header pins to length (Figure 10-14). This kit uses a length of 1 x 40, which is a row of 40 pins that is 1 row deep. Each pin has a notch in the plastic part that can be cut to divide the pins neatly. To secure the shield, you need lengths of 6 (analog in pins), 8 (power pins), 8 (digital pins), and 10 (digital pins). Use your clippers to cut the header pins to the correct length and you should be left with 8 spare pins. (Put these in a box for future use!) The pins should fit exactly because there is a 2.54mm (0.1 inch) pitch between them, which matches the board. You need to look for this same pitch if you are buying header pins of any other connectors separately.

Now that you're clear about where the header pins go, you can solder them in place. In the next section, I talk you through some soldering technique. Have a read through before you start.

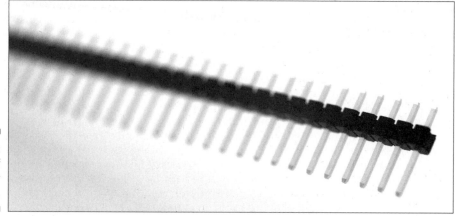

Figure 10-14:
Close up of
the header
pins.

Acquiring Your Soldering Technique

The first step with soldering is to make sure that your components are secure. It's common to try balancing your circuit board on whatever objects are closest to hand to arrange it in an accessible position, but if you do it's destined to fall over at some point, most likely when you have a hot soldering iron in your hand. As mentioned in the "Gathering What You Need for Soldering" section, earlier in this chapter, two good ways to secure your work are to use a third hand or adhesive putty. You can use the crocodile clips on the third hand to grip the plastic of the pins and the circuit board as well, holding them firmly at 90 degrees from one another. Similarly, you can hold the pins at 90 degress and press adhesive putty into the underside to hold them together. You can then press them into a rigid, weighty support to bring the board closer to you. I sometimes use a big reel of solder for the support.

A third way to secure your components might occur to you, and because it's very tempting, I describe it here so that you won't do it! You might think that the perfect way to lay out the pins would be to place them in the Arduino itself (with the long ends sticking into the sockets) and then place the circuit board on top. This approach holds everything at 90 degrees; however, because the pins are designed to connect to the Arduino and conduct electrical current, they can also conduct other things, such as heat. If they conduct the heat of your soldering iron, that heat can be passed through the board to the legs of the very sensitive microcontroller chip and damage it irreparably.

When you have your circuit board supported and ready, you can rotate it to a comfortable working angle, most likely the same angle that your iron is coming from (as shown in Figure 10-15).

Fire up your soldering iron. My Weller WES51 has a temperature range of 35–85 and the units show this as °F x 10, so the real range is 350–850 degrees F! The hotter you set it, the quicker it will melt solder to make joints, but it will also melt everything else faster, such as plastic parts and silicon chips. Always set your iron to the lowest convenient temperature. A good way to test this is to melt some solder. If it's taking a very long time to melt, make sure that you have a good amount of the surface area of the soldering iron's tip in contact with the solder, and if it's still not working, increase the temperature gradually, allowing time for it to get up to temperature. I normally set it to 650 degrees F (340 degrees C), which is hot enough, but not too hot.

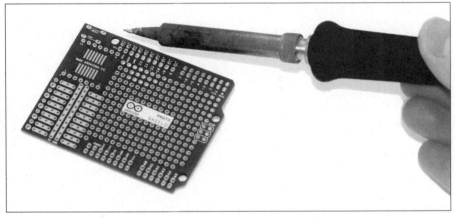

Figure 10-15:
Always arrange your work in a comfortable position.

Some quality soldering irons have a thermostat that tells you when you're up to temperature. The really fancy ones have a digital display. With the cheaper ones, you have to use your best judgment.

While your iron is getting up to temperature, you can wet your sponge. On some irons, the sponge is stuck down for "convenience," but it's particularly inconvenient when you need to wet it. I recommend unsticking it and taking it over to a basin rather than spilling water over your soldering iron and the surrounding area. The sponge should be damp but not full of water. The dampness stops the sponge from burning when you pass your iron across it. If the sponge is too wet, however, it can lower the temperature of the iron and the solder, meaning that the solder hardens or solidifies and can't be removed until it's up to temperature again.

Now you're ready you can start soldering. Follow these steps:

1. **Melt a small amount of solder on the tip of your iron, (called *tinning the tip*); see Figure 10-16.**

   The solder should stick to the edge and smoke. Generally, with a new or well-maintained iron, the solder latches onto the tip with no problem. If it does not stick to the edge of the tip, you may need to try rotating it to find a good patch that isn't oxidized. Failing that, you can use some tip cleaner to remove any layer that's built up. By pressing your hot iron into the tip cleaner and wiping away any build up as it loosens, you can restore your iron to its former glory.

   Tip cleaner is generally quite a nasty, toxic substance, and you should make sure not to ingest or inhale any of it.

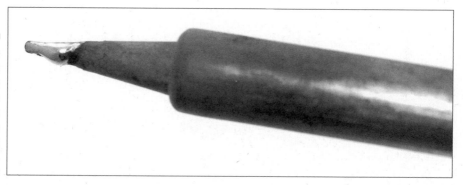

Figure 10-16: Tinning the tip helps to preserve your iron and makes soldering easier.

2. **When you have a blob of solder on your iron, wipe it off on a sponge to reveal a bright metallic tip on your iron.**

   The aim is to apply this freshly tinned edge of your iron (not the point) to the area that you are joining. Using the edge gives you more surface area and allows the joint to heat up quicker. It's also important to note that a variety of tips is available for soldering irons, and if you choose good ones, they are easily interchangeable, allowing you to suit them to different situations. Some are pointed, as in Figure 10-16, but there are also screwdriver tips, chisel tips, and beveled tips to provide different amounts of surface area for different situations.

3. **Starting on the first pin in one of the rows, apply the iron to the metal plate on the circuit board and the pin that is connecting to it.**

   This heats the board and pin, preparing them for the solder.

4. **With your other hand (the one not holding the iron), apply the solder to the point where the iron, the pin, and the metal plate all meet.**

   As the solder is heated, it melts and spreads to fill the gap, sealing the pin and the board together. To apply more solder, press it into the joint where it is melting; to apply less, simply pull it back out. You may need only a few millimeters of solder for small joints.

5. **When it has filled the area, remove the solder, but keep your iron there for a second or two longer.**

   This allows the solder to melt fully and fill any gaps for a solid joint.

6. **Remove your soldering iron by wiping it up the leg of the pin.**

   Any excess solder is directed upward into a point that can be cut off rather than sitting in a blob.

This entire process should take around 2–3 seconds. That probably sounds impossible, but after you get used to the rhythm, it's totally achievable. All it takes is practice.

Following the preceding steps should leave you with a neat, pyramid-shaped solder joint, and the metal pad on the circuit board should be completely covered. If you can see the hole that the pin has come through or have a blob of solder on the pin that is not connected to the circuit board, you need to reapply heat using the soldering iron, and maybe reapply a little solder as well.

After you solder the first pin, it's a good idea to do the pin at the other end of the row. By doing these two, you secure the row in place, and if it is not level or at 90 degrees, you can still straighten the row by heating up the solder at either end. If you find that you have too much solder, first try reapplying heat. Watch as the solder melts, and you should see it filling all the gaps. If you still have too much solder, you can use a solder sucker or copper braid (described in "Gathering What You Need to Solder," earlier in this chapter) to remove any excess and try again.

For examples of well-soldered joints versus bad ones, see the image at http://highfields-arc.co.uk/constructors/info/h2solder.htm.

When you are happy with the row, you can solder every pin in place and repeat this process for each section of header pins. For the pushbutton, simply place it in the position indicated on the top side of the circuit board and it should clip in because of the design of the pushbutton legs. Secure with adhesive putty if necessary and then turn the board over and repeat the same soldering technique as before. When you are done, do one last visual check to make sure that no solder joints are touching. Having two pins connected could cause a short circuit and damage your board, so check carefully. If in doubt, you can use the continuity test function on your multimeter to check consecutive pins. You shouldn't hear any beeps on pins that should not be joined.

Place the shield on top of your Arduino and check that it fits correctly. If it does, you're ready to solder your first circuit, which you find out about next.

Building Your Circuit

After you have a shield to work on (see "Assembling a Shield," earlier in this chapter), you can think about what circuit you want to build on it. Before you actually build that circuit, though, you should do some proper planning to avoid having to undo what you've done, which can be difficult. The best way to start is by prototyping the circuit on a solder-less breadboard. This is quick, easy, and — more important — not permanent. As covered in Chapters 7 and 8, throwing together a circuit and making sure that it works is simple. For this example, I use AnalogInOutSerial example (see Chapter 7) to demonstrate how you can transform a solderless breadboard into a soldered one.

Knowing your circuit

First, recreate the AnalogInOutSerial circuit on the breadboard as shown at the end of Chapter 7. Upload the sketch by choosing File➪Examples➪03. Analog➪AnalogInOutSerial. This should give you an LED that can be faded by twisting the potentiometer.

When you have this circuit working, take a look at the AnalogInOutSerial circuit again on the breadboard. One difference that you can immediately see is that the Proto Shield does not have the same rows and columns as the breadboard, except in one corner. This is specifically for ICs (integrated circuits) or chips, but can in fact be used for anything. The rest of the Proto Shield has individual holes that components can be soldered into. You can connect these with wires to join the various components.

The easiest way to convert the circuit to one that will work on the shield is to look at the circuit diagram. The lines that connect the components can be substituted for real wires and soldered directly to the correct pins. For the potentiometer, you need three wires: 5V, GND, and Analog 0. For the LED and resistor, you need two more: GND and Pin 9. It's always a good idea to draw the circuit first for clarity. It doesn't need to be as neat as the circuit diagram in the examples, but planning your circuit will save a lot of painful desoldering later. As the old carpentry saying goes, *measure twice, cut once* (or in this case, *sketch twice, solder once*).

Notice that the wires all go to holes next to the wire they need to connect with. Because you don't have enough space to comfortably fit the wires and the component legs in one hole, you need to get them close and then bridge the gap using the ends of the wire or the legs of the components.

Laying out your circuit

Now that you've drawn the circuit, you should lay it out so that you know what length to cut your wires. To secure the components to the board, insert them and bend the legs at 45 degrees. They should look something like that shown in Figure 10-17.

Figure 10-17:
An LED
secured
in a circuit
board.

Preparing your wire

You can see that the lengths of wire required are relatively short. If you have solid core wire, you can bend it neatly into shape to sit flat on the circuit board, using your needle-nose pliers. If you have multicore wire, it is easier to do an arc of wire up out of one hole and into the next. Remember to measure or estimate the distance and add a small amount on each end to fit into the hole before you cut your lengths. Strip back the wire and sit it in place to make sure that the length is correct. Note that sometimes the end of multicore wire can become frayed. If this happens, grip it between your thumb and forefinger and twist the end into a point. If you lightly coat the end in solder, you can prevent the wire from unravelling and tin it in preparation for soldering. When you are happy with the length, place the wires to one side.

Soldering your circuit

Now that you have all the components and wires, it's time to solder them in place. Earlier, you bent the component leg at 45 degrees, so the wires should still be hanging on. Because the resistor and LED are next to each other, you can use their legs to connect them, avoiding the use of another wire. Remember to check that your LED is the right way around. If required, use adhesive putty to further secure the components in place and then solder them as with the pin headers.

When all the components are in place, you can solder the wire. Insert the wire and bend to 45 degrees as before. When it is secured, you can solder it in place or bend it further to meet the component legs, bridging the gap as with the resistor and LED. As always, there is no right or wrong in the appearance of your result; it depends how neat you want to be. Some people prefer to wind the wire around the legs of the component to get a good grip; others prefer to join them side by side to get a clean joint. The choice is yours. As long as you have a good connection, you're in good shape.

Cleaning up

When you finish soldering, give the board a good check over for any loose connections. If all seems well, you can start neatening the board. Using your clippers, carefully remove the legs of the components from just above the solder joint, at the top of the pyramid. You can cut lower, but the solder is thicker and you risk tearing the metal contacts off the circuit board, which cannot be fixed. Remember, always hold or cover the piece of metal that you are clipping. If you don't, it can fly a great distance and seriously injure someone.

Using stripboard rather than a PCB

Specially designed shields are made to fit your Arduino perfectly but can often be relatively expensive. Stripboard, or perfboard as it's sometimes known, provides a cheap alternative that is highly versatile. Stripboard is a circuit board with strips of copper and a grid of perforated holes that you can use to lay out your circuit in a similar way as on a breadboard. An example of stripboard appears in the following figure.

The pitch of the holes and the layout of the copper strips can vary. The most useful pitch for Arduino-related applications is the same as the pitch on the Arduino pins, 0.1 inches (2.54mm), because that pitch allows you to build on the layout of your Arduino to make your own custom shields. You can buy stripboard in various arrangements of copper strip as well. It is commonly either long copper columns that run the length of the board or sets of columns three rows deep (usually called tri-board).

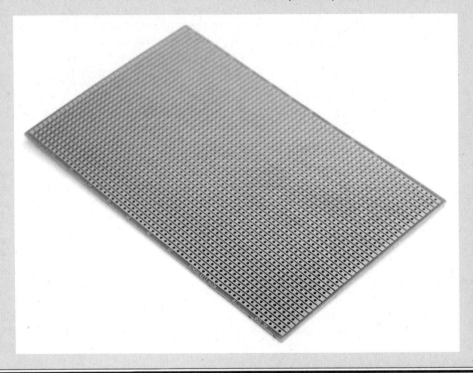

Testing your shield

Now that you have your shield with a completed circuit assembled on it, it's time to plug it in and try it. If everything is working correctly, you should have a neatly packaged dimmer circuit shield resembling something like Figure 10-18.

Figure 10-18: My new dimmer shield, ready to be taken out into the world!

Packaging Your Project

Now that your circuit is no longer at risk of falling apart, it's a good idea to look at protecting it from the outside world by boxing it up.

Enclosures

The simplest way to protect your circuit is by putting it in a box. In electronics terms, such a box is called an enclosure or project box. Generally you find a variety of plastic or metal enclosures in a vast array of shapes and sizes and finishes. The only task is to find the one that's right for you.

Many of the online suppliers (RS, Farnell, DigiKey, and others) have huge lists of possible enclosures, but you can't tell whether it's right without holding it in your hands. Many enclosures have accurate measurements for internal and external dimensions, but even with that there are usually omissions, such as the molded plastic for the screw fixings. My best advice is to find a retail store such as Maplin or Radio Shack and take an Arduino with you to see whether it will fit correctly with enough space for wires and any shields. Now you know what works and what to order next time.

Keep the following considerations in mind when boxing up your project.

- ✔ **The ability to access the USB for code changes.** You may have to unscrew your enclosure to update the code. If this is too time consuming, you may need to drill a hole big enough to plug the USB in from the outside.

- ✔ **Power to run the Arduino.** If your Arduino is not powered by USB, how is it powered? It could be an external power supply that plugs into the power jack, which needs a big enough hole for the plug. You could remove the plug and solder the bare wires to the Vin and Gnd pins if you're looking for something more permanent. Or you could even run it off a battery pack and only open it to charge every week or so.

- ✔ **The ability to access the inputs and outputs.** What use is an LED or a button if it's inside the box? Most projects need some contact with the outside world, if only to tell you that they're still working, and most components are often designed with this need in mind. The lip on an LED means that you can drill a 1.9-inch (5 mm) hole and push the front end through without it going all the way, and if you take the plastic or metal knob off a radio, you see that, too, is just a hole.

Always think carefully about the needs of your circuit before soldering it in place and boxing it up. Examine other cheap electronics around you to see what tricks the industry has been using. You may be amazed to find out that most the remote controls for remote control cars that give you forward, backward, left, and right are just a few simple pushbuttons underneath those complex-looking control sticks.

Wiring

To give you more flexibility with your wiring, consider attaching inputs, outputs, or power to flexible lengths of cable using terminal blocks, which are sometimes also known as connector strips, screw terminals or chocolate blocks ("choc blocks"). By doing this, you can fix the inputs and outputs to the enclosure rather than the circuit board. This approach gives you more flexibility and means that if you drill a hole slightly out of alignment, you won't need to de-solder or re-solder your circuit.

Following is a little more detail on adding wires to your project and selecting terminal blocks. This adds flexibility to your project and makes assembling and disassembling your project a lot easier.

Twisting

When you make wire connectors, I recommend twisting or braiding the wires together. This gives the wires extra strength if pulled on and, as a bonus, looks nice! To twist two wires together, cut them to length and grip one end in a power drill. Hold onto the other end of the two wires with your hand or a vice. Pull the wire taut enough to have no slack, but not too tight. Spin the drill until the wires are neatly twisted together, and you should be left with one twisted wire.

Braiding

If you have three wires, you can braid them in the same way that you braid hair. With three wires in your hand, hold them at one end facing forward. Pass the leftmost wire over the middle and under the rightmost. Keep repeating this process with the new left wire until you have braided the full length. This makes your project more robust and looks extra professional. Note that if you use the same color of wire for all three, you need to use the continuity tester on your multimeter to figure out which is which, so it's advisable to use different colors.

Terminal blocks

Terminal blocks come in a variety of sizes, depending on the amount of current passing through them, and are usually marked with the upper limit that they can maintain. When selecting one for your power supply, always read the current rating and choose a size with a bit of tolerance. If you have a 3A supply, choose a 5A terminal block. When connecting wires, especially multicore wires, you should tin the tip of the wire with a small amount of solder or fold the wire back under the insulation layer so that the screw grips the insulated side. This prevents the screw from cutting any of the strands of wire as it is tightened.

Securing the board and other elements

When you're happy with your cabling and have all the required holes, it's a good idea to secure your items so that they don't rattle around inside the box. To secure your Arduino, screw terminals, or stripboard, you can use Velcro-type tape or hot glue. If you have any loose wires, you can use cable ties to neatly tie them together.

Chapter 11

Getting Clever with Code

As you find different uses and needs for Arduino, you can refine your code to make it more accurate, responsive, and efficient. Also, by thinking about the code in your project, you may be able to avoid or minimize many of the unexpected results that can occur when dealing with physical hardware and the real world. In this chapter, you look at a few sketches that will help you fine-tune your project.

Blinking Better

Blink is most likely the first sketch you encountered. It's a magical moment when that first LED lights up, isn't it? But what if I told you it that it can get even better? The basic blink sketch presented in Chapter 4 performs its task well, with one significant drawback: It can't do anything else while blinking.

Take a look at it again:

```
/*
  Blink
  Turns on an LED on for one second, then off for one second, repeatedly.

  This example code is in the public domain.
*/

// Pin 13 has an LED connected on most Arduino boards.
```

```
// give it a name:
int led = 13;

// the setup routine runs once when you press reset:
void setup() {
  // initialize the digital pin as an output.
  pinMode(led, OUTPUT);
}

// the loop routine runs over and over again forever:
void loop() {
  digitalWrite(led, HIGH);    // turn the LED on (HIGH is the voltage level)
  delay(1000);                // wait for a second
  digitalWrite(led, LOW);     // turn the LED off by making the voltage LOW
  delay(1000);                // wait for a second
}
```

The loops can be summarized this way:

1. Turn the LED on.

2. Wait for a second.

3. Turn the LED off.

4. Wait for a second.

This delay or "waiting" is what can be problematic for a lot of people when they try to integrate the blink sketch with another bit of code. When the sketch uses the delay function, it waits for the amount of time specified (in this case, a second), during which it doesn't do anything else. Effectively, the sketch is twiddling its thumbs.

If you wanted to change something — for example, you wanted the LED to blink only when a light sensor was dark — you might think of writing the code in the loop section something like this:

```
void loop() {

sensorValue = analogRead(sensorPin);

if (sensorValue < darkValue) {
  digitalWrite(led, HIGH);    // turn the LED on (HIGH is the voltage level)
  delay(1000);                // wait for a second
  digitalWrite(led, LOW);     // turn the LED off by making the voltage LOW
  delay(1000);                // wait for a second
        }
}
```

This almost works. When the value threshold for a `darkValue` is crossed, the `if` loop starts and turns the LED on, waits for one second, and then turns it off and waits for one second. But because the sketch is occupied doing this blink for two seconds, the sketch cannot check to see if the light level becomes brighter again until the blink has finished.

The solution is to use a timer rather than pause the program. A timer or counter is like a clock that can be used to time events. For example, the timer can count from 0 to 1,000, and when it reaches 1,000 it can *do something*, and then start counting from 0 again. This can be especially useful for regularly timed events, such as checking a sensor every second — or in this case triggering an LED every second.

Setting up the BlinkWithoutDelay sketch

To complete this project, you need:

- ✔ An Arduino Uno
- ✔ An LED

Place the legs of the LED between pin 13 (long leg) and GND (short leg), as shown in Figures 11-1 and 11-2. This makes it a bit easier to see the blink in action. If you do not have an LED, look for the one fixed to your Arduino marked L. Upload the sketch to the correct serial port to see the LED blinking away as it would with the standard Blink sketch.

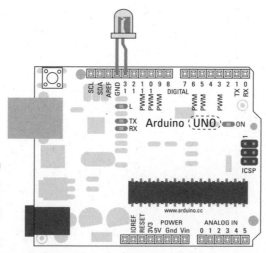

Figure 11-1:
All you need
is an LED in
pin 13.

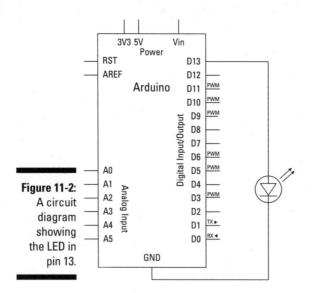

Figure 11-2:
A circuit
diagram
showing
the LED in
pin 13.

Find the BlinkWithoutDelay sketch by choosing File⇨Examples⇨02.Digital⇨
BlinkWithoutDelay and open it.

The complete code for the BlinkWithoutDelay sketch is as follows:

```
/* Blink without Delay

Turns on and off a light emitting diode(LED) connected
         to a digital pin,
         without using the delay() function.  This means that
         other code can run
         at the same time without being interrupted by the LED
         code.

The circuit:
 * LED attached from pin 13 to ground.
 * Note: on most Arduinos, there is already an LED on the
         board that's attached
         to pin 13, so no hardware is needed for this example.


created 2005
by David A. Mellis
modified 8 Feb 2010
by Paul Stoffregen

This example code is in the public domain.


http://www.arduino.cc/en/Tutorial/BlinkWithoutDelay
```

```
 */


// constants won't change. Used here to
// set pin numbers:

// the number of the LED pin
const int ledPin =  13;

// Variables will change:
int ledState = LOW;
// ledState used to set the LED

long previousMillis = 0;
// will store last time LED was updated

// the follow variables is a long because the time,
// measured in miliseconds,will quickly become a bigger
// number than can be stored in an int.
long interval = 1000;
// interval at which to blink (milliseconds)

void setup() {
  // set the digital pin as output:
  pinMode(ledPin, OUTPUT);
}

void loop()
{
  // here is where you'd put code that needs to be
  // running all the time.

  // check to see if it's time to blink the LED; that
  // is, if the difference between the current time and
  // last time you blinked the LED is bigger than the
  // interval at which you want to blink the LED.
  unsigned long currentMillis = millis();

  if(currentMillis - previousMillis > interval) {
    // save the last time you blinked the LED
    previousMillis = currentMillis;

    // if the LED is off turn it on and vice-versa:
    if (ledState == LOW)
      ledState = HIGH;
    else
      ledState = LOW;

    // set the LED with the ledState of the variable:
    digitalWrite(ledPin, ledState);
  }
}
```

This sketch is quite a bit longer than Blink and may seem more confusing, so walking through it one line at a time to see what's happening is a good idea.

Understanding the BlinkWithoutDelay sketch

First, in the declarations, a `const int` is used to set `ledPin` to 13 because it is a constant integer and does not change.

```
// constants won't change. Used here to
// set pin numbers:
const int ledPin = 13;        // the number of the LED pin
```

Next are the variables. `ledState` is set to `LOW` so that our LED starts the sketch in an off state.

```
// Variables will change:
int ledState = LOW;              // ledState used to set the LED
```

Then there is a new variable referred to as a `long` rather than an `int`. See the "Long and Unsigned Long" sidebar later in this chapter for more about `long`s. The first instance, `previousMillis`, is used to store the time in milliseconds so that you can monitor how much time has passed each time you do a loop.

```
long previousMillis = 0;         // will store last time LED was updated
```

The second variable, named `interval`, is the time in milliseconds between each blink, which is set to 1000 milliseconds, or 1 second.

```
long interval = 1000;          // interval at which to blink (milliseconds)
```

Long and unsigned long

Longs are for extra long number storage and can store a value from -2,147,483,648 to 2,147,483,647, whereas an `int` can store only -32,768 to 32,767. When measuring time in milliseconds, you need access to big numbers because every second is stored as 1,000 milliseconds. To get an idea of just how big a `long` value is, imagine the maximum amount of time that it could store. This could be written as 2,147,483.6 seconds, 35791.4 minutes, 596.5 hours, or approximately 24.9 days!

In some cases, you have no need for a negative range, so to avoid unnecessary calculations, you can use an `unsigned long` instead. An `unsigned long` is similar to a regular `long` but has no negative values. This gives your `unsigned long` a whopping range of 0 to 4,294,967,295.

In setup, you have only one pin to define as an OUTPUT. Pin 13 is referred to as ledPin, just as it is in the declarations.

```
void setup() {
  // set the digital pin as output:
  pinMode(ledPin, OUTPUT);
}
```

In the loop, things start to get more complicated. The code for the timer can be run at the end of every loop, so you can add your own code at the start of the loop so that it doesn't interfere with the timer. Following your code, the timer code begins, which declares another variable: an unsigned long to store the current value the timer in milliseconds. This uses the function millis() that returns the number of milliseconds since the current Arduino program began running. After approximately 50 days, this value resets to 0, but for most applications this is more than enough time.

```
unsigned long currentMillis = millis();
```

 Variables declared inside a loop or other functions are known as *local* variables. These exist only within the function in which they are declared (and other sub-functions contained inside), but cease to exist after the function is completed. They are redeclared the next time the function is called. If you have a variable that needs to be either read or written to by other functions or pieces of code, you should use a *global* variable and declare it at the start of the sketch before the setup loop.

Next you need to check the current millis() value to see how much time has passed. You do so using a simple if loop that subtracts the previous value from the current value to get the difference. If that difference is gr eater than the interval value, the sketch knows that it's time to blink. It's important that you also tell the code to reset the previousMillis, otherwise it'll measure the interval only once. This is what setting previous Millis = currentMillis does.

```
  if(currentMillis - previousMillis > interval) {
    // save the last time you blinked the LED
    previousMillis = currentMillis;
```

Because the LED could already be on or off, the code needs to check the state of the LED to know what to do. The state is stored in ledState, so another simple if statement can check the state and do the opposite: if LOW, then make HIGH; or if HIGH, then make LOW. The following code updates the variable ledState:

```
//  if the LED is off turn it on and vice-versa:
    if (ledState == LOW)
      ledState = HIGH;
    else
      ledState = LOW;
```

Now, all that is left to do is to write the newly updated state to the LED using `digitalWrite`:

```
    // set the LED with the ledState of the variable:
    digitalWrite(ledPin, ledState);
}
```

This code allows you to happily blink your LED while performing any number of other functions.

Taking the Bounce Out of Your Button

A strange occurrence that happens with pushbuttons is bouncing. The microcontroller on your Arduino can read a switch thousands of times per second, much faster than we are able to operate it. This is great in some ways because it ensures that the reading is instantaneous (as far as human perception can tell), but sometimes there is a moment of fuzziness when the contact on a switch is neither fully down nor fully up, which causes it to read on and off rapidly in quick succession until it reaches the correct state. This is bouncing. To remove this peculiarity, you have to ignore any sudden changes when the switch state changes using a timer. It's relatively simple and can greatly improve the reliability of your buttons. If you have just read the Blinking Better, note that this is a further use of timers for your inputs as well as outputs.

Setting up the Debounce sketch

Complete the circuit in Figure 11-3 to try out the Debounce sketch.

You need:

- An Arduino Uno
- A breadboard
- A pushbutton
- An LED
- A 10k ohm resistor
- Jump wires

Complete the circuit shown in Figures 11-3 and 11-4, using a breadboard to mount the pushbutton part of the circuit. The LED can be inserted straight into pin 13 and its neighboring GND pin.

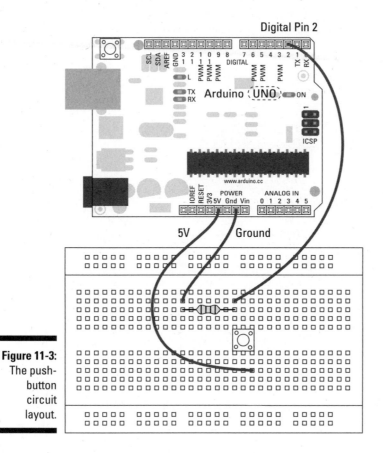

Figure 11-3:
The push-
button
circuit
layout.

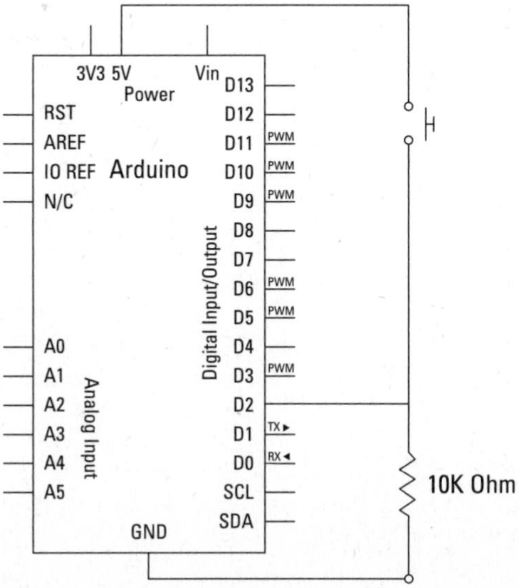

Figure 11-4:
A circuit
diagram of
the push-
button
circuit.

Build the circuit and choose File⇨Examples⇨02.Digital⇨Debounce to find the pushbutton Debounce sketch and open it. The complete code for the Debounce sketch is as follows:

```
/*
  Debounce

  Each time the input pin goes from LOW to HIGH (e.g. because of a push-button
  press), the output pin is toggled from LOW to HIGH or HIGH to LOW.  There's
  a minimum delay between toggles to debounce the circuit (i.e. to ignore
  noise).

  The circuit:
  * LED attached from pin 13 to ground
  * pushbutton attached from pin 2 to +5V
  * 10K resistor attached from pin 2 to ground

  * Note: On most Arduino boards, there is already an LED on the board
  connected to pin 13, so you don't need any extra components for this example.


  created 21 November 2006
  by David A. Mellis
  modified 30 Aug 2011
  by Limor Fried

  This example code is in the public domain.

  http://www.arduino.cc/en/Tutorial/Debounce
*/

// constants won't change. They're used here to
// set pin numbers:
const int buttonPin = 2;     // the number of the pushbutton pin
const int ledPin = 13;      // the number of the LED pin

// Variables will change:
int ledState = HIGH;         // the current state of the output pin
int buttonState;             // the current reading from the input pin
int lastButtonState = LOW;   // the previous reading from the input pin

// the following variables are long's because the time, measured in miliseconds,
// will quickly become a bigger number than can be stored in an int.
long lastDebounceTime = 0;  // the last time the output pin was toggled
long debounceDelay = 50;    // the debounce time; increase if the output
                            // flickers

void setup() {
  pinMode(buttonPin, INPUT);
  pinMode(ledPin, OUTPUT);
}

void loop() {
```

```
// read the state of the switch into a local variable:
int reading = digitalRead(buttonPin);

// check to see if you just pressed the button
// (i.e. the input went from LOW to HIGH), and you've waited
// long enough since the last press to ignore any noise:

// If the switch changed, due to noise or pressing:
if (reading != lastButtonState) {
  // reset the debouncing timer
  lastDebounceTime = millis();
}

if ((millis() - lastDebounceTime) > debounceDelay) {
  // whatever the reading is at, it's been there for longer
  // than the debounce delay, so take it as the actual current state:
  buttonState = reading;
}

// set the LED using the state of the button:
digitalWrite(ledPin, buttonState);

// save the reading.  Next time through the loop,
// it'll be the lastButtonState:
lastButtonState = reading;
}
```

When you have uploaded the sketch, you should have a reliable, debounced button. It can be difficult to see the effects, because if everything's working correctly, you should just see accurate button presses and responses from your LED.

Understanding the Debounce sketch

This sketch has quite a few variables. The first two are constants, used to define the input and output pins.

```
// constants won't change. They're used here to
// set pin numbers:
const int buttonPin = 2;     // the number of the pushbutton pin
const int ledPin = 13;       // the number of the LED pin
```

The next set of variables hold details about the button state. The ledState is set to HIGH so that the LED starts as being turned on; buttonState is left empty and holds the current state; lastButtonState holds the previous button state so that it can be compared with the current state.

```
// Variables will change:
int ledState = HIGH;        // the current state of the output pin
int buttonState;            // the current reading from the input pin
int lastButtonState = LOW;  // the previous reading from the input pin
```

Finally, there are two `long` variables to store time values. These are used in a timer to monitor the time between readings and prevent any sudden changes in values, such as those that occur during bounces.

```
// the following variables are long's because the time, measured in miliseconds,
// will quickly become a bigger number than can be stored in an int.
long lastDebounceTime = 0;  // the last time the output pin was toggled
long debounceDelay = 50;    // the debounce time; increase if the output
                            // flickers
```

Setup is straightforward and sets only the input and output pins.

```
void setup() {
  pinMode(buttonPin, INPUT);
  pinMode(ledPin, OUTPUT);
}
```

In the `loop`, a reading is taken from the button pin and is stored in a variable, in this case called `reading`:

```
void loop() {
  // read the state of the switch into a local variable:
  int reading = digitalRead(buttonPin);
```

`reading` is then checked against the `lastButtonState`. The first time this runs, `lastButtonState` is `LOW` because it was set in the variable declarations at the beginning of the sketch. In the `if` statement, the comparison symbol `!=` is used. This means: "If `reading` *is not* equal to the `lastButtonState`, then do something." If this change has occurred, `lastDebounceTime` is updated so that a fresh comparison can be made the next time the loop runs.

```
  // If the switch changed, due to noise or pressing:
  if (reading != lastButtonState) {
    // reset the debouncing timer
    lastDebounceTime = millis();
  }
```

If `reading` has been the same for longer than the debounce delay of 50 milliseconds, it can be assumed that the value is not erratic and can be forwarded to the `buttonState` variable.

```
  if ((millis() - lastDebounceTime) > debounceDelay) {
    // whatever the reading is at, it's been there for longer
    // than the debounce delay, so take it as the actual current state:
    buttonState = reading;
  }
```

The trusted value can then be used to trigger the LED directly. In this case, if the button is HIGH, it is closed, so the same HIGH value can be written to the LED to turn it on.

```
digitalWrite(ledPin, buttonState);
```

The current buttonState becomes the lastButtonState for the next loop and then it returns to the start.

```
lastButtonState = reading;
}
```

Some pushbuttons and triggers can be more or less reliable than others, depending on the way they're made or used. By using bits of code like this, you can sort out any inconsistencies and create more reliable results.

Making a Better Button

Buttons are usually very simple things. They are either on or off, depending on whether you're pressing them or not. You can monitor these changes and interpret them to make a button more intelligent than this. If you can tell when a button has been pressed, you don't need to constantly read its value and can instead just look for this change of state. This is a much better practice when connecting your Arduino to a computer, and efficiently sends the appropriate data as it is needed, rather than hogging the serial port.

Setting up the StateChangeDetection sketch

To make this circuit, you need:

- ✔ An Arduino Uno
- ✔ A breadboard
- ✔ A pushbutton
- ✔ A 10k ohm resistor
- ✔ An LED
- ✔ Jump wires

Using the layout and circuit diagrams shown in Figures 11-5 and 11-6, you can lay out a simple button circuit with an LED as an output. The hardware in this circuit is the same as the basic button sketch, but with the use of some simple code, you can make a button a lot more intelligent.

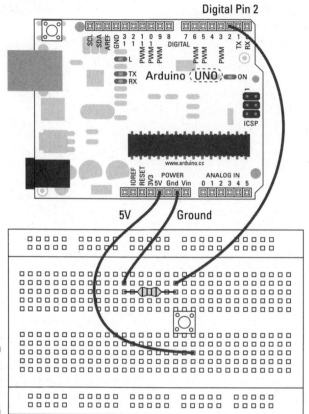

Figure 11-5:
A button circuit layout.

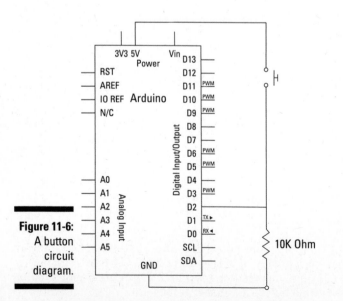

Figure 11-6:
A button circuit diagram.

Complete the circuit and open a new Arduino sketch. Choose File⇨Examples⇨
02.Digital⇨StateChangeDetection from the Arduino menu to load the sketch.

```
/*
  State change detection (edge detection)

  Often, you don't need to know the state of a digital input all the time,
  but you just need to know when the input changes from one state to another.
  For example, you want to know when a button goes from OFF to ON.  This is
  called state change detection, or edge detection.

  This example shows how to detect when a button or button changes from off to on
  and on to off.

  The circuit:
  * pushbutton attached to pin 2 from +5V
  * 10K resistor attached to pin 2 from ground
  * LED attached from pin 13 to ground (or use the built-in LED on
    most Arduino boards)

  created  27 Sep 2005
  modified 30 Aug 2011
  by Tom Igoe

This example code is in the public domain.

  http://arduino.cc/en/Tutorial/ButtonStateChange

  */

// this constant won't change:
const int  buttonPin = 2;      // the pin that the pushbutton is attached to
const int ledPin = 13;         // the pin that the LED is attached to

// Variables will change:
int buttonPushCounter = 0;   // counter for the number of button presses
int buttonState = 0;         // current state of the button
int lastButtonState = 0;     // previous state of the button

void setup() {
  // initialize the button pin as a input:
  pinMode(buttonPin, INPUT);
  // initialize the LED as an output:
  pinMode(ledPin, OUTPUT);
  // initialize serial communication:
  Serial.begin(9600);
}


void loop() {
  // read the pushbutton input pin:
  buttonState = digitalRead(buttonPin);
```

```
// compare the buttonState to its previous state
if (buttonState != lastButtonState) {
  // if the state has changed, increment the counter
  if (buttonState == HIGH) {
    // if the current state is HIGH then the button
    // wend from off to on:
    buttonPushCounter++;
    Serial.println("on");
    Serial.print("number of button pushes:  ");
    Serial.println(buttonPushCounter);
  }
  else {
    // if the current state is LOW then the button
    // wend from on to off:
    Serial.println("off");
  }
}
// save the current state as the last state,
//for next time through the loop
lastButtonState = buttonState;


// turns on the LED every four button pushes by
// checking the modulo of the button push counter.
// the modulo function gives you the remainder of
// the division of two numbers:
if (buttonPushCounter % 4 == 0) {
  digitalWrite(ledPin, HIGH);
} else {
  digitalWrite(ledPin, LOW);
}

}
```

Press the compile button to check your code. Compiling should highlight any grammatical errors and light up red if any are discovered. If the sketch compiles correctly, click Upload to send the sketch to your board. When the sketch is done uploading, choose the serial monitor and you should be presented with a readout showing when the button was turned on and off as well as how many times it was pressed. Also, the LED should illuminate every four button pushes to show that it's counting.

If nothing happens, try the following:

- Double-check your wiring.
- Make sure that you're using the correct pin number.
- Check the connections on the breadboard. If the jump wires or components are not connected using the correct rows in the breadboard, they will not work.

Understanding the StateChangeDetection sketch

In the StateChangeDetection sketch, the first action is that the variables for the sketch are declared. The input and output pins won't change, so they are declared as constant integers: pin 2 for the pushbutton and pin 13 for the LED.

```
// this constant won't change:
const int buttonPin = 2;    // the pin that the pushbutton is attached to
const int ledPin = 13;      // the pin that the LED is attached to
```

Other variables are needed to keep track of the pushbutton's behavior. One variable is a counter that keeps a running total of the number of button presses, and two other variables track the current and previous states of the pushbutton. These are used to monitor the button presses as the signal goes from HIGH to LOW or LOW to HIGH.

```
// Variables will change:
int buttonPushCounter = 0;   // counter for the number of button presses
int buttonState = 0;         // current state of the button
int lastButtonState = 0;     // previous state of the button
```

In setup, the pins are set to INPUT and OUTPUT accordingly. The serial port is opened for communication to display changes in the pushbutton.

```
void setup() {
   // initialize the button pin as a input:
   pinMode(buttonPin, INPUT);
   // initialize the LED as an output:
   pinMode(ledPin, OUTPUT);
   // initialize serial communication:
   Serial.begin(9600);
}
```

The first stage in the main loop is to read the state of the pushbutton.

```
void loop() {
   // read the pushbutton input pin:
   buttonState = digitalRead(buttonPin);
```

If this state is not equal to the previous value, which happens when the pushbutton is pressed, the program progresses to the next if () statement.

```
   // compare the buttonState to its previous state
   if (buttonState != lastButtonState) {
```

The next condition is to check whether the button is HIGH or LOW. If it is HIGH, the pushbutton has changed to on.

```
// if the state has changed, increment the counter
if (buttonState == HIGH) {
  // if the current state is HIGH then the button
  // wend from off to on:
```

This bit of code increments the counter and then prints a line on the serial monitor to show the state and the number of pushes. The counter is incremented on the downward part of the button press rather than the release.

```
buttonPushCounter++;
Serial.println("on");
Serial.print("number of button pushes:  ");
Serial.println(buttonPushCounter);
}
```

If the pushbutton went from HIGH to LOW, the button state is off, and this change of state is printed on the serial monitor, as shown in Figure 11-7.

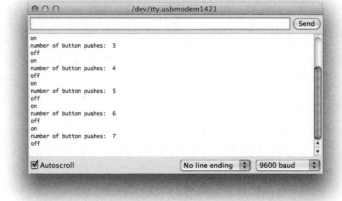

Figure 11-7:
The serial monitor provides a window into what your Arduino is experiencing.

```
else {
  // if the current state is LOW then the button
  // wend from on to off:
  Serial.println("off");
}
}
```

This piece of code allows you to click a pushbutton rather than have to hold it; the code also leaves plenty of room to add your own functionality to it.

Because a change has occurred, the current state becomes the last state in preparation for the next loop.

```
// save the current state as the last state,
//for next time through the loop
lastButtonState = buttonState;
```

At the end of the loop, a check is done to make sure that four button presses have occurred. If the total number of presses is divisible by four and equals 0, the LED pin is set to HIGH; if not the pin is set to LOW again.

```
// turns on the LED every four button pushes by
// checking the modulo of the button push counter.
// the modulo function gives you the remainder of
// the division of two numbers:
if (buttonPushCounter % 4 == 0) {
  digitalWrite(ledPin, HIGH);
} else {
  digitalWrite(ledPin, LOW);
}

}
```

You may find that the counter in this sketch can occasionally jump up, depending on the type and quality of pushbutton that you're using, and you may quite rightly ask, "Why doesn't this sketch include debouncing?" as explained in the previous section. The sketches in the Arduino examples are designed to help you understand many individual principles easily, to equip you for any situation. To include two or more techniques in one sketch may be good for the application, but would make it more difficult for you, the person learning, to understand how each element works.

It is possible to combine numerous examples to reap the benefits of each. Unfortunately, this is not covered in the context of this book, but it is best achieved by opening the two sketch examples side by side and combining them into one sketch, one line at a time, checking as you go that there are no repetitions of variables or omissions. The Compile shortcut (Ctrl+R or cmd+R) are very helpful for this task. Good luck!

Smoothing Your Sensors

Analog sensors can be highly accurate, allowing you to measure light levels or distance to a high degree of accuracy. Sometimes, however, they can be overly sensitive and flinch at the slightest change. If that's what you're looking for, that's great, but if not, you may want to smooth the results so that any erroneous readings don't spoil your results. Smoothing is effectively averaging your results so that any of these anomalies don't affect your reading as much. In Chapter 17 you also learn about showing these results on a bar graph, using Processing, which can be a great help for spotting inconsistencies.

Setting up the Smoothing sketch

For this example, you try smoothing on a light sensor.

For this sketch, you need:

- An Arduino Uno
- A breadboard
- An LED
- A light sensor
- A 10k ohm resistor
- A 220 ohm resistor
- Jump wires

Complete the circuit for reading a light-dependent resistor (LDR) as shown in Figures 11-8 and 11-9.

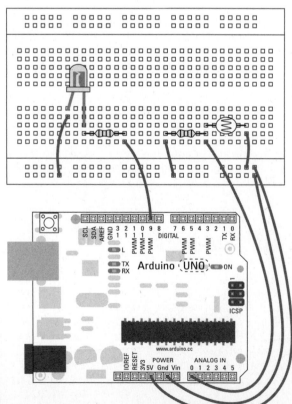

Figure 11-8:
The light sensor circuit layout.

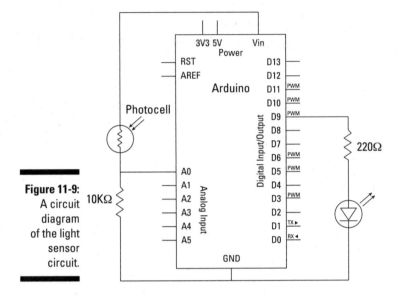

Figure 11-9:
A circuit
diagram
of the light
sensor
circuit.

Choose File➪Examples➪03.Analog➪Smoothing to find the sketch and upload it.

The sketch indicates that a potentiometer works for testing. This is true, but it is more difficult to see the effects of smoothing with a potentiometer because the mechanics of the device already make it quite a smooth analog input. Light, distance, and movement sensors are far more likely to need smoothing.

```
/*

  Smoothing

  Reads repeatedly from an analog input, calculating a running average
  and printing it to the computer.  Keeps ten readings in an array and
  continually averages them.

  The circuit:
    * Analog sensor (potentiometer will do) attached to analog input 0

  Created 22 April 2007
  By David A. Mellis  <dam@mellis.org>
  modified 9 Apr 2012
  by Tom Igoe
  http://www.arduino.cc/en/Tutorial/Smoothing

  This example code is in the public domain.


*/


// Define the number of samples to keep track of.  The higher the number,
```

```
// the more the readings will be smoothed, but the slower the output will
// respond to the input.  Using a constant rather than a normal variable lets
// use this value to determine the size of the readings array.
const int numReadings = 10;

int readings[numReadings];      // the readings from the analog input
int index = 0;                  // the index of the current reading
int total = 0;                  // the running total
int average = 0;                // the average

int inputPin = A0;

void setup()
{
  // initialize serial communication with computer:
  Serial.begin(9600);
  // initialize all the readings to 0:
  for (int thisReading = 0; thisReading < numReadings; thisReading++)
    readings[thisReading] = 0;
}

void loop() {
  // subtract the last reading:
  total= total - readings[index];
  // read from the sensor:
  readings[index] = analogRead(inputPin);
  // add the reading to the total:
  total= total + readings[index];
  // advance to the next position in the array:
  index = index + 1;

  // if we're at the end of the array...
  if (index >= numReadings)
    // ...wrap around to the beginning:
    index = 0;

  // calculate the average:
  average = total / numReadings;
  // send it to the computer as ASCII digits
  Serial.println(average);
  delay(1);          // delay in between reads for stability
}
```

This sketch gives you a nicely smoothed reading based on what the sensor is detecting. The smoothing is achieved by averaging a number of readings. The averaging process may slow down the number of readings per second, but because the Arduino is capable of reading these changes far faster than you are, the slowness doesn't affect how the sensor works in any noticeable way.

Understanding the Smoothing sketch

The start of the sketch declares the constants and variables. First is the number of readings to average, declared as `numReadings` with a value of 10.

```
const int numReadings = 10;
```

The next four variables are used to keep track of how many readings have been stored and to average them. These sensor readings are added to an array (or list), which is defined here as `readings`. The number of items in the `readings` array is defined in the square brackets. Because `numReadings` has already been declared, it can be used to set the array length to 10 (which are numbered, or "indexed," from 0 to 9).

```
int readings[numReadings];       // the readings from the analog input
```

Index is the common term for the current value and is used to keep track of how many loops or readings are taken. Because the index increases every time reading is taken, it can be used to store the results of that reading in the correct place in your array, before increasing to store the next reading in the next position in the array.

```
int index = 0;                   // the index of the current reading
```

The `total` variable provides a running total that is added to as readings are made. The `average` variable is where the average value is stored when the total is processed.

```
int total = 0;                   // the running total
int average = 0;                 // the average
```

The last variable is `inputPin`, the analog in pin that is being read.

```
int inputPin = A0;
```

In setup, the serial port is initialized to allow you to view the readings from the light sensor.

```
void setup()
{
  // initialize serial communication with computer:
  Serial.begin(9600);
```

Next in the code is a `for` loop, which is used to effectively reset the array. In the loop, a new local variable (`thisReading`) is initialized and made equal to zero. The variable `thisReading` is then compared to the length of the array. If it's less than the length of the array, the current reading the value in that part of the array is made equal to zero.

```
  // initialize all the readings to 0:
  for (int thisReading = 0; thisReading < numReadings; thisReading++)
    readings[thisReading] = 0;
}
```

In layman's terms, the code reads something like this: "Make a variable equal to 0, and if that variable is less than 10, make that same value in the array equal to zero; then increase the variable by one." As you can see, it is working through all the numbers 0 to 9 and setting that same position in the array to a zero value. After it reaches 10, the `for` loop ceases running and the code moves on to the main loop.

This type of automation is great for setting arrays. The alternative is to write them all as individual integer variables, which is a lot less efficient, both for you and the Arduino.

The first line of code in the main loop subtracts any reading in the current index of the array from the total. That value is replaced in this loop, so it is essential to remove it from the total first.

```
void loop() {
  // subtract the last reading:
  total= total - readings[index];
```

The next line obtains a new reading using `analogRead`, which is stored in the current index of the array, overwriting the previous value.

```
  // read from the sensor:
  readings[index] = analogRead(inputPin);
```

This reading is then added to the total to correct it.

```
  // add the reading to the total:
  total= total + readings[index];
```

```
  // advance to the next position in the array:
  index = index + 1;
```

It's important to check when the end of the array is reached so that the program doesn't loop forever without telling you your results. You can do this with a simple `if` statement: If the index value is greater than or equal to the number of readings that the sketch is looking for, set index back to zero. This `if` statement counts the index value from 0 to 9, as in setup, and then resets as soon as it reaches 10.

```
// if we're at the end of the array...
if (index >= numReadings)
  // ...wrap around to the beginning:
  index = 0;
```

To get the average from all the data in the array, the total is simply divided by the number of readings. This average is then displayed on the serial monitor for you to check. Because of the command used to display the message, this could also be referred to as "printing to the serial port." There is also a 1 millisecond delay at the end, which slows the program down considerably as well as helping to prevent erratic readings.

```
// calculate the average:
average = total / numReadings;
// send it to the computer as ASCII digits
Serial.println(average);
delay(1);          // delay in between reads for stability
}
```

Using simple procedures like this to average your results helps control unpredictable behavior in your projects. Averaging is especially useful if the sensor readings are directly linked to your output.

Calibrating Your Inputs

Think of calibrating your circuit as setting the thermostat in your home. Your furnace or boiler is capable of a range of temperatures, but depending on where you are in the world, different temperatures are appropriate. If you're in a mild climate, you may have the heating on only infrequently for a couple of months, but if you're in a cold climate, you may have the heating on every night for most of the year.

By calibrating the sensors on your Arduino project, you can tailor the sensor to its location. In this example, you learn how to calibrate a light sensor. Light, of course, is highly variable, whether you're inside, outside, in a well-lit room, or working by candlelight. Despite the huge variation, all these ranges of light can be sensed and interpreted by your Arduino as long as it knows the range that you're working to. The following sketch shows you how to calibrate a light sensor to its surroundings.

Setting up the Calibration sketch

For this example, complete the circuit shown in Figures 11-10 and 11-11 to calibrate your light sensor automatically.

You need:

- ✔ An Arduino Uno
- ✔ A breadboard
- ✔ An LED
- ✔ A light sensor
- ✔ A 10k ohm resistor
- ✔ A 220 ohm resistor
- ✔ Jump wires

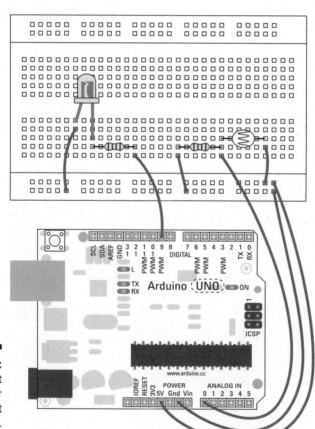

Figure 11-10:
The light
sensor
circuit
layout.

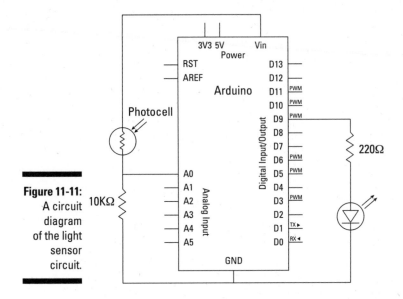

Figure 11-11:
A circuit
diagram
of the light
sensor
circuit.

Build the circuit and go to File⇨Examples⇨03.Analog⇨Calibration and to find the sketch. The code for this example is as follows:

```
/*
  Calibration

  Demonstrates one technique for calibrating sensor input.  The
  sensor readings during the first five seconds of the sketch
  execution define the minimum and maximum of expected values
  attached to the sensor pin.

  The sensor minimum and maximum initial values may seem backwards.
  Initially, you set the minimum high and listen for anything
  lower, saving it as the new minimum. Likewise, you set the
  maximum low and listen for anything higher as the new maximum.

  The circuit:
  * Analog sensor (potentiometer will do) attached to analog input 0
  * LED attached from digital pin 9 to ground

  created 29 Oct 2008
  By David A Mellis
  modified 30 Aug 2011
  By Tom Igoe

  http://arduino.cc/en/Tutorial/Calibration

  This example code is in the public domain.
```

```
*/

// These constants won't change:
const int sensorPin = A0;      // pin that the sensor is attached to
const int ledPin = 9;          // pin that the LED is attached to

// variables:
int sensorValue = 0;           // the sensor value
int sensorMin = 1023;          // minimum sensor value
int sensorMax = 0;             // maximum sensor value


void setup() {
  // turn on LED to signal the start of the calibration period:
  pinMode(13, OUTPUT);
  digitalWrite(13, HIGH);

  // calibrate during the first five seconds
  while (millis() < 5000) {
    sensorValue = analogRead(sensorPin);

    // record the maximum sensor value
    if (sensorValue > sensorMax) {
      sensorMax = sensorValue;
    }

    // record the minimum sensor value
    if (sensorValue < sensorMin) {
      sensorMin = sensorValue;
    }
  }

  // signal the end of the calibration period
  digitalWrite(13, LOW);
}

void loop() {
  // read the sensor:
  sensorValue = analogRead(sensorPin);

  // apply the calibration to the sensor reading
  sensorValue = map(sensorValue, sensorMin, sensorMax, 0, 255);

  // in case the sensor value is outside the range seen during calibration
  sensorValue = constrain(sensorValue, 0, 255);

  // fade the LED using the calibrated value:
  analogWrite(ledPin, sensorValue);
}
```

Upload the sketch, and let your Arduino settle with your normal ambient light levels for five seconds. Then try moving your hand over it. You should find it a lot more responsive than it is when it's just reading the analog value normally, and the LED should have a range from fully on when it is open to fully off when it is covered.

Understanding the Calibration sketch

The first part of the sketch lays out all the constants and variables. The constants are the pins that used for the light sensor and the LED. Note that the LED fades up and down, so it must use a PWM pin.

```
// These constants won't change:
const int sensorPin = A0;      // pin that the sensor is attached to
const int ledPin = 9;          // pin that the LED is attached to
```

The variables are used for the current sensor value and the minimum and maximum values of the sensor. You can see that sensorMin is initially set to a high value and sensorMax is set to a low one. This is because they must each work down and up, respectively, to set the minimum and maximum values.

```
// variables:
int sensorValue = 0;           // the sensor value
int sensorMin = 1023;          // minimum sensor value
int sensorMax = 0;             // maximum sensor value
```

In setup, quite a bit is going on. First, the usual pinMode sets pin 13 as an OUTPUT. This is followed by a digitalWrite to pin 13 to set it HIGH, which signals that the sensor is in its calibration phase.

```
void setup() {
   // turn on LED to signal the start of the calibration period:
   pinMode(13, OUTPUT);
   digitalWrite(13, HIGH);
```

For the first 5 seconds the sensor will calibrate. Because millis() starts counting the (milli)second that the program starts, the easiest way to count for 5 seconds is by using a while loop. The following code continues to check the value of millis(), and although this value is less than 5000 (5 seconds), it carries out the code inside the curly brackets.

```
   // calibrate during the first five seconds
   while (millis() < 5000) {
```

The brackets contain the calibration code. sensorValue stores the current sensor reading. If this reading is more than the maximum or less than the minimum, the values are updated. Because this happens during five seconds, you get a number of readings, and they all help to better define the expected range.

```
sensorValue = analogRead(sensorPin);

// record the maximum sensor value
if (sensorValue > sensorMax) {
  sensorMax = sensorValue;
}

// record the minimum sensor value
if (sensorValue < sensorMin) {
  sensorMin = sensorValue;
}
}
```

The LED pin is then written LOW to indicate that the calibration phase is over.

```
// signal the end of the calibration period
digitalWrite(13, LOW);
}
```

Now that the range is known, it just needs to be applied to the output LED. A reading is taken from the sensorPin. Because the reading is between 0 to 1024, it needs to be mapped to the LED's range of 0 to 255. sensorValue is converted to this new range using the map() function, using the sensorMin and sensorMax values from the calibration rather than the full range of 0 to 1024.

```
void loop() {
  // read the sensor:
  sensorValue = analogRead(sensorPin);

  // apply the calibration to the sensor reading
  sensorValue = map(sensorValue, sensorMin, sensorMax, 0, 255);
```

It is still possible for the sensor to read values outside those of the calibration, so sensorValue must be restricted using the constrain () function. This means that any values outside 0 to 255 are ignored. The calibration gives a good idea of the range of values, so any larger or smaller values are likely to be anomalies.

```
// in case the sensor value is outside the range seen during calibration
sensorValue = constrain(sensorValue, 0, 255);
```

All that is left to do is to update the LED with the mapped and constrained value by analog writing to the ledPin.

```
// fade the LED using the calibrated value:
analogWrite(ledPin, sensorValue);
}
```

This code should give you a better representation of your sensor's changing values relative to the environment you are in. The calibration runs only once when the program is started, so if the range still seems off, it's best to restart it or calibrate over a longer period. Calibration is designed to remove noise — erratic variations in the readings — so you should also make sure that the environment that is being measured does not have anything that you don't want to measure in it.

Chapter 12

Common Sense with Common Sensors

*I*n my experience of teaching, I often find that when people first have an idea, they get caught up in how to carry it out using a specific piece of hardware they've found instead of focusing on what they want to achieve. If Arduino is a toolbox with the potential of solving numerous problems, using the right tool for the right job is key.

If you go to any Arduino-related site, you're likely to see a list of sensors, and it can be a baffling experience trying to find the right ones for your project. A common next step is to search the web for projects similar to the one you want to do to see what other people have done. Other people's efforts and successes can be a great source of inspiration and knowledge, but these resources can also plunge you into a black hole of too many possible solutions, or solutions that are overkill for your needs.

In this chapter, you discover more about different sensors and how to use them, but also — and more important — *why* to use them.

Note that all prices given are approximate for buying an individual sensor to give you a rough idea of the cost. If you buy in bulk or do some thorough shopping around, you should be able to make considerable savings. Have a read of Chapters 19 and 20 for some places to start shopping.

Making Buttons Easier

The first sensor described in this book (in Chapter 7), and arguably the best, is the pushbutton. There are many kinds of pushbuttons, and switches are also included in this category. Generally, switches stick in their position in the same way that a light switch does, whereas buttons pop back. Some exceptions to this general rule are microswitches and toggle buttons. They are essentially the same electrically, and these differences are largely mechanical.

If you plan to use a button for your project, run through the following considerations:

- **Complexity:** In its simplest form, a pushbutton can be two metal contacts that are pushed together. At its most complex, it can be a set of carefully engineered contacts in an enclosed pushbutton. Pushbuttons tend to be mounted in enclosures that are designed around different uses. A pushbutton like the one in your kit is perfect for breadboard layouts and suited to prototyping. If it were used in the real world, it would need protecting. Take apart an old game console controller and you may well find an enclosed pushbutton inside. If you needed a more industrial button, such as an emergency stop button, the switch may be larger, more robust, and may even contain a bigger spring to handle the force of someone hitting or kicking it.

  The great thing about pushbuttons is that they never get really complicated, but the right spring or click to a button can make all the difference in the quality of your project, so choose wisely.

- **Cost:** The cost of a pushbutton varies greatly depending on the quality of the enclosure and the materials used. The prices on RS Components range from 9 cents (6p) for a microswitch to around $150 (£100) for an industrial stop button in an enclosure. It's very possible to use cheaper buttons for most applications with a bit of lateral thinking.

- **Where:** You can use buttons to detect presses from intentional human contact (or even unintentional, if you are clever with how you house the buttons). Museum exhibits are a great example of using buttons to register intentional human contact because people "get" how to use buttons. They're everywhere, and people use them every day without thinking. Sometimes it may seem clever to use subtler methods, but if in doubt, a button is always a safe option.

  You can also consider how you might apply the use of a button to what's already in place. For example, maybe you're monitoring how often a door is opened in your house. If you put a highly sensitive microswitch against the door when it's closed, that switch tells you every time the door moves away from it.

In Chapters 7 and 11 of this book, you learn how to wire a button circuit and to refine it. In the example in the following section of this chapter, you learn how to simplify the hardware of your button. By using a hidden feature of your Arduino, you can use a button with no additional hardware.

Implementing the DigitalInputPullup sketch

The basic button circuit is a relatively simple one, but it can be made simpler still by using a little-known function on your microcontroller. On the basic button example in Chapter 7 (see Figure 12-1) a *pull-down* resistor is connected to ground to make the button pin read LOW. Whenever pressed, the button is connects to 5V and goes HIGH. This behavior allows you to read the button's state as an input.

In the microcontroller, there is an internal *pull-up* resistor that can be activated to give you a constant HIGH value. When a button connected to ground is pressed, it grounds the current and sets the pin to LOW. This design gives you the same functionality as the basic example from Chapter 7, but the logic is inverted: HIGH is an open switch, and LOW is a closed switch. The wiring is, therefore, simpler because you eliminate the need for an extra wire and resistor.

To complete this example, you need:

✔ An Arduino Uno

✔ A breadboard

✔ A pushbutton

✔ An LED (optional)

✔ Jump wires

Complete the circuit shown in Figures 12-1 and 12-2 to try the new, simpler pushbutton using the Digital Pull-up sketch.

There is already an LED on the board linked to pin 13, but if you want to accentuate the output, an LED can be inserted straight into pin 13 and its neighbouring GND pin.

Complete the circuit and choose File⇨Examples⇨02.Digital⇨ DigitalIputPullup to find the Digital Input Pull-Up sketch.

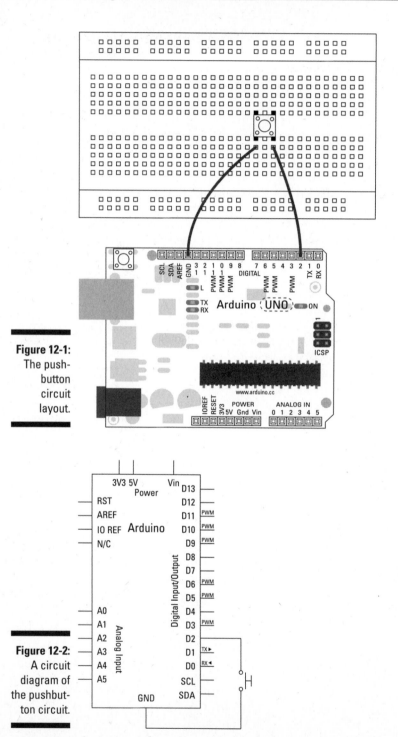

Figure 12-1:
The push-
button
circuit
layout.

Figure 12-2:
A circuit
diagram of
the pushbut-
ton circuit.

The smart ones among you notice that the title of this example has a typo. It's not uncommon in Arduino sketches to find typos, so I have left any words as they appear in the software to avoid confusion.

```
/*
  Input Pullup Serial

  This example demonstrates the use of pinMode(INPUT_PULLUP). It reads a
  digital input on pin 2 and prints the results to the serial monitor.

  The circuit:
  * Momentary switch attached from pin 2 to ground
  * Built-in LED on pin 13

  Unlike pinMode(INPUT), there is no pull-down resistor necessary. An internal
  20K-ohm resistor is pulled to 5V. This configuration causes the input to
  read HIGH when the switch is open, and LOW when it is closed.

  created 14 March 2012
  by Scott Fitzgerald

  http://www.arduino.cc/en/Tutorial/InputPullupSerial

  This example code is in the public domain

*/

void setup(){
  //start serial connection
  Serial.begin(9600);
  //configure pin2 as an input and enable the internal pull-up resistor
  pinMode(2, INPUT_PULLUP);
  pinMode(13, OUTPUT);

}

void loop(){
  //read the pushbutton value into a variable
  int sensorVal = digitalRead(2);
  //print out the value of the pushbutton
  Serial.println(sensorVal);

  // Keep in mind the pullup means the pushbutton's
  // logic is inverted. It goes HIGH when it's open,
  // and LOW when it's pressed. Turn on pin 13 when the
  // button's pressed, and off when it's not:
  if (sensorVal == HIGH) {
    digitalWrite(13, LOW);
  }
  else {
    digitalWrite(13, HIGH);
  }
}
```

Understanding the DigitalInputPullup sketch

The DigitalInputPullup sketch is similar to the standard button sketch but with a few changes. In setup, serial communication is started to monitor the state of the button. Next, the pinMode of the inputs and outputs is set. Pin 2 is your button pin, but instead of setting it to an INPUT, you use INPUT_PULLUP. Doing so activates the internal pull-up resistor. Pin 13 is set to be an output as an LED control pin.

```
void setup(){
  //start serial connection
  Serial.begin(9600);
  //configure pin2 as an input and enable the internal pull-up resistor
  pinMode(2, INPUT_PULLUP);
  pinMode(13, OUTPUT);

}
```

In the main loop, you read the value of the pull-up pin and store it in the variable sensorVal. This then prints to the serial monitor to show you what value is being read.

```
void loop(){
  //read the pushbutton value into a variable
  int sensorVal = digitalRead(2);
  //print out the value of the pushbutton
  Serial.println(sensorVal);
```

But because the logic is inverted, you need to invert your if () statement to make it correct. A HIGH value is open and a LOW value is closed. Inside the if () statement, you can write any actions to perform. In this case, the LED is being turned off, or set LOW, whenever the button pin is open, or pulled HIGH.

```
// Keep in mind the pullup means the pushbutton's
// logic is inverted. It goes HIGH when it's open,
// and LOW when it's pressed. Turn on pin 13 when the
// button's pressed, and off when it's not:
if (sensorVal == HIGH) {
  digitalWrite(13, LOW);
}
else {
  digitalWrite(13, HIGH);
}
}
```

This method is great for situations in which you don't have enough spare components around, and it allows you to make a switch with only a couple of wires, if necessary. This functionality can be used on any digital pins, but only for inputs.

Exploring Piezo Sensors

In Chapter 8, you learn how to make sound using a piezo buzzer, but you should know that you have another way to use the same hardware as an input rather than an output. To make a sound with a piezo, you put a current through it and it vibrates, so it follows that if you vibrate the same piezo, you generate a small amount of electrical current. This is commonly known as a *knock* sensor and is used to measure vibrations on the surface to which it is fixed.

Piezos vary in size, and that determines the scale of the vibrations that they can detect. Small piezos are extremely sensitive to vibrations and need very little to max out their range. Bigger piezos have a broader range, but more vibration is necessary for a reading to register. There are also specialised piezo sensors that are made to act as inputs to detect flex, touch, vibration, and shock. These cost slightly more than a basic piezo element but are usually made from a flexible film, which makes them a lot more robust.

When using a piezo, consider the following:

- ✔ **Complexity:** Piezos are relatively simple to wire, needing only a resistor to function in a circuit. The hardware of a piezo itself is also simple, and very little additional work on your part is necessary. Because the top half is made of a fragile ceramic, it is often enclosed in a plastic case, which makes it easier to mount and avoids any direct contact with the fragile solder joints on the surface of the piezo.

- ✔ **Cost:** Piezo elements are inexpensive, costing from around 40 cents (25p) for the cheapest elements without a casing to $15 (£10) for high-power piezo buzzers. As an input, a piezo element is preferable to the more specific piezo buzzer. The usual difference is a smaller form factor for buzzers, whereas elements usually have a broader base. The latter is preferable for the knock sensor because it gives you more area on the piezo as well as more contact with the surface that is being monitored.

  Piezos are much cheaper to purchase from the major electronics companies, but because these require you to browse their vast online catalogues, you might find it more useful to buy a selection from retail stores first, such as Maplin (UK) or RadioShack (US), where you can see the product in real life and get a feel for the different shapes, styles, and housings.

✔ **Where:** Knock sensors are not usually used as a direct input. Because they are so fragile, having people tapping on them all the time is risky. Instead, fix your piezo to a rigid surface such as wood, plastic, or metal and let that surface take the punishment. For example, a knock sensor mounted on a staircase could be very discreet and unobtrusive but still give highly accurate readings.

Piezos are simple and inexpensive sensors with a large variety of uses. You can use them to detect vibrations, or more directly in a homemade electric drum kit. This section's example shows you how to wire your own set of piezo knock sensors.

Implementing the Knock sketch

Knock sensors use a piezo element to measure vibration. When a piezo vibrates, it produces a voltage that can be interpreted by your Arduino as an analog signal. Piezo elements are more commonly used as buzzers, which inversely make a vibration when a current is passed through them.

You need:

✔ An Arduino Uno

✔ A breadboard

✔ A piezo

✔ A 1M ohm resistor

✔ Jump wires

Using the layout and circuit diagrams in Figures 12-3 and 12-4, assemble the circuit for the knock sensor. The hardware in this circuit is similar to the piezo buzzer sketch in Chapter 8, but with a few changes you can make this piezo element into an input as well.

Complete the circuit and open a new Arduino sketch. Choose File⇨Examples⇨06.Sensors⇨Knock from the Arduino menu to load the sketch.

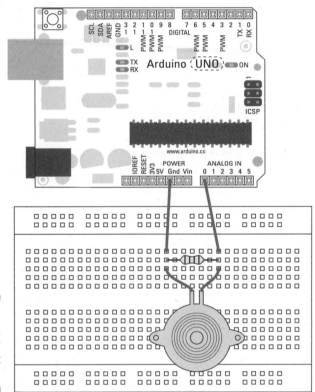

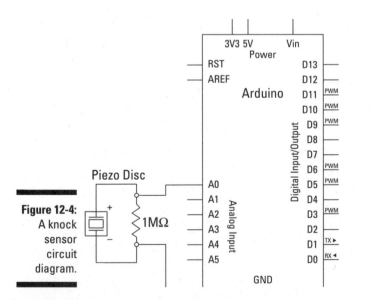

Figure 12-3: A knock sensor circuit layout.

Figure 12-4: A knock sensor circuit diagram.

```
/* Knock Sensor

  This sketch reads a piezo element to detect a knocking sound.
  It reads an analog pin and compares the result to a set threshold.
  If the result is greater than the threshold, it writes
  "knock" to the serial port, and toggles the LED on pin 13.

  The circuit:
   * + connection of the piezo attached to analog in 0
   * - connection of the piezo attached to ground
   * 1-megohm resistor attached from analog in 0 to ground

  http://www.arduino.cc/en/Tutorial/Knock

  created 25 Mar 2007
  by David Cuartielles <http://www.0j0.org>
  modified 30 Aug 2011
  by Tom Igoe

  This example code is in the public domain.

 */


// these constants won't change:
const int ledPin = 13;      // led connected to digital pin 13
const int knockSensor = A0; // the piezo is connected to analog pin 0
const int threshold = 100;  // threshold value to decide when the detected
                            // sound is a knock or not


// these variables will change:
int sensorReading = 0;       // variable to store the value read from the sensor
                            // pin
int ledState = LOW;          // variable used to store the last LED status, to
                            // toggle the light

void setup() {
 pinMode(ledPin, OUTPUT); // declare the ledPin as as OUTPUT
 Serial.begin(9600);         // use the serial port
}

void loop() {
  // read the sensor and store it in the variable sensorReading:
  sensorReading = analogRead(knockSensor);

  // if the sensor reading is greater than the threshold:
  if (sensorReading >= threshold) {
    // toggle the status of the ledPin:
    ledState = !ledState;
    // update the LED pin itself:
    digitalWrite(ledPin, ledState);
```

```
    // send the string "Knock!" back to the computer, followed by newline
    Serial.println("Knock!");
  }
  delay(100);  // delay to avoid overloading the serial port buffer
}
```

Press the Compile button to check your code. Doing so highlights any grammatical errors and lights them up in red when they are discovered. If the sketch compiles correctly, click Upload to send the sketch to your board. When it is done uploading, choose the serial monitor and give the surface that your piezo is on a good knock. If it's working, you should see "Knock!" on the serial monitor and the LED change with each successful knock.

If nothing happens, double-check your wiring:

✔ Make sure that you're using the correct pin number.

✔ Check the connections on the breadboard. If the jump wires or components are not connected using the correct rows in the breadboard, they will not work.

Understanding the Knock sketch

The first declarations are constant values, the LED pin number, the knock sensor pin number, and the threshold for a knock value. These are set and don't change throughout the sketch.

```
// these constants won't change:
const int ledPin = 13;       // led connected to digital pin 13
const int knockSensor = A0; // the piezo is connected to analog pin 0
const int threshold = 100;  // threshold value to decide when the
                            // detected sound is a knock or not
```

Two variables do change: the current sensor reading and the state of the LED.

```
// these variables will change:
int sensorReading = 0;       // variable to store the value read from the sensor
             pin
int ledState = LOW;          // variable used to store the last LED status,
                            // to toggle the light
```

In setup, the LED pin is set to be an output and the serial port is opened for communication.

```
void setup() {
 pinMode(ledPin, OUTPUT); // declare the ledPin as as OUTPUT
 Serial.begin(9600);       // use the serial port
 }
```

The first line in the loop is to read the analog value from the knock sensor pin.

```
void loop() {
  // read the sensor and store it in the variable sensorReading:
  sensorReading = analogRead(knockSensor);
```

This value is compared to the threshold value.

```
  // if the sensor reading is greater than the threshold:
  if (sensorReading >= threshold) {
```

If the value of sensorReading is greater than or equal to the threshold value, the LED's state is switched between 0 and 1 using the !, the NOT symbol. The ! symbol in this case is used to return the opposite Boolean value of whatever the ledState variable currently is. As you know, Booleans are either 1 or 0 (true or false), the same as the possible values of ledState. This line of code could be written as "make ledState equal to whatever value it is not."

```
    // toggle the status of the ledPin:
    ledState = !ledState;
```

The ledState value is then sent to the LED pin using digitalWrite. The digitalWrite function interprets a value of 0 as LOW and 1 as HIGH.

```
    // update the LED pin itself:
    digitalWrite(ledPin, ledState);
```

Finally, the word "Knock" is sent to the serial port with a short delay, for stability.

```
    // send the string "Knock!" back to the computer, followed by newline
    Serial.println("Knock!");
  }
  delay(100);  // delay to avoid overloading the serial port buffer
}
```

Utilizing Pressure, Force, and Load Sensors

Three closely related kinds of sensors are commonly confused: *pressure, force,* and *load* sensors. These three sensors are actually extremely different in how they behave and what data they can give you, so it's important to know the difference so that you pick the one that's right for your situation. In this section, you learn about the different definitions of each of these sensors, as well as where you use them and why you use one over the other.

Consider the following as you plan:

✔ **Complexity:** As you might expect, complexity increases depending on how accurate you need to be:

- *Pressure pads* are designed to detect when pressure is applied to an area, and they come in quite a variety of both quality and accuracy. The simplest pressure pads are often misnamed and are really the equivalent of big switches. Inside a simple pressure pad are two layers of foil separated by a layer of foam with holes in it. When the foam is squashed, the metal contacts touch through the foam and complete the circuit. This means that instead of measuring pressure or weight, the pad is actually detecting when there is enough weight to squash the foam. These pads do a fine job and are similar to the mechanisms found inside dance mats — ample proof that you don't need to overthink your sensors!

- For more precision, you may want to use *force sensors*, which measure the force applied by whatever is put on them within their range. Although force sensors are accurate enough to detect a change in weight, they are not accurate enough provide a precise measurement. Force sensors are usually flexible, force-sensitive resistors; that is, resistors that are made on a flexible PCB, that change their resistance when force is applied. The resistor itself is on the flexible circuit board, and although it can tolerate extremely high forces and loads, protecting it from direct contact is a good idea to prevent it from bending, folding, or tearing.

- With pressure pads at one end of the spectrum, at the other are *load sensors*. An example of a load sensor is found in your bathroom scale. Load sensors can accurately measure weight up to their limit. They work in much the same way as force sensors by changing resistance as they bend. In most cases, a load sensor is fixed to a rigid piece of metal and monitors changes as the metal is put under strain. The changes are so minute that they often require an amplification circuit known as a Wheatstone Bridge. Incorporating this kind of sensor is more complex than the others, but you can find material on the Internet that can walk you thorough the process.

✔ **Cost:** The cost of each sensor is relatively low, even for the most sensitive ones. A cheap pressure pad can set you back $3 (£2), for all the materials to make a DIY one, to $12 (£8), for an inexpensive, entry-level pressure mat available from most electronics stores and suppliers. Force sensitive resistors range from $8 to $23 (£5 to £15), but cover a much smaller area than a pressure pad, so you may need quite a few of them to cover a large area. Load sensors are also relatively cheap at around $11 (£7), most likely because they are so widespread that mass production has knocked the price down. There may be an extra cost in time to plan and make the additional circuitry.

✔ **Where:** The real challenge with all these sensors is housing them to prevent damage. In the case of the pressure pad and the force-sensitive resistors, placing a good layer of upholstery foam on the side that the force is coming from is a good idea. Depending on the density of the foam, it should dampen enough of the force to protect the sensor but still compress it enough for a good reading. Underneath the sensors, you want to have a solid base to give you something to push against. This could just be the floor or surface that the sensor is placed on or a sheet of MDF/ plywood could be attached to the underside of the sensor. It's a good idea to protect the exterior of your pressure sensor as well, so consider something a bit more sturdy than foam on the exterior. For a soft finish, upholstery vinyl is a great option. If you plan to have people walk on the surface, for example, a layer of wood on the top to sandwich the foam is a good option to spread the load and can easily be replaced, if needed. In the case of load sensors, they require very little movement and should be connected to or placed in direct contact with a ridged surface. In the case of your bathroom scales, it may take some trial and error to place the sensor in the correct location to get an accurate reading. Sometimes multiple sensors are used to get an average reading across the surface.

Picked a sensor? Now you need to figure out how to use it:

✔ *Pressure pads* are an extremely simple circuit, the same as for a pushbutton. The hardware of a pressure pad is also easy enough that you can make one yourself using two sheets of foil, a sheet of foam, a cover, and a couple of wires. As an alternative to foil, a great material to use is conductive fabric or conductive thread, which are a lot more flexible than foil.

✔ *Force sensors* are also relatively easy to use and can take the place of other analog sensors, such as light or temperature sensors, in simple Arduino circuits. The ranges of force may vary, but whatever the range, you can scale the force to your needs quite simply in the code.

✔ *Load sensors* are probably the most complex sensor if they are being used for accurate reading, as with a set of weight scales. They require extra circuitry and an amplifier for the Arduino to read the minute changes in resistance. This topic is outside the scope of this book, so if you want to know more, get friendly with Google.

Force sensors are just like any other variable resistor and can easily be switched with potentiometer or light-dependant resistors as needed. In this section's example, you learn how to use force-sensitive resistors to make an Arduino piano keyboard using the toneKeyboard sketch.

Implementing the toneKeyboard sketch

You may think of pushbuttons as the perfect input for a keyboard, but force-sensitive resistors give you much more sensitivity to touch. Rather than detect just a press, you can also detect the intensity of the key press in the same way as on a traditional piano.

You need:

- ✔ An Arduino Uno
- ✔ A breadboard
- ✔ Three force-sensitive resistors
- ✔ Three 10k ohm resistors
- ✔ One 100 ohm resistor
- ✔ A piezo element
- ✔ Jump wires

Using the layout and circuit diagrams in Figures 12-5 and 12-6, lay out the force-sensitive resistors and the piezo to make your own keyboard.

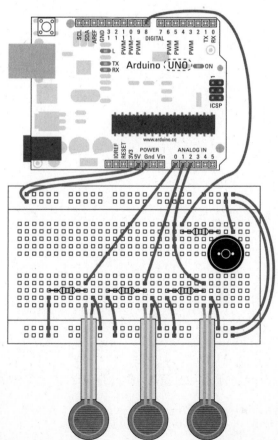

Figure 12-5:
A button circuit layout.

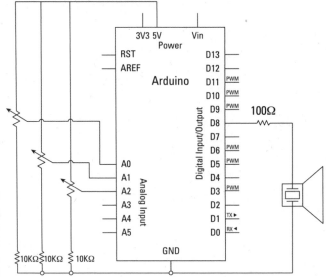

Figure 12-6:
A button
circuit
diagram.

Complete the circuit and open a new Arduino sketch. Choose File➪Examples➪
02.Digital➪toneKeyboard from the Arduino menu to load the sketch.

```
/*
  keyboard

  Plays a pitch that changes based on a changing analog input

  circuit:
  * 3 force-sensing resistors from +5V to analog in 0 through 5
  * 3 10K resistors from analog in 0 through 5 to ground
  * 8-ohm speaker on digital pin 8

  created 21 Jan 2010
  modified 9 Apr 2012
  by Tom Igoe

This example code is in the public domain.

  http://arduino.cc/en/Tutorial/Tone3

  */

#include "pitches.h"

const int threshold = 10;     // minimum reading of the sensors that generates a
                              // note

// notes to play, corresponding to the 3 sensors:
```

```
int notes[] = {
  NOTE_A4, NOTE_B4,NOTE_C3 };

void setup() {

}

void loop() {
  for (int thisSensor = 0; thisSensor < 3; thisSensor++) {
    // get a sensor reading:
    int sensorReading = analogRead(thisSensor);

    // if the sensor is pressed hard enough:
    if (sensorReading > threshold) {
      // play the note corresponding to this sensor:
      tone(8, notes[thisSensor], 20);
    }
  }
}
```

Press the Compile button to check your code. The compiler should highlight any grammatical errors and light them up in red when they are discovered. If the sketch compiles correctly, click Upload to send the sketch to your board. When it is done uploading, try the keys to make sure they're working. If they are, you're ready to play.

If nothing happens, double-check your wiring:

- ✔ Make sure that you're using the correct pin number.
- ✔ Check the connections on the breadboard. If the jump wires or components are not connected using the correct rows in the breadboard, they won't work.

Understanding the toneKeyboard sketch

The toneKeyboard sketch uses the same table of notes as the Melody sketch in Chapter 8. The first line includes `pitches.h`, which should be open in a separate tab next to the main sketch.

```
#include "pitches.h"
```

A low threshold of 10 (out of a possible 1024) is set to avoid any low readings resulting from background vibrations.

```
const int threshold = 10;     // minimum reading of the sensors that generates a
                              // note
```

The notes for each sensor are stored in an array with values (0,1 and 2) that correspond to the analog input pin numbers (A0, A1 and A2). You can change these the note values that are contained in this array manually using the look-up table on `pitches.h`. Simply copy and paste new note values in the change the note of each sensor.

```
// notes to play, corresponding to the 3 sensors:
int notes[] = {
  NOTE_A4, NOTE_B4,NOTE_C3 };
```

In setup, you have nothing to define because the analog input pins are set to be inputs by default.

```
void setup() {

}
```

In the main loop, a `for ()` loop cycles through the numbers 0 to 2.

```
void loop() {
  for (int thisSensor = 0; thisSensor < 3; thisSensor++) {
```

The value of the `for ()` loop is used as the pin number, and its value is stored temporarily to `sensorReading`.

```
    // get a sensor reading:
    int sensorReading = analogRead(thisSensor);
```

If the reading is greater than the threshold, it is used to trigger the correct note assigned to that input.

```
    // if the sensor is pressed hard enough:
    if (sensorReading > threshold) {
      // play the note corresponding to this sensor:
      tone(8, notes[thisSensor], 20);
    }
  }
}
```

Because the loop happens so quickly, any delay in reading each sensor is unnoticeable.

Sensing with Style

Capacitive sensors detect changes in electromagnetic fields. Every living thing has an electromagnetic field — even you. Capacitive sensors are extremely useful because they can detect human contact and ignore other environmental factors. You are probably familiar with high-end capacitive sensors because they are present in nearly all smartphones, but they have actually been around since the late 1920s. You can find Arduino kits with capacitive sensors, such as Capacitive Touch Keypads, that you can hook up easily. But it's just as easy to make your own capacitive sensors with an Arduino and an antenna.

Consider the following in your plans:

✔ **Complexity:** Because all that is required is an antenna, you can be quite creative with what the antenna is and where it is placed. Short pieces of wire or copper tape are great for simple touch sensors. The piece of copper tape suddenly becomes a touch switch, meaning that you don't even need a pushbutton to get the same functionality. You could even connect the antenna to a bigger metal object such as a lamp, turning it into a touch lamp.

If the antenna is made from a reel of wire or a piece of foil, you can extend the range of the sensor beyond touch, which is known as a projected capacitive sensor. This means that you can detect a person's hand a couple of inches away from the antenna, which creates a lot of new possibilities for hiding sensors behind other materials. These discreet capacitive sensors are now commonly seen in many recent consumer electronics to remove the physical buttons and maintain the sleek shape of the product. The electronics can also under layers of other material and be perfectly protected from the outside world.

Capacitive touch sensors are easy to make. The real difficulty is with projected field sensors to determine the range of the field. The best way to determine this range is by experimentation, testing to see whether the field that you are generating is far reaching enough.

✔ **Cost:** A capacitive touch kit designed for a specific purpose costs around $15 to $23 (£10 to £15). The kit should perform its job well, but it will be limited to the design of the interface. There is a capacitive sensor breakout board from Sparkfun for around $10 (£6.50) that lets you control up to 12 capacitive sensors. You have to wire your own touch pads, but you're free to design an interface that suits your purpose.

The cheapest option is to use the CapSense library for Arduino, which allows you to make a capacitive sensor with an antenna and no additional hardware! This means that you could spend a few cents (or pence) for an antenna or repurpose an old one.

✔ **Where:** Capacitive touch sensors can work with any conductive metal, so if you can design an attractive metal exterior, the only work will be to connect that exterior to your Arduino. If you're looking for something more discreet, you may want to experiment with different layers of wood or plastic to hide your metal antenna. A thin layer of plywood allows the metal to be close to the surface, able to trigger the sensor. By covering the antenna with a non-conductive surface, you also give it a seemingly magical property, ensuring that people are left guessing at how it works.

Getting the CapSense library

The CapSense library is available from GitHub. GitHub is an online repository of software that manages different versions and allows you to see who has updated the software, and how. It's an excellent system for sharing and collaborating on code projects. You can find the Arduino platform on GitHub; check it out if you're curious about any changes. To get the library:

1. **Point your Web browser to the GitHub CapSense page at** `https://github.com/moderndevice/CapSense`.

2. **On the CapSense page, click the Download This Repository as a Zip File button.**

   The button is marked with a cloud and the word ZIP.

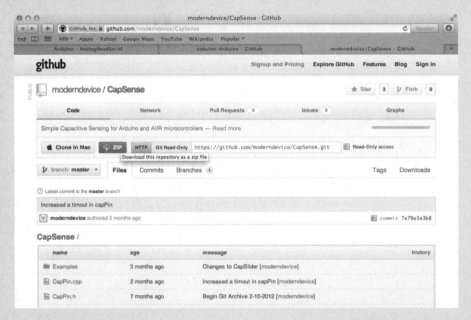

This downloads the latest version of the library to your downloads folder or a folder you specify.

3. **Rename the folder "CapSense."**

   Inside the folder, you should see a number of files ending in `.h` and `.cpp` as well as an Examples folder.

4. **Move the entire folder to your Arduino libraries directory.**

This should be the same directory that your sketches are saved to, for example: Username/Documents/Arduino/libraries. If you don't have a libraries directory, create one.

Your can find your Arduino Save directory by choosing Arduino➪Preferences from the Arduino menu bar. After the CapSense library is inside this folder, it will be available the next time you run Arduino.

5. Start or restart Arduino and go to Sketch⇨Import Library in the Arduino menu.

Look for CapSense under the Contributed libraries section. If you don't find it, check your directories and spelling and then restart Arduino.

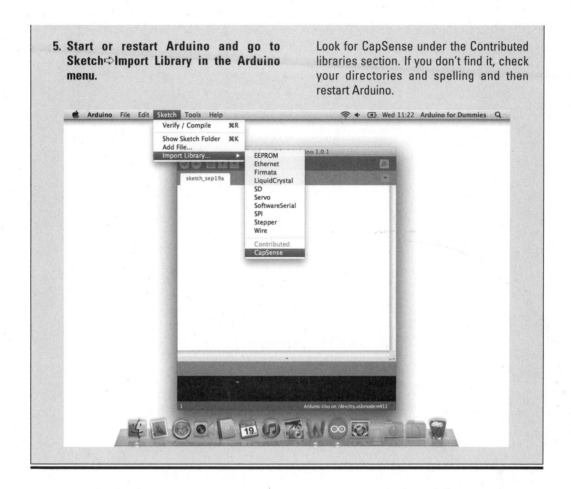

The easiest way to make a capacitive sensor is to use the CapSense library by Paul Badger. By using the CapSense library (I explain how in the "Getting the CapSense Library" sidebar), you can do away with mechanical switches altogether and replace them with highly robust capacitive touch sensors or capacitive presence detectors.

Implementing the CapPinSketch sketch

For this project, you need:

- ✔ An Arduino Uno
- ✔ A wire antenna
- ✔ Crocodile clips (optional)

As you can see from the photo in Figure 12-7, very little work is needed. You can simply have a wire antenna connected to pin 5 and you can enlarge this by connecting that to any other conductive surface. Crocodile clips are useful to latch onto different antennas quickly and easily.

Figure 12-7:
A photo of a DIY capacitive sensor.

If the CapSense library is recognized, the Examples folder inside it should be, too. Build the circuit and choose File➪Examples➪CapSense➪Examples➪Cap PinSketch from the Arduino menu to load the sketch.

```
#include <CapPin.h>

/* CapPin
 * Capacitive Library CapPin Demo Sketch
 * Paul Badger 2011
 * This class uses the built-in pullup resistors read the capacitance on a pin
 * The pin is set to input and then the pullup is set,
 * A loop times how long the pin takes to go HIGH.
 * The readPin method is fast and can be read 1000 times in under 10 mS.
 * By reading the pin repeated you can sense "hand pressure"
 * at close range with a small sensor. A larger sensor (piece of foil/metal)
 * will yield larger return values and be able to sense at more distance. For
 * a more sensitive method of sensing pins see CapTouch
 * Hook up a wire with or without a piece of foil attached to the pin.
 * I suggest covering the sensor with mylar, packing tape, paper or other insulator
```

```
 * to avoid having users directly touch the pin.
 */

CapPin cPin_5 = CapPin(5);    // read pin 5

float smoothed;

void setup()
{

  Serial.begin(115200);
  Serial.println("start");
 // slider_2_7.calibrateSlider();

}

void loop()
{


  delay(1);
  long total1 = 0;
  long start = millis();
  long total =  cPin_5.readPin(2000);


  // simple lowpass filter to take out some of the jitter
  // change parameter (0 is min, .99 is max) or eliminate to suit
  smoothed = smooth(total, .8, smoothed);

Serial.print( millis() - start);        // time to execute in mS
Serial.print("\t");
Serial.print(total);                    // raw total
Serial.print("\t");
Serial.println((int) smoothed);         // smoothed
  delay(5);
}

// simple lowpass filter
// requires recycling the output in the "smoothedVal" param
int smooth(int data, float filterVal, float smoothedVal){

  if (filterVal > 1){      // check to make sure param's are within range
    filterVal = .999999;
  }
  else if (filterVal <= 0){
    filterVal = 0;
  }

  smoothedVal = (data * (1 - filterVal)) + (smoothedVal  *  filterVal);

  return (int)smoothedVal;
}
```

Press the Compile button to check your code. Compiling highlights any grammatical errors, which light up in red when they are discovered. If the sketch compiles correctly, click Upload to send the sketch to your board. When it is done uploading, open the serial monitor and touch or approach the antenna. You should see two values racing down the screen. On the left is the raw value that is being read; on the right is the same reading after smoothing.

If nothing happens, double-check your wiring:

✔ Make sure that you're using the correct pin number.

✔ Check the connections on the breadboard. If the jump wires or components are not connected using the correct rows in the breadboard, they will not work.

Understanding the CapPinSketch sketch

At the start of the sketch in the declarations, a new `CapPin` object is named. Notice that `cPin_5` is the name and that it is assigned to pin 5 using `CapPin(5)`.

```
CapPin cPin_5 = CapPin(5);   // read pin 5
```

A float named `smoothed` is declared to store the processed value of the sensor.

```
float smoothed;
```

In `setup`, serial communication is started on the fastest baud rate available to Arduino 115200, and the message "start" is sent to indicate to you that the serial port is connected.

```
void setup()
{

  Serial.begin(115200);
  Serial.println("start");
```

What is a float?

A *float,* or floating point number, is any number with a decimal point. Variables can be set to floating point numbers instead of integers. This is preferable in some situations, such as in this case where you are taking extremely precise readings of capacitance. However, processing floats takes much more time than integers and should, therefore, be avoided if possible.

This commented line is not used in this sketch, but is referenced in some of the other CapSense examples. It can be uncommented to include further calibration functions that are in the library, but is not be covered in this example:

```
// slider_2_7.calibrateSlider();

}
```

In this sketch, many variables are declared locally. Because they are not needed outside the loop, they are removed after each loop and redeclared at the start of the next loop.

First, a one-millisecond delay occurs to help improve stability of the reading:

```
void loop()
{


  delay(1);
```

Next, the long variable total1 is declared. This variable can look confusing because the lowercase *L* and the numeral one look the same in most fonts. Incidentally, this variable does not appear to be used in this sketch. It may well be leftover from a previous version.

```
  long total1 = 0;
```

The next long variable is set to the current millis () value. Because this is a local variable, this value is reset on each loop.

```
  long start = millis();
```

The specific function .readPin() reads your capacitive pin.

```
  long total = cPin_5.readPin(2000);
```

If you want to explore in more depth what's happening, look at CapPin.cpp in the CapSense library. At first this looks baffling, but by finding the line that follows, you can see that the value relates to the number of samples that the Arduino is taking of the capacitance reading:

```
long CapPin::readPin(unsigned int samples)
```

Editing the inner workings of libraries is not advised for beginners, but it is good to have a look at them to know what's happening in your code and try to gain a better understanding of them.

A smoothing function is also included in the sketch. This function takes the raw reading from the sensor, the smoothing value, and then the output variable. At present, it is set to 0.8, but go ahead and experiment with this value to find the appropriate amount of smoothing for your application. This amount is dependent on how fast the loop is completed and how many readings are made in that time, so bear that in mind if you expect to add a lot of other controls or outputs.

```
// simple lowpass filter to take out some of the jitter
// change parameter (0 is min, .99 is max) or eliminate to suit
smoothed = smooth(total, .8, smoothed);
```

Finally, the values are printed to the serial port to be monitored. `millis()` – `start` gives the time that is taken to carry out the reading. If more samples are taken or any delays are added to the code, these activities increase the time to complete the loop and, therefore, the reaction time of the sensor.

```
Serial.print( millis() - start);        // time to execute in mS
```

Tabs are used to neatly space the values. The total and smoothed values are both printed for comparison. You may notice a slight delay in the response time of the smoothed value. This delay shows you that your Arduino is reading many more values to do the smoothing, which takes time. This is barely noticeable when the sensor is in use because the baud rate is so high.

```
Serial.print("\t");
Serial.print(total);                    // raw total
Serial.print("\t");
Serial.println((int) smoothed);         // smoothed
  delay(5);
}
```

At the bottom of the sketch outside the main loop is an additional function. This is referred to as a *lowpass filter* and gives you the smoothed result. You can see that rather than starting with `void` as is the case in `setup ()` and `loop ()`, the function starts with `int`, which means that an integer value is returned. Starting with `int` indicates that when this function is called, it is possible to assigned its return value to a variable.

```
// simple lowpass filter
// requires recycling the output in the "smoothedVal" param
int smooth(int data, float filterVal, float smoothedVal){

  if (filterVal > 1){        // check to make sure param's are within range
    filterVal = .999999;
```

```
  }
  else if (filterVal <= 0){
    filterVal = 0;
  }

  smoothedVal = (data * (1 - filterVal)) + (smoothedVal  *  filterVal);

  return (int)smoothedVal;
}
```

Tripping Along with Lasers

Laser trip wires are made up of two parts, a laser light source and a light sensor. As you know from the movies, when the beam is broken an alarm sounds and the henchmen come running. With an Arduino, you can make a laser trip wire very simply and trigger anything you want from it. Rather than buy a state-of-the-art security system, you can build one yourself using a few simple components. You're on your own for the henchmen, though.

✔ **Complexity:** Lasers are a difficult subject area because of the potential risks of working with them. But rather than risk your eyesight or spend a few years studying, why not use something that's already been tested, certified, and turned into a product? Laser pens or laser pointers are widely available and relatively cheap. These are usually Class 1 lasers, the lowest class, and are visible and safe under all conditions of normal use, but you're still advised to check the specifications of your laser to ensure that it is appropriate for the audience and the environment. Adults are normally sensible enough not to look directly into the laser, but with children, you want to err on the side of caution and find another sensor.

Because a laser beam is so precise, it's best to choose one with a fairly large sensor so that you have a large area to aim for. The only added complexity of this sensor may be powering the laser. A laser pointer is usually battery powered (because it's not much use with a huge plug on the end), so you may need to replace the batteries every few days or wire a power supply of equal value to the battery compartment.

To make them useful in the outside world, I recommend that you house both the laser and the light sensor in enclosures. A nice touch is to mount the enclosures on mini tripods to give you some flexibility when aligning them.

✔ **Cost:** For around $15 (£10) you can purchase a small, discreet laser pointer from RadioShack, in the United States, or Maplin in the United Kingdom. Battery life and beam color are the main differences between pointers. The light sensor costs around 75 cents to $2.50 (50p to £1.50), depending on the size. If you opt for an enclosure, it may cost around $6 (£4). A mini tripod is around $9 (£6).

✔ **Where:** If you have a fixed location for your tripwire, mounting the enclosure on either side of a doorway is simple. The best position is as low to the floor as possible to avoid eye contact with the laser. If you're not sure where you want it or want to try a few ideas, keep it mobile and take your tripod-mounted trip wire with you wherever it's needed. Laser tripwires make especially good camera triggers, which you can read more about in the bonus chapter at www.dummies.com/go/arduinofd.

The laser trip wire is a refinement of a conventional light sensor. By providing a more intense, controlled light source, you can increase the accuracy of a simple light sensor.

In this example, you use a laser to make your light sensor achieve its full potential. By using the DigitalInOutSerial circuit, you can monitor the levels of your sensor when the laser is hitting it and look for the change when the laser is obscured. From this reading, you can trigger any number of outputs.

Implementing the AnalogInOutSerial sketch

You need:

✔ An Arduino Uno

✔ A breadboard

✔ A light sensor

✔ An LED

✔ A 10k ohm resistor

✔ A 220 ohm resistor

✔ Jump wires

Complete the circuit from the layout in Figures 12-8 and 12-9 to make the receiver side of the circuit. The laser pen can be battery powered or wired to a power supply of equal voltage as the batteries. For more detail on choosing a power supply, head over to Chapter 15.

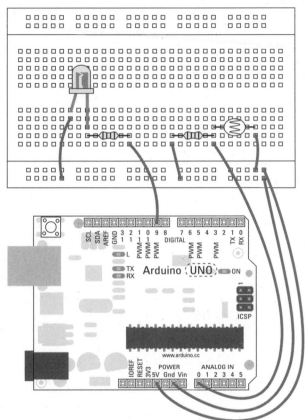

Figure 12-8:
Analog input
and LED
output cir-
cuit layout.

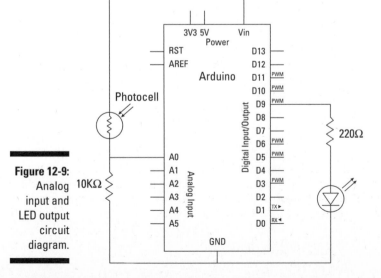

Figure 12-9:
Analog
input and
LED output
circuit
diagram.

Choose File⇨Examples⇨03.Analog⇨AnalogInOutSerial from the Arduino menu to load the sketch.

```
/*
  Analog input, analog output, serial output

  Reads an analog input pin, maps the result to a range from 0 to 255
  and uses the result to set the pulsewidth modulation (PWM) of an output pin.
  Also prints the results to the serial monitor.

  The circuit:
  * potentiometer connected to analog pin 0.
    Center pin of the potentiometer goes to the analog pin.
    side pins of the potentiometer go to +5V and ground
  * LED connected from digital pin 9 to ground

  created 29 Dec. 2008
  modified 9 Apr 2012
  by Tom Igoe

  This example code is in the public domain.

  */

// These constants won't change.  They're used to give names
// to the pins used:
const int analogInPin = A0;  // Analog input pin that the potentiometer is
                  attached to
const int analogOutPin = 9; // Analog output pin that the LED is attached to

int sensorValue = 0;        // value read from the pot
int outputValue = 0;        // value output to the PWM (analog out)

void setup() {
  // initialize serial communications at 9600 bps:
  Serial.begin(9600);
}

void loop() {
  // read the analog in value:
  sensorValue = analogRead(analogInPin);
  // map it to the range of the analog out:
  outputValue = map(sensorValue, 0, 1023, 0, 255);
  // change the analog out value:
  analogWrite(analogOutPin, outputValue);

  // print the results to the serial monitor:
  Serial.print("sensor = " );
  Serial.print(sensorValue);
  Serial.print("\t output = ");
  Serial.println(outputValue);

  // wait 2 milliseconds before the next loop
```

```
// for the analog-to-digital converter to settle
// after the last reading:
delay(2);
}
```

Press the Compile button to check your code. The compiler highlights any grammatical errors, which light up in red when they are discovered. If the sketch compiles correctly, click Upload to send the sketch to your board. When it is done uploading, mount your laser so that it hits the center of the light sensor. On the serial monitor, you should see analog values at the high end of the range (1024 max). When you obstruct the beam, that range should drop, and the change should be shown by the LED as well. Experiment with the values in the map function to determine the best range of values.

When the value drops below a certain threshold, you can trigger any of a variety of actions — you have a highly sensitive trip wire sensor.

If nothing happens, double-check your wiring:

- ✔ Make sure that you're using the correct pin number.
- ✔ Check the connections on the breadboard. If the jump wires or components are not connected using the correct rows in the breadboard, they do not work.

Understanding the AnalogInOutSerial sketch

For more details on the workings of this sketch, see the notes in AnalogInOutSerial in Chapter 7. You can also find suggestions for different sketches to provide smoothing and calibration in Chapter 11.

Detecting Movement

A Passive Infrared (PIR) sensor is a common sensor in some homes and most commercial buildings. You may have seen this sensor in the corner of a room, blinking red every once in a while. It registers heat given off by people, animals, or other heat sources as infrared radiation. Infrared radiation is invisible to the human eye but is easy for the sensor to distinguish. The sensor itself is similar to the sensor found in a digital camera, but without the complex lenses to capture a detailed picture. Essentially, a PIR sensor is somewhere between a high-resolution light sensor and a low-resolution camera. Simple lenses are usually fitted to PIR sensors to give them a wider viewing angle.

Most commonly, this type of sensor is used for motion detection in burglar alarms. Rather than detect motion, it actually detects changes in temperature. Temperature changes can trigger an alarm system or something more interesting (henchmen!), but the sensor is purely a way of monitoring changes in an environment.

You have two ways to get a PIR sensor. The first is to take apart a PIR burglar alarm, which is likely pre-packaged with a lens and a sensor, which may be difficult to identify. The second method is to buy one specifically intended for microcontroller projects. This most often comes with a basic, ping-pong-ball-styled lens and a bare circuit board underneath. The latter is easier to work with because all the details are known and it is detailed later in this section.

Consider the following during planning:

- **Complexity:** It can be tricky to hack an existing PIR sensor made for a specific system. Because it needs to communicate with that system, however, the sensor usually has clearly marked connections on the back. One of the benefits of using an existing sensor is that it is prepackaged, which reduces the amount of time you have to spend putting components together. Prepackaged systems are designed to be easy to install, so you may also be able to use manual calibration, by way of a potentiometer or screwdriver slot, which can be a huge benefit for on-the-fly calibration rather than having to re-upload.

  If you're using a PIR sensor that is not prepackaged, it should be a lot more straightforward on the hardware and software side but requires some careful thought concerning the housing. Some PIR sensors have their own on-board logic and operate like a switch, going HIGH when movement occurs over the threshold. This kind of sensor needs calibration to identify change from the norm.

- **Cost:** A household PIR sensor costs between $15 and $45 (£10 and £30). The main expense is the housing, usually designed to be discreet or look suitably high-tech. Bare PIR sensors cost a fraction of the price at around $10 (£6.50), but need a suitable housing to be of any real use.

- **Where:** Many housings allow you to neatly fit the sensor against a wall, or you might consider using mini tripods for direction, as suggested in the previous section of this chapter. Some of the tripod mounts also come with a suction-cup mount, which is perfect for fixing your sensor to glossy surfaces such as glass.

Most PIR sensors come ready for action, needing only power. They calibrate themselves based on what they can see and then send a HIGH or LOW value when they detect change. This makes them extremely easy to program because you are dealing with the same signals as with a pushbutton.

Implementing the DigitalReadSerial sketch

In this example, you learn how to use the SE-10, a PIR sensor available from all the major Arduino retailers. This particular PIR sensor has three wires: red, brown, and black. The red wire is the power source and should be connected to 5V. Oddly, the black wire is the signal wire and not the ground (see Figure 12-10; the black is the leftmost wire, brown is in the middle, and red is on the right). Brown should be wired to ground and black to pin 2.

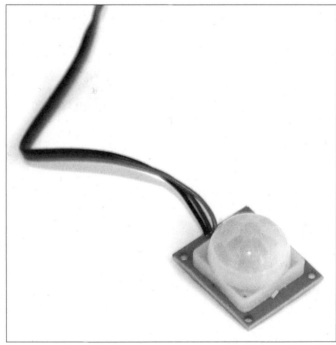

Figure 12-10:
The SE-10, with its strangely colored wires.

The signal pin is known as an open-collector and needs to be pulled HIGH to start with. To do so, you use a 10k resistor to connect it to 5V as well. The pin, therefore, reads HIGH when no motion occurs and is pulled to LOW when there is motion.

You need:

- ✔ An Arduino Uno
- ✔ A breadboard
- ✔ An SE-10 PIR Motion Sensor
- ✔ A 10k ohm resistor
- ✔ Jump wires

Lay out the circuit as in the layout and circuit diagrams shown in Figures 12-11 and 12-12.

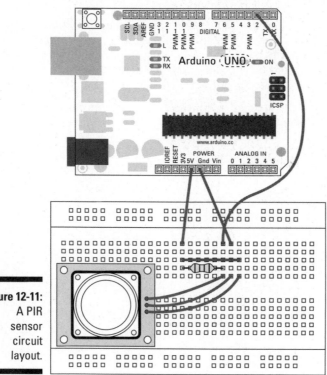

Figure 12-11:
A PIR sensor circuit layout.

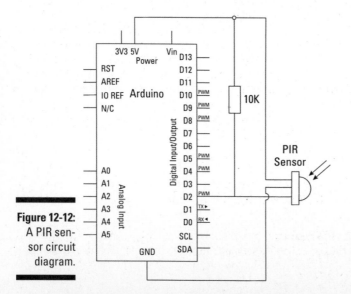

Figure 12-12:
A PIR sensor circuit diagram.

Complete the circuit and choose File⇨Examples⇨01.Basics⇨DigitalReadSerial from the Arduino menu to load the sketch. This sketch is intended for a push-button but follows the same principles. If you want to make the sketch more specific, you can save it with a more appropriate name and variable names.

```
/*
  DigitalReadSerial
  Reads a digital input on pin 2, prints the result to the serial monitor

  This example code is in the public domain.
 */

// digital pin 2 has a pushbutton attached to it. Give it a name:
int pushButton = 2;

// the setup routine runs once when you press reset:
void setup() {
  // initialize serial communication at 9600 bits per second:
  Serial.begin(9600);
  // make the pushbutton's pin an input:
  pinMode(pushButton, INPUT);
}

// the loop routine runs over and over again forever:
void loop() {
  // read the input pin:
  int buttonState = digitalRead(pushButton);
  // print out the state of the button:
  Serial.println(buttonState);
  delay(1);        // delay in between reads for stability
}
```

Press the Compile button to check your code. Doing so highlights any grammatical errors and turns them red when they are discovered. If the sketch compiles correctly, click Upload to send the sketch to your board. When it is done uploading, affix the PIR sensor to a surface that is free of movement and open the serial monitor. Opening the serial monitor resets the sketch and the sensor calibrates itself in the first 1 to 2 seconds. When movement is detected, you should see the buttonState value change from 1 (no movement) to 0 (movement).

If nothing happens, double-check your wiring:

- ✔ Make sure that you're using the correct pin number.

- ✔ Check the connections on the breadboard. If the jump wires or components are not connected using the correct rows in the breadboard, they will not work.

- ✔ Try restarting the PIR sensor by disconnecting and reconnecting the GND wire, and be sure that it does not move during or after calibration.

Understanding the DigitalReadSerial sketch

The only variable to declare is pin 2, the `pushButton` pin, or in this case the `pirSensor` pin.

```
// digital pin 2 has a pushbutton attached to it. Give it a name:
int pushButton = 2;
```

In setup, the serial port is opened and set to a baud rate of 9600; the input pin is set to an output.

```
// the setup routine runs once when you press reset:
void setup() {
  // initialize serial communication at 9600 bits per second:
  Serial.begin(9600);
  // make the pushbutton's pin an input:
  pinMode(pushButton, INPUT);
}
```

In the `loop ()`, the input pin is read and its value stored in `buttonState`. This value reads `HIGH` when no movement is occurring because the pull-up resistor is providing a voltage from the 5V pin. When there is movement, the open-collector grounds the voltage and reads `LOW`.

```
// the loop routine runs over and over again forever:
void loop() {
  // read the input pin:
  int buttonState = digitalRead(pushButton);
```

The value of the input is then printed to the serial monitor.

```
  // print out the state of the button:
  Serial.println(buttonState);
  delay(1);        // delay in between reads for stability
}
```

This is one example of how to use existing code for different hardware. From this point, it is possible to trigger different outputs based on the **_HIGH_** or **_LOW_** signal of the PIR sensor. For the ease of use and clarity of other people using your code, you should rename variables to more appropriate names, add your own comments, and save the sketch so that you can easily distinguish it.

Measuring Distance

Two sensors for measuring distance are extremely popular: the infrared proximity sensor and the ultrasonic range finder. They work in similar ways and achieve pretty much the same thing, but it's important to pick the right sensor for the environment you're in. An infrared proximity sensor has a light source and a sensor. The light source bounces infrared light off objects and back to the sensor, and the time it takes the light to return is measured to indicate how far away an object is.

An ultrasonic range finder fires out high frequency sound waves and listens for an echo when they hit a solid surface. By measuring the time that it takes a signal to bounce back, the ultrasonic range finder can determine the distance travelled.

Infrared proximity sensors are not as accurate and have a much shorter range than ultrasonic range finders.

Consider the following during planning:

✔ **Complexity:** Both of these sensors are designed to be extremely easy to integrate with Arduino projects. In the real world, they're used for similar electronics applications, such as proximity meters on the back of cars that beep as you approach the curb. Again, the main complexity is housing them effectively. Infrared proximity sensors such as those made by Shape have useful screw holes on the outside of the body of the sensor. Maxbotix makes ultrasonic range finders that do not have these mounts, but their cylindrical shape makes them simple to mount in a surface by drilling a hole through.

✔ **Cost:** Infrared proximity sensors cost in the region of $15 (£10) and have a range up to about 59 inches (150 cm) or less. Ultrasonic range finders have a far greater possible range and accuracy but an equally great price, costing between $27 (£18) for a sensor that can read up to 254 inches (645 cm) and $100 (£65) for a more weather-resistant model that can read up to 301 inches (765 cm).

✔ **Where:** A common application for these sensors is monitoring presence of a person or an object in a particular floor space, especially when a pressure pad would be too obvious or easy to avoid, or when a PIR sensor would measure too widely. Using a proximity sensor lets you know where someone is in a straight line from that sensor, making it a very useful tool.

IR proximity sensors are okay in dark environments but perform terribly in direct sunlight. The MaxBotix Ultrasonic Range Finder is one of my favorite and most reliable sensors. When using ultrasonic range finders, you can also choose how wide or narrow a beam you want. A large, teardrop-shaped sensor is perfect for detecting large objects moving in a general direction, whereas narrow beams are great for precision measurement.

Implementing the MaxSonar sketch

In this example, you learn how to measure precise distances using a MaxBotix LV-EZ0. The EZ0, EZ1, EZ2, EZ3 and EZ4 all work the same way, but each has a slightly narrower beam, so choose the appropriate one for your project.

The range finder needs some minor assembly. To use the range finder in your circuit, you either need to solder on header pins to use it on a breadboard, or solder on lengths of wire.

You have three ways to connect your range finder: using analog, pulse width, or serial communication. In this example, you learn how to measure the pulse width and convert that to distance. The analog output can be read straight into your analog input pins but provide less accurate results than pulse width. This example does not cover serial communication.

You need:

- ✔ An Arduino Uno
- ✔ An LV-EZ0 Ultrasonic Range Finder
- ✔ Jump wires

Complete the circuit from the layout and circuit diagrams in Figures 12-13 and 12-14. The connections for the range finder are clearly marked on the underside of the PCB. The 5V and GND connections provide power for the sensor and should be connected to the 5V and GND supplies on your Arduino. The PW connection is the pulse width signal that will be read by pin 7 on your Arduino. Make sure that your distance sensor is affixed to some sort of base pointed in the direction that you want to measure.

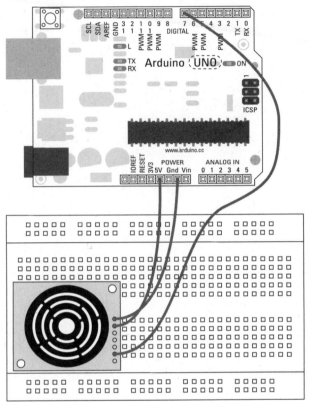

Figure 12-13:
An LV-EZ0
circuit
layout.

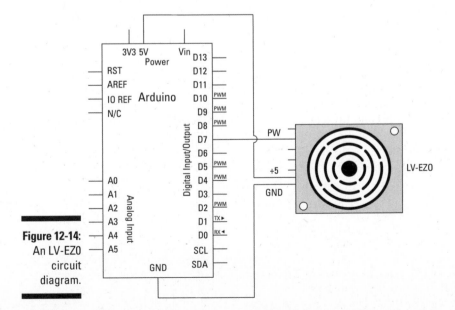

Figure 12-14:
An LV-EZ0
circuit
diagram.

You can find the MaxSonar code by Bruce Allen in the Arduino playground at www.arduino.cc/playground/Main/MaxSonar, along with some additional notes and functions. Create a new sketch, copy or type the code into it, and save it with a memorable name, such as myMaxSonar.

```
//Feel free to use this code.
//Please be respectful by acknowledging the author in the code if you use or
          modify it.
//Author: Bruce Allen
//Date: 23/07/09
//Digital pin 7 for reading in the pulse width from the MaxSonar device.
//This variable is a constant because the pin will not change throughout
          execution of this code.
const int pwPin = 7;
//variables needed to store values
long pulse, inches, cm;

void setup() {
  //This opens up a serial connection to shoot the results back to the PC
          console
  Serial.begin(9600);
}

void loop() {

  pinMode(pwPin, INPUT);

    //Used to read in the pulse that is being sent by the MaxSonar device.
  //Pulse Width representation with a scale factor of 147 uS per Inch.

  pulse = pulseIn(pwPin, HIGH);
  //147uS per inch
  inches = pulse/147;
  //change inches to centimetres
  cm = inches * 2.54;

  Serial.print(inches);
  Serial.print("in, ");
  Serial.print(cm);
  Serial.print("cm");
  Serial.println();

  delay(500);

}
```

Press the Compile button to check your code. The compiler highlights any grammatical errors, turning them red when they are discovered. If the sketch compiles correctly, click Upload to send the sketch to your board. When it is done uploading, open the serial monitor and you should see the distance measured in inches and centimeters. If the value is fluctuating, try using an object with a bigger surface.

This sketch allows you to accurately measure distance in a straight line. Test this with a tape measure and make adjustments to the code if you find discrepancies.

If nothing happens, double-check your wiring:

✔ Make sure that you're using the correct pin number.

✔ Check the connections on the breadboard. If the jump wires or components are not connected using the correct rows in the breadboard, they will not work.

Understanding the MaxSonar sketch

In the declarations, pin 7 is defined as the `pwPin`.

```
//This variable is a constant because the pin will not change throughout
          execution of this code.
const int pwPin = 7;
```

`long` variables are used to store the pulse width and distances in inches and centimeters. Notice that you can declare all three in a list if they have no value.

```
//variables needed to store values
long pulse, inches, cm;
```

In setup, the serial connection is opened to print the results.

```
void setup() {
  //This opens up a serial connection to shoot the results back to the PC
          console
  Serial.begin(9600);
}
```

In the main `loop ()`, the `pwPin` is set as an input. You can set the input in the `loop ()` but can also move it to `setup ()`.

```
void loop() {

  pinMode(pwPin, INPUT);
```

You use the function `pulseIn` to return the length of time it takes the pulse to return to the sensor in microseconds, or µS.

```
  //Used to read in the pulse that is being sent by the MaxSonar device.
  //Pulse Width representation with a scale factor of 147 uS per Inch.

  pulse = pulseIn(pwPin, HIGH);
```

A pulse travels 1 inch every 147 µS, so you can calculate the number of inches from the time. From this information, a simple conversion outputs the distance in different units.

```
//147uS per inch
inches = pulse/147;
//change inches to centimetres
cm = inches * 2.54;
```

The results are printed to the serial monitor, with a `Serial.println` at the end to start a new line in between each reading.

```
Serial.print(inches);
Serial.print("in, ");
Serial.print(cm);
Serial.print("cm");
Serial.println();
```

A delay is added to slow down the readings for legibility, but you can remove the delay if responsiveness is more important.

```
    delay(500);

}
```

This provides you with an accurate distance reading that you can incorporate into your own projects. A simple way to make use of this is with an `if` statement. For example:

```
if (cm < 50) {
// do something!
}
```

Testing, Testing . . . Can Anybody Hear This?

Sound is another way to detect presence, and the best way to do it is with an electret microphone. It's common to think of sounds in their analog form as recognizable noises, but a lot of the sounds we hear every day have undergone or will undergo an analog to digital conversion. By converting sound into a digital signal, it's possible to interpret it on a computer or an Arduino. An electret microphone is similar to the microphones found in computer headsets and is extremely sensitive, but needs an amplifier in order for the Arduino to register the readings.

Consider the following during your planning:

- ✔ **Complexity:** There are plenty of electret mics to choose from, but by far the easiest is Sparkfun's Breakout Board for Electret Microphone. It comes preassembled with the mic mounted on a circuit board and with an amplifier, and can easily be wired up to an Arduino as an analog input. It is possible to use electret mics from other headsets or desktop microphones, but these need their own amplifier to be of any use. There is some work involved to make the correct housing for the mic to protect it from the environment or human contact, but this could simply be an enclosure with a hole.

- ✔ **Cost:** The microphone itself is extremely cheap at 90 cents (61p) from Sparkfun (or distributors of their products). The breakout board costs $7.50 (£5.10), which is not a huge expense for the amount of labor saved.

- ✔ **Where:** As an ambient sensor, the mic could be placed just about anywhere to map the noise levels of a room. If you're listening for a specific noise like a door slamming, it may be best to place the microphone near that source to get a clear reading.

One unusual use for a mic that I have encountered is monitoring someone's breath. As the mic measures the amplitude or volume of the sound, it's perfect for this application. By placing the mic at the end of a tube it's even possible to monitor the length and intensity of breaths as the air rushes past the mic.

Electret mics are great for measuring the amplitude or volume of noise. This can be a trigger for a variety of outputs.

Implementing the AnalogInOutSerial sketch

In this example, you monitor sound levels wherever you are using an electret mic. This simple sensor can be read as an analog input into your Arduino.

You need:

- ✔ An Arduino Uno
- ✔ A Breakout Board for Electret Microphone
- ✔ Jump wires

Complete the circuit from the layout and circuit diagrams in Figures 12-15 and 12-16 to connect the mic as your input and the LED as your output. The Electret Mic breakout board requires a small amount of soldering to use on a breadboard or connect to your Arduino. You can either solder on a set of three header pins or solder on a length of wire, depending on your situation.

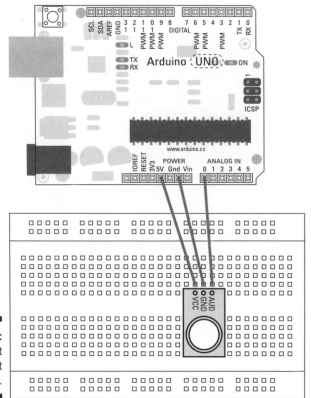

Figure 12-15:
An electret
mic circuit
layout.

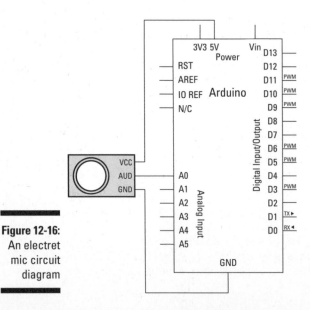

Figure 12-16:
An electret
mic circuit
diagram

Choose File⇨Examples⇨03.Analog⇨AnalogInOutSerial from the Arduino menu to load the sketch.

```
/*
  Analog input, analog output, serial output

  Reads an analog input pin, maps the result to a range from 0 to 255
  and uses the result to set the pulsewidth modulation (PWM) of an output pin.
  Also prints the results to the serial monitor.

  The circuit:
  * potentiometer connected to analog pin 0.
    Center pin of the potentiometer goes to the analog pin.
    side pins of the potentiometer go to +5V and ground
  * LED connected from digital pin 9 to ground

  created 29 Dec. 2008
  modified 9 Apr 2012
  by Tom Igoe

  This example code is in the public domain.

  */

// These constants won't change.  They're used to give names
// to the pins used:
const int analogInPin = A0;  // Analog input pin that the potentiometer is
                 attached to
const int analogOutPin = 9; // Analog output pin that the LED is attached to

int sensorValue = 0;        // value read from the pot
int outputValue = 0;        // value output to the PWM (analog out)

void setup() {
  // initialize serial communications at 9600 bps:
  Serial.begin(9600);
}

void loop() {
  // read the analog in value:
  sensorValue = analogRead(analogInPin);
  // map it to the range of the analog out:
  outputValue = map(sensorValue, 0, 1023, 0, 255);
  // change the analog out value:
  analogWrite(analogOutPin, outputValue);

  // print the results to the serial monitor:
  Serial.print("sensor = " );
  Serial.print(sensorValue);
  Serial.print("\t output = ");
```

```
Serial.println(outputValue);

// wait 2 milliseconds before the next loop
// for the analog-to-digital converter to settle
// after the last reading:
delay(2);
}
```

Press the Compile button to check your code. Doing so highlights any gram-matical errors and turns them red when they are discovered. If the sketch compiles correctly, click Upload to send the sketch to your board. When it is done uploading, open the serial monitor to see analog values in the range of 0 to 1024.

If nothing happens, double-check your wiring:

- Make sure that you're using the correct pin number.
- Check the connections on the breadboard. If the jump wires or compo-nents are not connected using the correct rows in the breadboard, they will not work.

See what range of values you get from different noises in your environment and how sensitive or over sensitive the mic is. Another sketch to consider is the Smoothing sketch in Chapter 11.By using if statements, you can perform actions whenever the sound level crosses a threshold.

Understanding the AnalogInOutSerial sketch

For more details on the workings of this sketch, see the notes in AnalogInOutSerial in Chapter 7. You can also find suggestions for different sketches to provide smoothing and calibration in Chapter 11.

Part IV
Unlocking Your Arduino's Potential

The 5th Wave   By Rich Tennant

© RICHTENNANT

"I'm kind of busy. I told my neighbor I'd fix his PS2 so he could play extra games on it."

In this part . . .

Part IV is all about how to do more with your Arduino project. You learn how to use the Arduino Mega 2560, which can control more outputs than a regular Uno. You also learn how additional hardware can allow your Uno board to do much more than you thought possible, with shift registers and PWM drivers. With this knowledge, you could animate huge numbers of LEDs to create your own version of the Las Vegas Strip (or the Blackpool Illuminations, for my British friends) and control an army of servo motors to create your very own robot walker to do your bidding!

Chapter 13

Becoming a Specialist with Shields and Libraries

In This Chapter

▶ Finding out about shields

▶ Looking at the range of shields available

▶ Understanding libraries

---

*T*he further you progress in learning about Arduino, the more you want to do, and it's natural to want to run before you can walk. The areas that interest you may be highly specialized in themselves and require a huge investment of time to understand. Perhaps the most important thing about Arduino is the Arduino community, which is where you can get help when you want go further.

The traditional viewpoint that is hammered into us in education is to protect our ideas for dear life. Thankfully, many people in the Arduino community have seen past that limitation and are kind enough to share their hard work. By sharing this knowledge, the Arduino community helps the hardware and software become available to more people, who find new and interesting uses for it. If these people in turn share their results, the community continues to grow and eventually makes even the most difficult projects achievable. In this chapter, you find out more about how powerful shared resources such as shields and libraries can be, even for beginners.

Looking at Shields

Shields are pieces of hardware that sit on top of your Arduino, often to give it a specific purpose. For example, you can use a shield to make it easier to connect and control motors or even to turn your Arduino into something as complex as a mobile phone. A shield may start out as an interesting bit of hardware that an enthusiast has been experimenting with and wants to share with the community. Or an enterprising individual (or company) may design a shield to make a specific application easier based on demand from the Arduino community.

Shields can be very simple or very complex. They are sold preassembled or as kits. Kits allow you more freedom to assemble the shield as you need it to be. Some kits require you to assemble the circuitry of the boards, although more complex shields may already be largely assembled, needing only header pins.

Shields allow you to use your Arduino for more than one purpose and to change that purpose easily. They neatly package the electronics for that circuit in the same footprint as an Arduino. They are stackable to combine different functionalities. But they all have to use the same pins on the Arduino, so if you stack shields, watch out for those that need to use the same pins. They always connect the GND pins, too, because any communication by your Arduino and another device needs a common GND.

Considering combinations

In theory, shields could be stacked on top of each other forever, but you should take some points into consideration before combining them:

- ✔ **Physical size:** Some shields just don't fit on top of one another. Components that are higher than the header sockets may touch the underside of any board on top of it. This situation, which can cause short circuits if a connection is made that shouldn't be, can seriously damage your boards.

- ✔ **Obstruction of inputs / outputs:** If an input or output is obstructed by another shield, it becomes redundant. For example, there's no point having a Joystick Shield or an LCD Shield under another shield because no more than one can be used.

- ✔ **Power requirements:** Some hardware requires a lot of power. Although it is all right for shields to use the same power and ground pins, there is a limit to the amount of current that can flow through the other input/output (I/O) pins: 40mA per pin and 200mA max. between all I/O pins. Exceed this, and you run the risk of seriously damaging your board and any other attached shield. In most cases, you can easily remedy this problem by powering your Arduino and shields from an external power supply so that the current isn't passed through the Arduino. Make sure to use a common GND if you're communicating between a board using I2C, SPI, or serial.

- ✔ **Pins:** Some shields require the use of certain pins. It's important to make sure that shields aren't doubling up on the same pins. In the best case, the hardware will just be confused; in the worst case, you can send voltage to the wrong place and damage your board.

- ✔ **Software:** Some of these shields need specific libraries to work. There can be conflicts in libraries calling on the same functions, so make sure to read up on what's required for your shield.

✔ **Interference with radio/WiFi/GPS/GSM:** Wireless devices need space to work. Move antennas or aerials away from the board to get a clear signal. If an antenna is mounted on the board, it's generally a bad idea to cover it. Always try to place wireless shields at the top of the stack.

Reviewing the field

To give you an idea of available shields, this section covers some of the most interesting and useful shields on the market shows you where to look for more information.

Note that all prices were current at the time this book was written and are liable to change, but I've included them to give you an idea of the cost. Links to products may also change, so always try searching for the product if the link is broken. Technical information is gathered from the manufacturers websites, but you should always check the details yourself to make sure that you are buying what you need. Boards are revised occasionally, so always keep an eye out for the latest versions.

Finally, a lot of feedback on all of these products is available online, so always read the comments and forums to get a good understanding of what you're buying.

This range of shields covers a vast number of different uses and the huge potential of Arduino projects. For many projects, a shield is all you need, but a shield is also an excellent stepping stone for proving a concept before refining or miniaturizing your project.

Prices provided are from a range of distributors to show the approximate value of the items. If you're a savvy shopper or looking to buy in bulk, you may also be able to reduce the cost further.

Proto Shield Kit Rev3

Made by: Arduino

Price: £8.95 from RS Components; $12.95 from Mouser

Pins used: None

The Proto Shield (shown in Figure 13-1) is a platform for building custom circuits on your Arduino. Many shields listed in this chapter add a specific function to your Arduino, but with a Proto Shield, you can decide how to use it. Take your existing breadboard layouts and solder them to the surface of the Proto Shield to make your project much more durable. Proto Shields also come in a larger size to match the Arduino Mega's footprint. Another handy feature of these shields is the handy space to attach SMD parts, which can be difficult to do otherwise.

The Proto Shield is either sold fully assembled or as a kit that requires soldering.

You can find details about the shield on the Arduino product page (`http://arduino.cc/en/Main/ArduinoProtoShield`).

Figure 13-1:
A fully
assembled
Proto
Shield.

ProtoScrew Shield

Made by: WingShield Industries

Price: £9.94 from Proto-Pic; $14.95 from SparkFun

Pins used: None

The ProtoScrew Shield is extremely similar to the regular Proto Shield but has large screw terminals connected to the pins as well. This feature is great for applications that have lots of inputs that may need changing or swapping, or just for easier assembly and disassembly. Changing a piece of wire is much easier with screw terminals than with soldering, so bear this in mind when planning your next project.

The ProtoScrew Shield is sold as a kit and requires soldering.

You can find more details on the SparkFun products page (www.sparkfun.com/products/9729).

Adafruit Wave Shield v1.1

Made by: Adafruit

Price: £18.00 from Oomlou; $22.00 from Adafruit

Pins used: 13, 12, 11, 10, 5, 4, 3, 2 on the Uno R3

The Wave Shield (see Figure 13-2) is a relatively cheap kit that allows you to play sounds or music with your Arduino. The Wave Shield allows you to play .WAV files directly from an SD card, making it easy to upload and change the sound files from your computer. To use the shield, you need the WaveHC library available from the product page or Google Code (http://code.google.com/p/wavehc/).

The Wave Shield is sold as a kit and requires soldering. The SD card reader must use pins 13, 12, and 11 because they support high-speed serial peripheral interface (SPI), which is a protocol needed to transfer data quickly. Pin 10 is used to communicate with the SD card reader, and pins 5, 4, 3, and 2 are used to talk to the digital to analog converter (DAC), which converts a digital music signal into an analog voltage.

For more details, visit the product page on Adafruit's website (www.adafruit.com/products/94), where you can find a thorough tutorial as well (www.ladyada.net/make/waveshield/).

Figure 13-2: A fully assembled Wave Shield.

MP3 Player Shield

Made by: SparkFun

Price: £23.95 from HobbyTronics; $39.95 from SparkFun

Pins used: 13, 12, 11, 9, 8, 7, 6, 5, 4, 3, 2 on the Uno R3

Turn your Arduino into an MP3 player with this easy-to-assemble shield! Not only can it decode MP3 files, it's also capable of decoding Ogg Vorbis, AAC, WMA, and MIDI. The MP3 Shield also has a MicroSD card reader for ease of uploading files, and it has a 3.5mm mini jack that you can plug into most speaker systems.

The MP3 Player Shield (shown in Figure 13-3) is assembled, but requires minor soldering to attach the header pins or header sockets. The SD card reader uses pins 13, 12, and 11. You use pin 9 to talk with the SD card reader. Use pins 8, 7, 6, and 2 talk to the MP3 Audio Decoder VS1053B, and you use 4 and 3 for additional midi functionality.

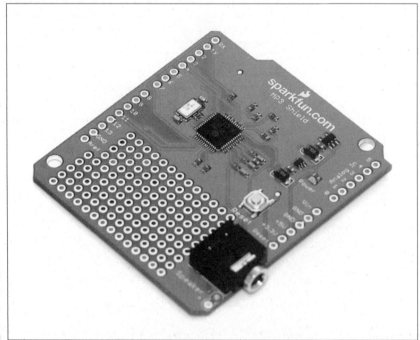

Figure 13-3:
An MP3
shield kit.

For more details, visit the SparkFun products page (www.sparkfun.com/products/10628). There is also a tutorial page to get you started (www.sparkfun.com/tutorials/295), but this was written quite a while ago and is out of date. Thankfully, the comments beneath the tutorial address many of the issues with this guide, and one user has even written a library to make your life easier. This is a great example of the Arduino community supporting the products that already exist.

Always read the comments and forum entries on products and kits. These comments often contain a lot of detail on the ease (or lack of) of a specific product. This is also the place to voice your own problems. Just be sure that you're not repeating something that's solved further down the page; otherwise, you'll be advised to read the manual!

MIDI Shield

Made by: SparkFun

Price: £13.90 from HobbyTronics; $19.95 from SparkFun

Pins used: Uses pins 7, 6, 4, 3, 2, A1, A0 on the Uno R3

MIDI is short for Musical Instrument Digital Interface, and it revolutionized the music industry in the 1980s. Despite being relatively old now, MIDI is still a good standard to connect instruments, computer, stage effects, and other hardware and so is still widely used. With the MIDI shield, you can interface with anything that can send or receive MIDI data and incorporate it into your Arduino project.

The MIDI Shield is sold as a kit and requires soldering.

For more details, visit the Sparkfun product page (www.sparkfun.com/products/9595). You can find some excellent general tutorials on MIDI available at (http://arduino.cc/en/Tutorial/Midi and http://itp.nyu.edu/physcomp/Labs/MIDIOutput). A lot of excellent reference material is at (www.tigoe.net/pcomp/code/communication/midi/ and http://hinton-instruments.co.uk/reference/midi/protocol/).

RGB LCD Shield w/16 x 2 character display

Made by: Adafruit

Price: £15.36 from Adafruit; $24.95 from Adafruit

Pins used: Uses pins A4 and A5 on the Uno R3

This handy LCD (liquid crystal display) shield packages everything you need onto one board. LCDs are found in older mobile phones and Nintendo GameBoys (wow, that sounds old already). They use a film that sits over a solid-colored surface that is usually backlit. The pixels of this film can be turned on or off to make shapes, text, or graphics, and this is what you control with your Arduino. At the center of the shield is an RGB LCD display, so instead of being stuck with just one color, you can choose from *any* RGB color. The RGB backlight is controlled directly from your Arduino. The display is a 16 x 2 character display (no graphics), and you can write two rows of 16 characters. Depending on which display you choose, your display is either colored text on a dark background (negative) or dark text on a colored background (positive). You have a variety of LCD character displays with various backlighting and dimensions from which to choose, so be sure to shop around.

The RGB LCD Shield is sold as a kit and requires soldering. Instead of using nine pins or more, the LDC, backlight, and the buttons all use just two. By using the I2C to communicate with the shield, you can use use only an analog pin 4, which is the data (SDA) line, and analog pin 5, which is the clock (SCL) line. This protocol is used in many devices, so it is extremely useful to know about. For more details on I2C, check John Boxall's excellent tutorial at `http://tronixstuff.wordpress.com/2010/10/20/tutorial-arduino-and-the-i2c-bus/`.

For more details, check out the Adafruit products page (`http://adafruit.com/products/714`) and tutorial (`http://learn.adafruit.com/rgb-lcd-shield`).

Shields are also available that use the same technology but don't limit you to just letters and numbers. If you're looking to display your own graphics, you might want to use the SparkFun Color LCD shield, which uses a Nokia 6100 screen, or the larger TFT Touch Shield.

TFT Touch Shield

Made by: Adafruit

Price: £56.74 from Proto-PIC; $59.00 from Adafruit

Pins used: 5, 6, 7, 8, 9, 10, 11, 12, 13, A0, A1, A2, A3

If an LCD display isn't enough for you, try this TFT Touch Shield to add full color and touch input to your project. This display is a TFT LCD screen (a variation on a standard LCD screen that uses thin-film transistor (TFT) technology to improve the image quality) with a resolution of 240 x 320 pixels and 18-bit colors, giving you 262,144 different shades. The screen is also fitted with a resistive touch screen to register finger presses anywhere on the surface of the screen.

The TFT Touch Shield is sold fully assembled and requires no soldering, so it can simply be plugged on top of your Arduino. The Touch Shield needs a lot of pins to function and leaves you with only digital pins 2 and 3 and analog pins 4 and 5. Pin 12 is also available if you are not using the microSD reader.

Check out the products page at `www.adafruit.com/products/376` and a full tutorial at `http://learn.adafruit.com/2-8-tft-touch-shield`. Adafruit has also very kindly written a complete library for the TFT to draw pixels, shapes and text (`https://github.com/adafruit/TFTLCD-Library`) and a library for the touch screen that detects x, y, and z horizontal movement, vertical movement, and pressure (`https://github.com/adafruit/Touch-Screen-Library`).

Joystick Shield

Made by: SparkFun

Price: £8.94 from Proto-PIC; $12.95 from SparkFun

Pins used: 2, 3, 4, 5, 6, A0, A1

The Joystick Shield (shown in Figure 13-4) has all the functions of a modern game controller on a single Arduino-compatible board. Not only does it give you four pushbuttons to assign to various functions, it also has a hidden button in the control stick itself. With the ergonomic control stick, you can smoothly transition between *x* and *y* axes to perform movements with great accuracy.

The Joystick Shield is sold as a kit and requires soldering. The Joystick Shield uses only five digital pins and two analog pins, leaving many other Arduino pins free for other uses. It has five pushbuttons, using digital pins 2 to 6. The movement of the joystick is measured using two potentiometers: analog 0 maps the *x* or horizontal movement; analog 1 maps the *y* or vertical movement.

Figure 13-4:
A Joystick
Shield.

You can find more details on the SparkFun product page (www.sparkfun.com/products/9760). You can also see in-depth assembly tutorial (www.sparkfun.com/tutorials/161) and quick-start guide (www.sparkfun.com/tutorials/171).

Gameduino

Made by: James Bowman

Price: £41.99 from Cool Components; $52.95 from SparkFun

Pins used: 9, 11, 12, 13

The Atmel AVR processor in your Arduino is much more powerful than the 8-bit game consoles of the 1980s, so James Bowman decided to make his own shield to harness this power and created a game adapter for Arduino: the Gameduino (see Figure 13-5). With the Gameduino, you can output graphics to a monitor, projector, or any VGA-compatible display, using the VGA connector on the board. Output audio using the 3.5mm mini jack connector. You can pair this shield with the Joystick Shield described in the previous section to create an all-in-one console and controller.

Figure 13-5: A Gameduino, which plays nicely with a Joystick Shield.

The Gameduino is sold fully assembled and ready to use. The Gameduino is treated as an SPI (Serial Peripheral Interface) peripheral by the Arduino, and four pins are used for communication. For more details, on SPI peripherals go to (`http://en.wikipedia.org/wiki/Serial_Peripheral_Interface_Bus`). You can find Arduino-specific reading at `http://arduino.cc/en/Reference/SPI`. For reference, pin 9 is SEL or SS (slave select), 11 is MOSI (master output, slave input), 12 is MISO (master input, slave output), and 13 is SCK or SCLK: serial clock.

A wealth of resources is available on the Gameduino product page (`http://excamera.com/sphinx/gameduino/`). To get started, download the example sketches to see what's possible from `http://excamera.com/sphinx/gameduino/samples/`. Many specifics of the Gameduino require a lot of reading to fully understand and should be considered advanced work. Good luck!

Adafruit Motor/Stepper/Servo Shield Kit v1.0

Made by: Adafruit

Price: £16.00 from Oomlout; $19.50 from Adafruit

Pins used: 3, 4, 5, 6, 7, 8, 9, 10, 11, 12

Love motors? Want to try them all? Then this shield is the one for you. The Adafruit Motor/Stepper/Servo Shield is aptly named and allows you to run all those motors you love. You can connect up to two 5V hobby servos, two stepper motors, or four bidirectional DC motors. The screw terminals make attaching and switching motors as needed easy. When dealing with motors, it's always important to make sure that you have enough current to drive them all, so a handy screw terminal is on the shield to allow you to power your motors independently of your Arduino.

The Adafruit Motor/Stepper/Servo Shield Kit is sold as a kit and requires soldering. If any DC or stepper motors are in use, pins 4, 7, 8 and 12 are needed to operate the chip that drives them all (74HC595). Pins 3, 5, 6, or 11 control the speed of each individual DC or stepper motor. Pins 9 and 10 control any servos that are connected. This leaves you with digital pins 2 and 13 as well as a full complement of analog input pins, which you can use as digital pins if needed.

You can find many details on the Adafruit product page (`www.adafruit.com/products/81`). A full, in-depth tutorial is on ladyada.net (`www.ladyada.net/make/mshield/`). Be aware of how much load is on the motor because the shield is designed to provide up to 600 mA per motor, with 1.2A peak current. If you're approaching 1A, include a heat sink on the motor driver to dissipate the heat.

Also, the nice people at Adafruit provide an easy-to-use library for your motor project (www.ladyada.net/make/mshield/download.html). Happy motoring!

Motor Shield R3

Made by: Arduino

Price: £18.90 from RS Components; $36.25 from Arduino Store

Pins used: 3, 8, 9, 11, 12, 13, A0, A1

The Arduino Motor Shield is the official motor shield designed by the Arduino team. It can control a modest number of motors, either two DC motors or one unipolar stepper motor, but it can cope with high currents of up to 2A per channel, allowing some heavy lifting. It's also compatible with the TinkerKit, which is ideal for situations in which wire stripping and soldering aren't an option, or for quickly experimenting with using different sensors to control your motors.

The Arduino Motor Shield Rev3 is sold fully assembled and ready to use. The pins on the Arduino Motor Shield are divided into A and B channels. You can use each channel for two individual DC motors to provide four functions: direction, speed, brake and current sensing. Pins 12 and 13 control the direction of each channel, respectively; pins 3 and 11 control the speed of each motor using pwm; pins 9 and 8 are used to break the motor suddenly, rather than allowing it to slow down; and analog pins 0 and 1 can be used read the current draw of the motor on each channel, outputting 3.3V at the maximum rated current of 2A.

To power the motors, you need to use an external power supply that can be connected using the screw terminals on the shield. It's also worth noting that headers on top of the board are for the TinkerKit modules and are not so easy to use without the correct connectors.

To find out more about the Arduino Motor Shield, head over to the product page at the Arduino store (http://store.arduino.cc/ww/index.php?main_page=product_info&cPath=11_5&products_id=204). You can find even more more detail about the shield on the Arduino site (http://arduino.cc/en/Main/ArduinoMotorShieldR3). Curious about TinkerKit modules? Visit www.tinkerkit.com.

LiPower Shield

Made by: SparkFun

Price: £23.57 from Proto-PIC; $29.95 from SparkFun

Pins used: 3

If you want to make your Arduino project more mobile, batteries are the answer. Rather than use bulky AA or AAA battery packs, the LiPower Shield allows you to use rechargeable lithium batteries instead. Although lithium batteries are rated only as 3.7V, some clever hardware steps them up to 5V to make them sufficient to power your Arduino.

The LiPower Shield is assembled but requires minor soldering to attach the header pins or header sockets. Because the LiPower shield is there to provide power and not consume it, only one pin is in use. Pin 3 can be configured as an alert interrupt pin to signal whenever the battery drops to 32 percent or lower.

For more details, check out the SparkFun product page (www.sparkfun. com/products/10711). You find interesting notes on the hardware around the difficulties with charging lithium batteries, so make sure to read all the comments below the product description.Many other smaller lithium break-out boards are available that supply the standard 3.7V, such as the Lithium Polymer USB Charger and Battery by SparkFun (www.sparkfun.com/ products/9876) and the USB/DC Lithium Polymer battery charger 5-12V - 3.7/4.2v by Adafruit (www.adafruit.com/products/280). These breakout boards are perfect when paired with an appropriate low-voltage Arduino, such as the Pro Micro - 3.3V/8Mhz (www.sparkfun.com/products/ 10999) or the Arduino Pro 328 - 3.3V/8MHz (www.sparkfun.com/products/ 10914). These are useful when trying to reduce the size of your Arduino project.

GPS Shield Retail Kit

Made by: SparkFun

Price: £60.59 from Cool Components; $79.95 from SparkFun

Pins used: 0, 1 or 2, 3 (default)

Using the GPS Shield (Figure 13-6), it's quick and easy to incorporate location data into your project. Find your location to within a few meters, maybe to create GPS art or to map all your movements over the month. This shield is also great for giving you an extremely accurate time.

The GPS Shield comes assembled but requires minor soldering to attach the header pins or header sockets. Data from the GPS module can either be set to UART to directly send location data to the Arduino's hardware RX and TX pins, 0 and 1, or set to DLINE to send the data to digital pins 2 and 3 (default). Code can be sent to the Arduino only when it is set to DLINE.

Note that the retail kit is sold with a GPS module and header pins. This shield is designed for the EM-406a module (www.sparkfun.com/products/465).

You can use other modules, such as the EM-408 and EB-85A, but you need to buy the appropriate socket separately.

For more details, visit the SparkFun product page (www.sparkfun.com/products/10710). There is also a great GPS Shield Quickstart Guide to get you going in no time; go to (www.sparkfun.com/tutorials/173/). SparkFun also has an excellent GPS buying guide (www.sparkfun.com/pages/GPS_Guide).

Figure 13-6:
The
Sparkfun
GPS Shield
with the
EM-406a.

GPS Logger Shield Kit v1.1

Made by: Adafruit

Price: £20.53 from Proto-PIC; $19.50 from Adafruit

Pins used: 10, 11, 12, 13 and any two other pins

The GPS Logger Shield lets you track and store location information using the Global Positioning System. You can find your location within a few meters. Use it to create GPS art or to map all your movements over the month. It's also great for giving you an extremely accurate time. This data is stored on an SD card as a .txt file which can then be overlaid onto Google Maps or visualized in some other way.

With the (ever increasing) size of SD cards, you are able to store much more data than your Arduino can on its own internal memory. This is especially useful because it keeps your data-logging device mobile without the need for a computer, meaning that you can leave that bulky laptop at home and send your GPS device out into the world!

The Adafruit GPS Logger Shield Kit is sold as a kit and requires soldering. Pins 10, 11, 12, and 13 are used for communication with the SD card. The GPS module actually requires only a few pins, which are connected by using jump wires to whichever pins you would prefer. RX and TX pins must be connected to two digital pins, such as 2 and 3. You can enable other optional functions, such as a signalling LED to indicate when data is logged, a pin to monitor the pulse from the GPS synchronization clock, and a pin to detect when an SD card is in the slot.

Note that you need to buy a GPS module and SD separately. This shield is designed for the EM-406a module (www.adafruit.com/products/99) but works with a variety of modules (listed at http://ladyada.net/make/gpsshield/modules.html).

Get the shield and more information on Adafruit (www.adafruit.com/products/98). You can view an in-depth tutorial on Ladyada's site (www.ladyada.net/make/gpsshield/) that details everything from construction of the kit through to the Arduino code, along with uses for the GPS data.

Wireless Proto Shield and Wireless SD Shield

Made by: Arduino

Price: £12.22 and £15.92 from RS Components; $27 and $36 from Arduino Store

Pin requirements: 0 and 1 for the Wireless Proto Shield; 0, 1, 4, 11, 12, 13 for the Wireless Shield SD

The Arduino Wireless Proto Shield lets you create a network of wireless devices using XBee radio modules. These highly versatile, reliable, and affordable modules are used to link multiple Arduino boards to create your very own wireless sensor network. The Wireless Shield SD also gives you the ability to store any data you might be collecting from your network and visualize it later on a computer. Each shield also has ample space to add a number of sensors or actuators to your project.

The Wireless Shield and Wireless Shield SD are sold fully assembled and ready to use. The shield talks with either the sketch on the Arduino or through the Arduino to a computer using USB. Using the serial select switch, you can toggle between these two modes. If you have the Wireless Shield

SD, pins 4, 11, 12 and 13 are used to communicate with it and are therefore unavailable for any other function.

Note that you need to purchase the XBee module separately. The XBee 1mW Chip Antenna - Series 1 (802.15.4) is a good one to start with and is available from RS Components (http://uk.rs-online.com/web/p/zigbee-ieee-802154/0102715/) and SparkFun (www.sparkfun.com/products/8664). SparkFun has an excellent XBee buying guide that is extremely helpful if you're starting in the world of wireless networks (www.sparkfun.com/pages/xbee_guide).

The Arduino product page has more detail on the shield (http://arduino.cc/en/Main/ArduinoWirelessShield), and there is a tutorial for simple communication using the XBee 1mW Chip Antenna - Series 1 (802.15.4) on the Arduino site (http://arduino.cc/en/Guide/ArduinoWirelessShield).

Ethernet Shield R3 and Ethernet Shield R3 with PoE

Made by: Arduino

Price: £25.42 and £36.82 from RS Components; $45.95 and $59.95 from SparkFun

Pin requirements: 4, 10, 11, 12, 13

The Ethernet Shield (shown in Figure 13-7) allows your Arduino to talk to the Internet without the need for a computer in the middle. Your Arduino can, therefore, either use or contribute to the wealth of data on the Internet. It may be monitoring Twitter for hashtags or uploading sensor data for the world to see. The shield even has a microSD card reader to allow you to save results or store files to distribute over the network. The R3 is the latest version of this shield and adds a few extra pins to make the shield compatible with the Uno R3.

The Ethernet Shield R3 with Power-over-Ethernet (PoE) includes an extra module that runs diagonally across the board. This is a PoE module and allows you to power your Arduino using the Ethernet cable. This requires a Category 5 (CAT5) Ethernet cable, conforming to the IEEE 802.3af PoE standard and a port that supports PoE. In many cases, a conventional house hub or router does not support PoE, but it's a good feature to be aware of.

The Ethernet Shield R3 and Ethernet Shield R3 with PoE are sold fully assembled and ready to use. Pins 4, 11, 12, and 13 are used to communicate with the SD card on the shield, so they should not be used for any other function.

Get more details on the Arduino product page (http://arduino.cc/en/Main/ArduinoEthernetShield) as well as information in the Ethernet library (http://arduino.cc/en/Reference/Ethernet).

Figure 13-7:
An Ethernet
Shield
(without PoE
module).

WiFi Shield

Made by: Arduino

Price: £74.39 from Proto-PIC; $84.95 from SparkFun

Pin requirements: 4, 7, 10, 11, 12, 13

The WiFi Shield (shown in Figure 13-8) allows you to connect wirelessly to a hub or hotspot. It's especially useful when you don't have access to an Ethernet port or want a degree of mobility for your project, or to access or put information on the Internet. The shield even has a microSD card reader to allow you to save results or store files to distribute over the network.

The WiFi Shield is sold fully assembled and ready to use. The Arduino talks with both the WiFi Shield's processor and the microSD card reader using the SPI bus, pins 11, 12, and 13. You use pin 10 to select the processor on the WiFi Shield (HDG104) and pin 4 to select the microSD card reader. Use pin 7 for handshaking — the process of setting up communication between two devices, in this case the Arduino and the WiFi Shield.

Find more details on the WiFi Shield on the Arduino product page (http://arduino.cc/en/Main/ArduinoWiFiShield). There is an excellent tutorial for getting started with the WiFi Sshield on the Arduino site (http://arduino.cc/en/Guide/ArduinoWiFiShield) and details of the

WiFi library on the Arduino Reference page (http://arduino.cc/en/
Reference/WiFi).

Figure 13-8:
The Arduino
WiFi Shield.

Cellular Shield with SM5100B

Made by: SparkFun

Price: £66.17 from Proto-PIC; $99.95 from SparkFun

Pin requirements: 0, 1 or 2, 3 (default)

The Cellular Shield (Figure 13-9) turns your modest Arduino into a functional
mobile phone. With this shield, you can send and receive calls, text messages, and even data. All you need is a prepaid SIM card and an antenna, and
you're ready to communicate with the world. By using Serial.print, you can
send the correct codes to talk to the SM5100B.

The Cellular Shield with SM5100B is sold fully assembled and ready to use.
You need to purchase an antenna with an SMA connector; SparkFun offers the
Quad-band Cellular Duck Antenna SMA (www.sparkfun.com/products/
675). The Arduino talks with the SM5100B using either the RX and TX pins 0
and 1 or pins 2 and 3 using the SoftwareSerial library. By default, this is set to 2
and 3 but can be changed by removing the solder jumper on the board.

The SIM card should have enough credit to perform the actions you're trying to do. Those offering unlimited text messages are especially useful. Other optional extras are a mic and speaker; without them, you can call and hang up but won't be able to do any more than that.

Find more details on the SparkFun products page (www.sparkfun.com/products/9607). That page has an example sketch, but for a real introduction, I recommend heading over to John Boxall's site (http://tronixstuff.wordpress.com/2011/01/19/tutorial-arduino-and-gsm-cellular-part-one/). He has some excellent resources available through his introduction to GSM, so make sure to have a good read.

Figure 13-9:
The Cellular Shield ready to connect people.

Geiger Counter – Radiation Sensor Board
Made by: Liberium

Price: £110.80 from Cooking Hacks; $170 from MicroController Pros

Pin requirements: 2, 3, 4, 5, 6, 7, 8, 9, 10, 11, 12, 13

The Radiation Sensor Board is probably one of the most impressive Arduino shields. It allows you to monitor radiation levels in the environment. This board was made to help the people of Japan monitor radiation levels following the radiation leakages in Fukushima in March 2011. The Geiger counter can use various Geiger tubes to detect different types and levels of radiation. There is also an LCD display, LED, and piezo speaker for feedback.

This shield uses Geiger tubes that operate at dangerously high voltages (400V–1000V), so it requires extreme care. It is best to keep the Radiation Sensor Board in an enclosure to keep it out of human contact. Radiation is dangerous, but so is electricity. If you don't know what you're doing, don't mess around.

The piezo speaker and LED are connected to pin 2, which triggers an interrupt with every pulse that the Geiger tube generates. Depending on the tube used and the number of pulses or counts per minute (cpm), you can determine the actual radiation level in Sieverts per hour. Pins 3 to 8 are used for the LCD display to generate the sensor readings in detail. Pins 9 to 13 are used for the LED bar to give clear visual feedback of the radiation level. The first three LEDs are green, and the last two are red, showing that a high and potentially dangerous level of radiation is being approached.

More details on this project can be found on the Cooking Hacks product page (`www.cooking-hacks.com/index.php/documentation/tutorials/geiger-counter-arduino-radiation-sensor-board`).

Staying current

Many other great shields are available, and new and improved ones are being released all the time. You can take some actions to keep up to date, though.

Check the stores regularly for the latest products. It's a bit like browsing in a DIY shop; you never know what you'll find.

- **Arduino Store** (`http://store.arduino.cc`)
- **Adafruit**(`www.adafruit.com`)
- **Maker Shed** (`www.makershed.com`)
- **Seeed Studio** (`www.seeedstudio.com`)
- **SparkFun**(`www.sparkfun.com`)

Also, check Arduino-related blogs regularly. Blogs and news pages on Arduino-related sites often show off new kits or new and interesting applications of older hardware, so they're always worth checking for a spot of inspiration.

- **Arduino Blog** (`http://arduino.cc/blog`)
- **Adafruit** (`www.adafruit.com/blog`)
- **Hack A Day** (`http://hackaday.com`)

✔ **Make** (http://blog.makezine.com)

✔ **Seeed Studio** (www.seeedstudio.com/blog)

✔ **SparkFun** (www.sparkfun.com/news)

Some people have made efforts to document the various shields. Check these sites:

✔ **Arduino Playground** (www.arduino.cc/playground/Main/SimilarBoards#goShie)

✔ **Arduino Shield List** (http://shieldlist.org)

Browsing the Libraries

Basic sketches can get you quite a long way, but when you get more advanced you need to know about libraries. Libraries provide extra functionality to your sketch, either to use specific hardware or to incorporate more complex functions in software. In the same way that you'd go to a physical library to learn something new, you include libraries in your code to teach your Arduino something new. By including a library in a sketch you can quickly and easily access functions to help you achieve your goals.

Getting started with complex hardware or software can be a difficult thing to do. Luckily a lot of people have taken the time to document their progress and have released libraries, often with examples, that can be easily integrated into your own sketches. From this it's possible to get something working, get to grips with it, and hopefully gain a better understanding of it. This is the learn-by-doing approach of Arduino that allows you to make a lot of progress quickly and easily with hardware or software that would otherwise be a huge challenge.

Reviewing the standard libraries

This section covers is a selection of the libraries included in the current release of Arduino at the time of writing (1.0.1). The standard libraries cover a wide range of subject areas and are usually popular topics that have been heavily documented. You can find these libraries by choosing Sketch⇨Import Library. Choosing a library includes one line at the top of your current sketch, such as #include <EEPROM.h>. Before you understand a library, you should try an example of it. You'll find examples at the bottom of the menu that appears at File⇨Examples.

Here is a brief description of what library does:

- ✔ **EEPROM** (http://arduino.cc/en/Reference/EEPRO): Your Arduino has Electrically Erasable Programmable Read-Only Memory (EEPROM), which is permanent storage similar to the hard drive in a computer. Data stored in this location stays there even if your Arduino is powered down. Using the EEPROM library, you can read from and write to this memory.

- ✔ **Ethernet** (http://arduino.cc/en/Reference/Ethernet): After you have your Ethernet Shield, the Ethernet library allows you to quickly and easily start talking to the Internet. When you use this library, your Arduino can either act as a server that is accessible to other devices or as a client that requests data.

- ✔ **Firmata** (http://arduino.cc/en/Reference/Firmata): Firmata is one way to control your Arduino from software on a computer. It is a standard communication protocol, which means that rather than write your own communication software, you can use the library to allow easy communication between hardware and software.

- ✔ **LiquidCrystal** (http://arduino.cc/en/Reference/LiquidCrystal): The LiquidCrystal library helps your Arduino talk to most liquid crystal displays. The library is based on the Hitachi HD44780 driver, and you can usually identify these displays by their 16-pin interface.

- ✔ **SD** (http://arduino.cc/en/Reference/SD): The SD library allows you to read from and write to SD and microSD cards connected to your Arduino. SD cards need to use SPI to transfer data quickly, which happens on pins 11, 12, and 13. You also need to have another pin to select the SD card when it's needed.

- ✔ **Servo** (http://arduino.cc/en/Reference/Servo): The Servo library allows you to control up to 12 servo motors on the Uno R3 (and up to 48 on the Mega). Most "hobby" servos turn 180 degrees, and using this library, you can specify the degree that you want your servo(s) to turn to.

- ✔ **SPI** (http://arduino.cc/en/Reference/SPI): The Serial Peripheral Interface (SPI) is a method of communication allowing your Arduino to communicate very quickly with one or more devices over a short distance. This could be could be receiving data from sensors, talking to peripherals such as an SD card reader, or communicating with another microcontroller.

- ✔ **SoftwareSerial** (http://arduino.cc/en/Reference/Software Serial): The Software Serial library allows you to use any digital pins to send and receive serial messages instead of, or in addition to, the usual hardware pins, 0 and 1. This is great if you want to keep the hardware pins free for communication to a computer, allowing you to have a permanent debug connection to your project while still being able to upload new sketches, or to send duplicate data to multiple serial devices.

- **Stepper** (http://arduino.cc/en/Reference/Stepper): The stepper library allows you to control stepper motors from your Arduino. This code also requires the appropriate hardware to work, so make sure to read Tom Igoe's notes on the subject (www.tigoe.net/pcomp/code/circuits/motors/stepper-motors/).

- **WiFi** (http://arduino.cc/en/Reference/WiFi): The WiFi library is based on the Ethernet library listed previously, but with alterations specific to the WiFi Shield to allow you to wirelessly connect to the Internet. The WiFi library also works well with the SD library, allowing you to store data on the shield.

- **Wire** (http://arduino.cc/en/Reference/Wire): The Wire library allows your Arduino to communicate with I2C devices (also known as TWI, or two-wire interface). Such devices could be addressable LEDs or a Wii Nunchuk, for example.

Installing additional libraries

Many libraries aren't included in the Arduino software. Some libraries are for completely unique applications such as specific hardware or functions; others are refinements or adaptations of existing libraries. Luckily, Arduino makes including these incredibly easy, so you can quickly try them all to see which are right for your needs.

Libraries are usually be distributed as .zip files that have the same name as the library; for example, the capacitive sensing library CapSense should be distributed as CapSense.zip and should contain a folder of the same name when unzipped. It may also be distributed as a version, such as CapSense-1.0.1 or CapSense_20120930. Distributing it as a version allows you to keep track of the current version so that you can use the latest or a specific revision. Whichever version you are using, be sure to name the library folder with the library name CapSense.

Inside the folder there are files ending in .h and .cpp, such as CapPin.h and CapPin.cpp, and maybe even an Examples folder. If your .zip file contains only loose .h and .cpp files, you should place them in a folder with a library name. Sometimes you may find many .h and .cpp files that all perform different functions in the library, so make sure they're all inside the folder.

In the latest release of Arduino (1.0.1 at time of writing), it's easy to include libraries. Simply move the library folder into your Arduino sketch folder.

In Mac OSX, it will look like this:

```
~/Documents/Arduino/libraries/CapSense/CapPin.h
~/Documents/Arduino/libraries/CapSense/CapPin.cpp
~/Documents/Arduino/libraries/CapSense/examples
```

In Windows, it will look like this:

```
My Documents /Arduino/libraries/CapSense/CapPin.h
My Documents /Arduino/libraries/CapSense/CapPin.cpp
My Documents /Arduino/libraries/CapSense/examples
```

After the library is installed, restart Arduino and choose Sketch➪Import Library to check that your library is in the list, as shown in Figure 13-10. The libraries does not function if the files are not in the correct folder structure or if the names are changed, so be sure to check this if you cannot see the library there.

Figure 13-10: The Arduino menu shows the library in the Import Library drop-down list.

If the library has an Examples folder, you should also be able to see the examples in File➪Examples under the name of the library, as in Figure 13-11.

That's all there is to installing a library. Removing a library is as simple as taking the library folder in question out of the Arduino sketch folder.

Figure 13-11:
If there are examples with the library, you should also be able to see them in the menu.

Obtaining contributed libraries

A long list of community-contributed libraries appears on the Arduino libraries page (http://arduino.cc/en/Reference/Libraries), and an exhaustive list appears on the Arduino Playground (http://arduino.cc/playground/Main/LibraryList).

CapSense and TimerOne are two commonly used and helpful libraries to start with as you get familiar with contributed libraries:

✔ **CapSense (**www.arduino.cc/playground/Main/CapSense**):** CapSense is a library that allows you to make one or many pins on your Arduino into capacitive sensors. This allows you to make simple touch, pressure, or presence detection sensors quickly and easily with very little hardware.

The Arduino Playground page has a lot of useful information, but a more recent version of the code can be found on GitHub (https://github.com/moderndevice/CapSense).

✔ TimerOne (`http://playground.arduino.cc//Code/Timer1`): TimerOne or Timer1 uses a hardware timer on your Arduino to perform timed events at regular intervals. It's a great library for reading sensor data regularly without interrupting what's going on in the main loop. There is a page on the Arduino Playground and an up-to-date version of the library on Google Code (`http://code.google.com/p/arduino-timerone/`).

If you're really keen to understand libraries more and maybe even write your own, check out this introduction to writing your own libraries on the Arduino page at `http://arduino.cc/en/Hacking/LibraryTutorial`.

Chapter 14

Sensing More Inputs and Controlling More Outputs

· ·

· ·

An individual input and output is great, and sometimes that's all that is necessary for your project. Often, however, you want to sense or control with a lot of inputs and outputs all at one time. Many of the most well-known digital art and installations are actually very simple at heart; the real complexity is in instructing those simple actions to occur hundreds, and maybe even thousands, of times.

In this chapter, you find out how to perform lots of activities simultaneously with your Arduino. You might accomplish this by using a bigger board, such as the Arduino Mega 2560, or by using additional hardware to allow your regular Arduino Uno to do more than it can on its own. You learn about the pros and cons of each of these methods to equip you with the right knowledge to help you build a monster of an Arduino project.

Controlling Multiple LEDs

One of the simplest ways to extend your Arduino project is by using a bigger board: the Arduino Mega 2560. This monster of a board, shown in Figure 14-1, gives you a many more pins to play with than a typical Arduino board does: 54 digital I/O pins, 15 PWM capable pins, and 16 analog input pins. With the Mega 2560, you have a lot more space for all kinds of inputs and outputs. But that's not all. The Mega has four hardware serial ports, allowing it to communicate with multiple serial devices simultaneously. This capability is great for keeping the USB serial line free for communication with a computer without disturbing any connections to serial devices.

Figure 14-1:
An Arduino
Mega 2560.

This communication is all possible because of the ATmega2560 microprocessor on the board. If you compare the Mega 2560 to an Uno, the first difference you notice is physical. If you look at the chip on an Uno R3, you see that ATmega328 is shaped like a millipede — a form known as dual in-line package (also known as DIP and DIL) because of the two parallel lines of pins. More specifically, this is a plastic dual in-line package (PDIP). If you look at the center of your Mega 2560, you see a diamond-shaped computer chip known as a quad flat package (QFP) because of the four sets of pins and the very flat profile of the chip. Specifically, this one is a thin quad flat package (TQFP), and it has many other variations. You see both chips in Figure 14-2.

The physical form isn't the only difference; the names of the chips are also slightly different. The microcontroller names are printed on top of the chip: the Uno reads ATMEGA328P-PU and the Mega shows ATMEGA2560 16-AU (both names are visible in Figure 14-2). These are product numbers that relate to the amount of memory on the chip. The two important numbers to understand are 328 and 2560, which relate to the amount of flash memory that each microcontroller has — 32KB and 256KB, respectively. Flash memory is used to store your sketches, so you can see that the Mega 2560 has more than seven times the space of the Uno, which can be especially useful for programs that are storing a lot of data, such as strings.

Figure 14-2:
PDIP and
TQFP.

To familiarize yourself with the Mega, take a look at the layout of the board with the pins labeled shown in Figure 14-3. Much of the board is similar to the Uno, but you have to pay special attention to the block of pins at the end to make sure that you don't use the extra 5V and GND pins rather than the digital pins. Also, some shields need modification to work with the Mega 2560, so read the instructions carefully.

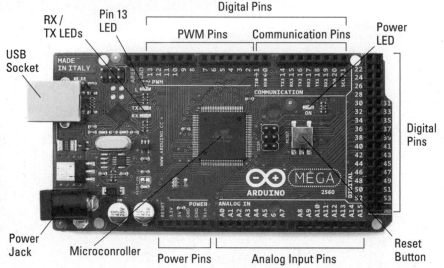

Figure 14-3:
The Mega 2560 board layout with labels.

USB Socket · RX / TX LEDs · Pin 13 LED · Digital Pins · PWM Pins · Communication Pins · Power LED · Digital Pins · Power Jack · Microconroller · Power Pins · Analog Input Pins · Reset Button

Implementing the AnalogWriteMega sketch

In this example, you learn how to make a Nightrider-style LED bar. Because the Mega 2560 has 15 possible PWM pins, it's perfect for precise control of many analog outputs. The AnalogWriteMega sketch allows you to smoothly transition between LEDs.

For this project, you need:

✔ An Arduino Mega 2560

✔ A breadboard

✔ Twelve LEDs

✔ Twelve 220 ohm resistors

✔ Jump wires

This circuit is all about repetition, so it's a good idea to find a pack of color-coded jump wires or carefully cut and strip lengths of equipment wire, preferably single core. When choosing LEDs and resistors, be sure to do your calculations. Standard 3mm or 5mm LEDs in most kits require a voltage of around 2.5V and a current of around 25mA, and the Arduino's digital pins are capable of providing a maximum of 5V.

In an equation, this means:

(5V - 2.5V) / 0.025A = 100 ohms

A 100 ohm resistor is an exact match for running the LED up to the maximum recommended power, but by using a 220 ohm resistor, you keep the LED well within its limits, which allows it to operate longer. A general rule when choosing a resistor is to pick the nearest available resistor that is above the calculated resistance. If you feel that your LEDs just aren't bright enough, you can find resistors that are closer to the optimum resistance, find higher brightness LEDs, or find a higher power LED that consumes closer to 5V.

After you have your LEDs, resistors, and jump wires, assemble the circuit as shown in Figures 14-4 and 14-5. The circuit is basically 12 of the same, smaller circuits, each of the Arduino Mega pins being connected to a 220 ohm resistor, then onto the anode (long leg) of the LED, with the cathode (short leg) being connected to ground.

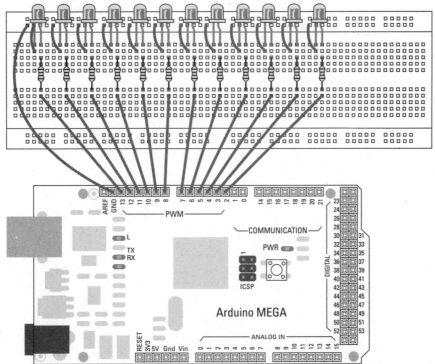

Figure 14-4:
Lots of LEDs
wired up to
your Mega.

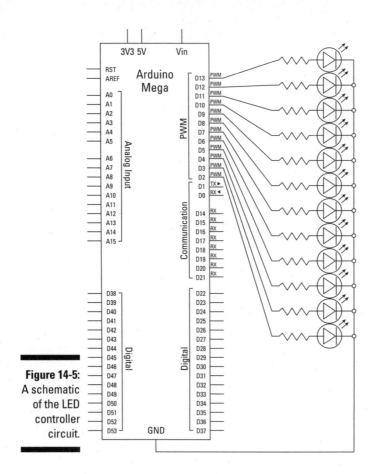

Figure 14-5:
A schematic
of the LED
controller
circuit.

After you've assembled your circuit, you want to find the appropriate sketch. From the Arduino menu, choose File➪Examples➪03.Analog➪AnalogWriteMega to display a sketch for doing lots of analogWrite() functions on the Mega. The code for the sketch is as follows:

```
/*
  Mega analogWrite() test

  This sketch fades LEDs up and down one at a time on digital pins 2 through 13.
  This sketch was written for the Arduino Mega, and will not work on previous
  boards.

  The circuit:
  * LEDs attached from pins 2 through 13 to ground.

  created 8 Feb 2009
```

```
   by Tom Igoe

  This example code is in the public domain.

  */
// These constants won't change.  They're used to give names
// to the pins used:
const int lowestPin = 2;
const int highestPin = 13;


void setup() {
  // set pins 2 through 13 as outputs:
  for (int thisPin =lowestPin; thisPin <= highestPin; thisPin++) {
    pinMode(thisPin, OUTPUT);
  }
}


void loop() {
  // iterate over the pins:
  for (int thisPin =lowestPin; thisPin <= highestPin; thisPin++) {
    // fade the LED on thisPin from off to brightest:
    for (int brightness = 0; brightness < 255; brightness++) {
      analogWrite(thisPin, brightness);
      delay(2);
    }
    // fade the LED on thisPin from brithstest to off:
    for (int brightness = 255; brightness >= 0; brightness--) {
      analogWrite(thisPin, brightness);
      delay(2);
    }
    // pause between LEDs:
    delay(100);
  }
}
```

If your sketch uploads correctly, you see each LED fade up and then down in sequence, and then return to the start again.

If you don't see this happening, double-check your wiring:

✔ Make sure that you're using the correct pin numbers.

✔ Check the connections on the breadboard. If the jump wires or components are not connected using the correct rows in the breadboard, they don't work.

✔ Check that your LEDs are the right way around, with the digital pin going to a resistor to the long leg and the short leg going to ground.

Understanding the AnalogWriteMega Sketch

This sketch is similar to fading a single LED, as in the basic AnalogWrite sketch (see Chapter 7), but involves a lot of repetition. Using `for` loops it's possible to perform a lot of repetitive tasks without writing the same code for each LED.

At the start of this sketch, you declare the constant integers. Rather than declare 12 separate values, you can declare the lowest and highest pin because the board has 12 PWM pins all in a row, from pin 2 to pin 13. The other three PWM pins are 44, 45, and 46, so they're not quite as conveniently spaced for the sketch.

```
const int lowestPin = 2;
const int highestPin = 13;
```

In setup, the pins are set to be outputs using a `for` loop. Because the pins are in one unbroken row, the `for` loop can simply count up through each pin from the first to the last and set each of them to OUTPUT. Inside the `for` loop, the local variable `thisPin` is declared as an integer equal to the `lowestPin`; this is your start point. The variable `thisPin` is then compared to `highestPin`. If `thisPin` is less than or equal to (<=) `highestPin`, the digital pin of the same number is set as an output and `thisPin` is incremented by one for the next loop. This process quickly and effectively sets all your pins to an output with two lines of code rather than 12.

```
void setup() {
  // set pins 2 through 13 as outputs:
  for (int thisPin =lowestPin; thisPin <= highestPin; thisPin++) {
    pinMode(thisPin, OUTPUT);
  }
}
```

In the main `loop`, there are `for` loops within `for` loops! You can see where each loop sits by the indentation of the `for` loop code. To format your code automatically, choose Tools⇨Auto Format (or press Ctrl+T on Windows or ⌘+T on a Mac). If you get confused, move the cursor to the right side of a {} curly brace to see the other corresponding curly brace highlighted. This is helpful but can be incorrect if you have too few curly braces, so make sure that you have them in the right places. Start with the first or highest level `for` loop, which contains the other two loops. The highest loop counts through the pins 2 to 13 in order, each time incrementing the value `thisPin` until it reaches 14.

```
void loop() {
  // iterate over the pins:
  for (int thisPin =lowestPin; thisPin <= highestPin; thisPin++) {
    // fade the LED on thisPin from off to brightest:
```

The first loop gives you the current pin number, so it can be used again in the next two `for` loops. The first of these loops creates another loop with the local variable brightness. This brightness, too, is incremented, counting from 0 to 255, one value at a time. Every time the brightness is incremented, an `analogWrite` is run with the current brightness value, with a short delay of 2mS before increasing the brightness again.

```
for (int brightness = 0; brightness < 255; brightness++) {
  analogWrite(thisPin, brightness);
  delay(2);
}
```

After the brightness has reached its maximum PWM value of 255, the next `for` loop returns to 0. This is done exactly the same way, but instead counts down one point of brightness at a time.

```
for (int brightness = 255; brightness >= 0; brightness--) {
  analogWrite(thisPin, brightness);
  delay(2);
}
```

At the end of the second `for` loop, a 100mS delay occurs before the sketch returns to the higher level `for` loop. The next loop round the LED (as held in the variable `thisPin`) moves on one and repeats the same task until it reaches pin 13. After pin 13, the criteria of the `for` loop is no longer true, so it exits and starts the main loop from scratch, completing the sketch and ready to start again.

```
  // pause between LEDs:
  delay(100);
  }
}
```

This sketch fades up and down each LED from pin 2 to 13 and works well to check that the circuit is functioning. This isn't the most interesting of applications, though, so in the next section you learn how to do more with this setup.

Tweaking the AnalogWriteMega sketch

Animating a string of LEDs can be great fun. There is a huge difference between blinking them on and off and animating them, which really has to be seen in the flesh (or LED) to be appreciated.

The first step is to change the sequence to make it more interesting. By adding another `for` loop and commenting out the delay, you can create an animation that loops nicely. Create a new sketch, type the code that follows, and save it with a memorable name, such as myLedAnimation. Alternatively, you can open the AnalogWriteMega sketch, make the changes (indicated by the arrows in the margin), and choose File➪Save As to save the sketch with a new name.

It's also a good habit to update the comments of your sketch as you modify it, as shown in the code that follows.

```
/*
myLedAnimation

  This sketch fades LEDs up one at a time on digital pins 2 through 13
  and then down one at a time on digital pins 13 through 2.

  This sketch was written for the Arduino Mega, and will not work on previous
  boards.

  The circuit:
  * LEDs attached from pins 2 through 13 to ground.

  Original code by Tom Igoe (2009) - Mega analogWrite() test
  Modified by [Your_Name] (20__)

*/

const int lowestPin = 2;
const int highestPin = 13;


void setup() {

  for (int thisPin =lowestPin; thisPin <= highestPin; thisPin++) {
    pinMode(thisPin, OUTPUT);
  }
}

void loop() {

  for (int thisPin =lowestPin; thisPin <= highestPin; thisPin++) {
```

```
      // fade the LED on thisPin from off to brightest:
      for (int brightness = 0; brightness < 255; brightness++) {
        analogWrite(thisPin, brightness);
        delay(2);
      }
    }

    for (int thisPin =highestPin; thisPin >= lowestPin; thisPin--) {

      for (int brightness = 255; brightness >= 0; brightness--) {
        analogWrite(thisPin, brightness);
        delay(2);
      }
      // pause between LEDs:
// delay(100);
    }
}
```

When you run the changes, you get a row of LEDs that light up quickly one at a time. After the row is full, each LED dims until all are off; then the whole sequence repeats.

That's fun, but you can do even more. This next bit of code transforms your LED display into something similar to KITT, David Hasselhoff's companion from Knight Rider.

Create a new sketch, type the following code, and save it with a memorable name, such as myKnightRider. Alternatively, open the AnalogWriteMega sketch, make the changes (indicated by the arrows in the margin), and choose File⇨Save As to save the sketch with a new name.

```
/*
myKnightRider

  This sketch quickly fades each LED up then down on digital pins 2 through 13
  and returns on 13 through 2, like KITT from Knight Rider.
  Unfortunately it won't make your car talk.

  This sketch was written for the Arduino Mega, and will not work on previous
  boards.

  The circuit:
  * LEDs attached from pins 2 through 13 to ground.

  Original code by Tom Igoe (2009) - Mega analogWrite() test
Modified by [Your_Name] (20__)

  */
```

```
// These constants won't change.  They're used to give names
// to the pins used:
const int lowestPin = 2;
const int highestPin = 13;


void setup() {
  // set pins 2 through 13 as outputs:
  for (int thisPin =lowestPin; thisPin <= highestPin; thisPin++) {
    pinMode(thisPin, OUTPUT);
  }
}


void loop() {
  // iterate over the pins:
  for (int thisPin =lowestPin; thisPin <= highestPin; thisPin++) {
    // fade the LED on thisPin from off to brightest:
    for (int brightness = 0; brightness < 255; brightness++) {
      analogWrite(thisPin, brightness);
      delay(2);
    }
    for (int brightness = 255; brightness >= 0; brightness--) {
      analogWrite(thisPin, brightness);
      delay(2);
    }
}

for (int thisPin =highestPin; thisPin >= lowestPin; thisPin--) {
  // fade the LED on thisPin from brightest to off:
  for (int brightness = 0; brightness < 255; brightness++) {
    analogWrite(thisPin, brightness);
    delay(2);
  }
  for (int brightness = 255; brightness >= 0; brightness--) {
    analogWrite(thisPin, brightness);
    delay(2);
  }
    // pause between LEDs:
  // delay(100);
  }
}
```

This sketch gives you an awesome LED animation, with the row of LEDs lighting up one at a time, moving from left to right, and then repeating. You can tweak it further by adjusting the delay() times and brightness values to get the timing just right. For more inspiration give "KITT from Knight Rider" a Google and you'll find a lot of videos of people doing similar.

Controlling Lots of LEDs by Shifting Out

Sometimes even the Mega 2560 with its 70 pins isn't enough, and you need options that allow you to have even more inputs and outputs. Luckily, you can obtain chips that allow you to increase the number of outputs your Arduino can control. One such chip is a shift register.

Many types of shift registers are available. A popular one is the 74HC595, which is described as an "8-bit serial-in, serial or parallel-out shift register with output latches; 3 state" on its datasheet (http://www.nxp.com/documents/data_sheet/74HC_HCT595.pdf). The "8-bit" part refers to the number of outputs that can be controlled, so to understand how the shift register works, you must first look at binary, bits, and bytes, which I explain in the "Making sense of binary, bits, and bytes" sidebar. The 74HC595 is shown in Figure 14-6.

Figure 14-6:
A 74HC595 shift register.

Making sense of binary, bits, and bytes

The binary number system uses only two values: 0 or 1. Because it uses only two values, it is also known as base-2. Decimal numbers that you use are usually referred to as base-10 and use 0 to 9; hexadecimal numbers are base-16, and use 0 to 9 and A to F.

But how is binary useful when you're trying to talk to lots of things and have only two options? The answer is that you use a lot of binary values.

If you take a base-2 binary number such as 10101101, you can determine its value in base-10 using a simple lookup table. Binary is typically read from right to left. Because binary is base-2, each value is the binary value multiplied by 2 to the power of (2^x), where x is equal to the order of the bit, starting at 0 on the right. For example, as shown below the fourth binary value is equal to $1 \times (2 \times 2 \times 2) = 8$.

Binary	1	0	1	0	1	1	0	1	
Calculation	1×2^7	0×2^6	1×2^5	0×2^4	1×2^3	1×2^2	0×2^1	1×2^0	Total
Decimal	128	0	32	0	8	4	0	1	173

As you can see, extremely large numbers can be formed using only zeros and ones. In this case, you have eight binary values with a total decimal value of 255. When talking about memory, each binary value takes one *bit* of memory, and each group of eight bits is referred to as a *byte*. To give you an idea of scale, a blank Arduino sketch uses 466 bytes; an Uno can store a maximum of 32,256 bytes, and a Mega can store a maximum of 258,048 bytes.

Figure 14-7 shows a diagram of the pins on the 74HC595. The pin names are explained in Table 14-1.

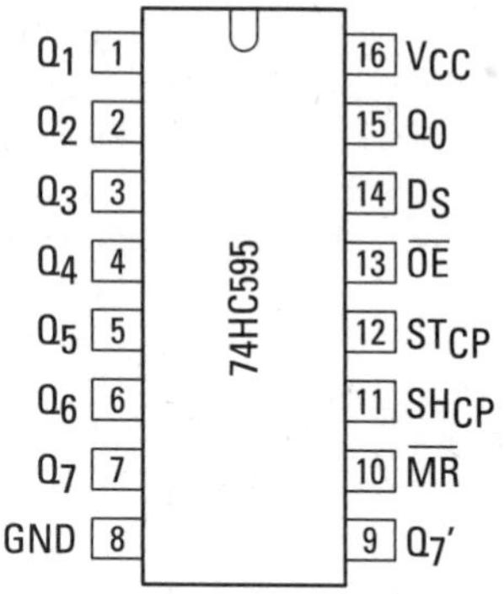

Figure 14-7:
A diagram
of the pins
on the
74HC595.

In the case of the 74HC595, there are eight output pins and, conveniently, there are also eight bits in a byte. The values are sent one bit at a time to the shift register. When the clock pin (SH_CP) is set HIGH, all the bits shift one place forward, the last pin "shifts out" and a new pin takes its value from the serial data input (DS). The bits are all stored in the register until the latch pin (ST_CP) is pulled HIGH and the values are sent to the outputs.

Table 14-1		74HC595 Pins
Pin	*Description*	*Use*
Q0–Q7	Output pins	These are linked to your LEDs.
GND	Ground	This is linked to your Arduino's ground.
Q7′	Serial out	Serial out is used to shift data to another 74HC595.
MR	Master Reclear, active low	This clears the shift register if pulled LOW.
SH_CP	Shift register clock pin	If pulled HIGH, this shifts all the values forward one.
ST_CP	Storage register lock pin (latch pin)	When pulled HIGH, it outputs the new shift register values. This must be pulled HIGH straight after SH_CP goes low again.
OE	Output enable, active low	This enables the output when grounded and disables it when HIGH.
DS	Serial data input	This is the input pin for the new serial data.
Vcc	Positive voltage supply	This is the voltage supply for the LEDs.

The total value in eight bits (or one byte or a decimal number from 0 to 255) represents every combination of the register, and that is how the shift register communicates its outputs. If you send 11111111, all output pins go HIGH; if you send 10101101, pins 0, 2, 3, 5 and 7 go HIGH. You can also cascade the 74HC595s, meaning that you can add multiple chips to extend the number of outputs further by using the serial out pin (Q7). Doing so gives you more registers to shift bits of data into. If you send 16 bits (ortwo bytes or a decimal number from 0 to 511), the bits flow through to the first register and into the second as they are shifted.

Implementing the shiftOutCode, Hello World sketch

In this example, you look at shifting out using a single 74HC595 to control eight LEDs. The LEDs count up in binary from 0 to 255.

You need:

✔ An Arduino Uno

✔ A big breadboard

✔ A 74HC595

✔ Eight LEDs

✔ Eight 220 ohm resistors

✔ Jump wires

The 74HC595 is placed across the gap in the center of the breadboard and should be an exact fit. That's because your breadboard was designed with this placement in mind. The gap in the center allows you to easily connect wires to both sides of the chip, keeping each side of pins separate from one another. Moreso for this example than some others, it is a good idea to have a power and ground rail on each side of the board. To that end, you want to link the Arduino's 5V and ground pins to each of the two tracks on both sides of the board, as shown in the Figure 14-8 circuit layout.

The layout of the pins is quite straightforward, except that the first pin — pin 0 — is on the opposite side of the board from the others. For this example, it's a good idea to use lots of color-coded jump wires or equipment wire to keep track of where the connections are going. Complete the circuit as shown in Figures 14-8 and 14-9.

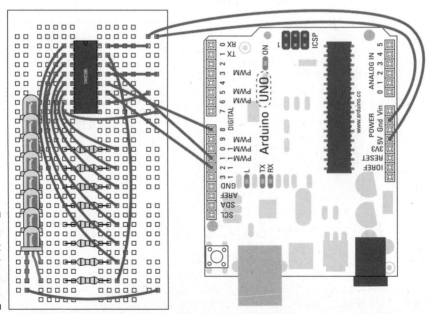

Figure 14-8:
A circuit layout for using a 74HC595.

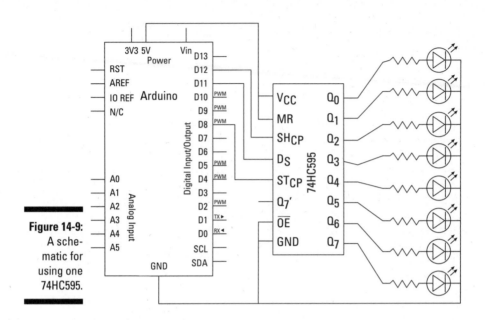

Figure 14-9:
A schematic for using one 74HC595.

After your circuit is assembled, you need the appropriate software to use it. Create a new sketch by typing the code that follows and saving it with a memorable name, such as myShiftOut. Alternatively, you can find this example at http://arduino.cc/en/Tutorial/ShftOut11.

```
//************************************************************//
// Name    : shiftOutCode, Hello World
// Author  : Carlyn Maw,Tom Igoe, David A. Mellis
// Date    : 25 Oct, 2006
// Modified: 23 Mar 2010
// Version : 2.0
// Notes   : Code for using a 74HC595 Shift Register    //
//         : to count from 0 to 255
//************************************************************

//Pin connected to ST_CP of 74HC595
int latchPin = 8;
//Pin connected to SH_CP of 74HC595
int clockPin = 12;
////Pin connected to DS of 74HC595
int dataPin = 11;


void setup() {
  //set pins to output so you can control the shift register
  pinMode(latchPin, OUTPUT);
```

```
  pinMode(clockPin, OUTPUT);
  pinMode(dataPin, OUTPUT);
}

void loop() {
  // count from 0 to 255 and display the number
  // on the LEDs
  for (int numberToDisplay = 0; numberToDisplay < 256; numberToDisplay++) {
    // take the latchPin low so
    // the LEDs don't change while you're sending in bits:
    digitalWrite(latchPin, LOW);
    // shift out the bits:
    shiftOut(dataPin, clockPin, MSBFIRST, numberToDisplay);

    //take the latch pin high so the LEDs will light up:
    digitalWrite(latchPin, HIGH);
    // pause before next value:
    delay(500);
  }
}
```

You should see your row of LEDs counting up in binary from 0 to 255. Usually, binary is read from right to left, with the least significant bit (LSB), 1, on the right and the most significant bit, in this case 128, on the left. Work out the first few numbers to see whether the pattern looks right. Table 14-2 shows you numbers 0 to 9.

Table 14-2	Decimal to Binary
Decimal	*Binary*
0	00000000
1	00000001
2	00000010
3	00000011
4	00000100
5	00000101
6	00000110
7	00000111
8	00001000
9	00001001

If you don't see this happening, double-check your wiring:

- Check the connections on the breadboard. If the jump wires or components are not connected using the correct rows in the breadboard, they will not work.

- Make sure that your LEDs are oriented correctly, in the right order, and that the Arduino pins are wired to the correct 74HC595 pins.

Understanding the shiftOutCode, Hello World sketch

At the start of the sketch, the three pins needed to control the shift register are declared. Pin 8 is the latch pin, used to output the values from the register; pin 12 is the clock pin, used to shift the bits along by one pin; pin 11 is used to send new data into the register.

```
//Pin connected to ST_CP of 74HC595
int latchPin = 8;
//Pin connected to SH_CP of 74HC595
int clockPin = 12;
////Pin connected to DS of 74HC595
int dataPin = 11;
```

In setup, you simply set the pinMode of each pin to OUTPUT.

```
void setup() {
    //set pins to output so you can control the shift register
    pinMode(latchPin, OUTPUT);
    pinMode(clockPin, OUTPUT);
    pinMode(dataPin, OUTPUT);
}
```

You immediately notice that the loop() is quite small for the seemingly complicated task explained earlier. A for() loop is used to count from 0 to 255. A local variable called numberToDisplay is the current number.

```
void loop() {
    // count from 0 to 255 and display the number
    // on the LEDs
    for (int numberToDisplay = 0; numberToDisplay < 256; numberToDisplay++) {
```

The latch pin is set LOW so that it doesn't output the value of the register while you are changing it.

```
// take the latchPin low so
// the LEDs don't change while you're sending in bits:
digitalWrite(latchPin, LOW);
```

The `shiftOut` function is included in Arduino for this exact purpose and requires four parameters. The first is `dataPin`; the second is `clockPin`; the third is the order of the bits, either most significant bit (`MSBFIRST`) or least significant bit (`LSBFIRST`); the fourth parameter is the value to display, which is the local variable `numberToDisplay`. This function takes the value and handles all the pulses to convert it to a combination of pins that fills the buffer.

```
// shift out the bits:
shiftOut(dataPin, clockPin, MSBFIRST, numberToDisplay);
```

All that is left to do is to set the latch pin `HIGH` again to send the updated values to the LEDs.

```
//take the latch pin high so the LEDs will light up:
digitalWrite(latchPin, HIGH);
```

There is a brief pause of half a second by using the delay function, before the program returns to the start of the `for` loop and incrementing the number by one.

```
// pause before next value:
delay(500);
  }
}
```

This cycle continues until the `for` loop reaches 255, which sets all the LEDs `HIGH`, then returns to 0 and repeats the count. This is great for counting in binary, but not much else. In the next section, I refine the code to let you address the LEDs individually.

Tweaking the shiftOutCode, Hello World sketch

The previous binary method is great for understanding how the shift register works, but what if you want to turn on a specific pin without converting it to binary? This code uses the same circuit as described previously but allows you to select LEDs individually from the serial port.

Start by creating a new sketch by typing out the code that follows and saving it with a memorable name, such as mySerialShiftOut. Alternatively, find this example at http://arduino.cc/en/Tutorial/ShftOut12.

```
/*
  Shift Register Example
  for 74HC595 shift register

  This sketch turns reads serial input and uses it to set the pins
  of a 74HC595 shift register.

  Hardware:
  * 74HC595 shift register attached to pins 2, 3, and 4 of the Arduino,
  as detailed below.
  * LEDs attached to each of the outputs of the shift register

  Created 22 May 2009
  Created 23 Mar 2010
  by Tom Igoe

  */

//Pin connected to latch pin (ST_CP) of 74HC595
const int latchPin = 8;
//Pin connected to clock pin (SH_CP) of 74HC595
const int clockPin = 12;
////Pin connected to Data in (DS) of 74HC595
const int dataPin = 11;

void setup() {
  //set pins to output because they are addressed in the main loop
  pinMode(latchPin, OUTPUT);
  pinMode(dataPin, OUTPUT);
  pinMode(clockPin, OUTPUT);
  Serial.begin(9600);
  Serial.println("reset");
}

void loop() {
  if (Serial.available() > 0) {
    // ASCII '0' through '9' characters are
    // represented by the values 48 through 57.
    // so if the user types a number from 0 through 9 in ASCII,
    // you can subtract 48 to get the actual value:
    int bitToSet = Serial.read() - 48;

  // write to the shift register with the correct bit set high:
    registerWrite(bitToSet, HIGH);
  }
}

// This method sends bits to the shift register:

void registerWrite(int whichPin, int whichState) {
```

```
// the bits you want to send
  byte bitsToSend = 0;

  // turn off the output so the pins don't light up
  // while you're shifting bits:
  digitalWrite(latchPin, LOW);

  // turn on the next highest bit in bitsToSend:
  bitWrite(bitsToSend, whichPin, whichState);

  // shift the bits out:
  shiftOut(dataPin, clockPin, MSBFIRST, bitsToSend);

    // turn on the output so the LEDs can light up:
  digitalWrite(latchPin, HIGH);

}
```

After the sketch is done uploading, click the serial monitor button to open the window. The first word should be "reset," which is displayed in setup when the sketch starts. Enter numbers between 0 and 7 and click Send (or press Return) to turn on different LEDs in the row.

In this piece of code, you convert the binary addressing system to a decimal one, and instead of having to enter all the binary combinations, you can just pick out individual addresses of each LED by entering a decimal number from 0 to 7.

In the main loop, the if statement checks to see whether there is any data to read. Serial.available is the buffer or storage for incoming bytes, so the if statement is true and then progress only if data has been sent.

```
  if (Serial.available() > 0) {
```

Characters sent through the serial port are sent as ASCII characters, and when they are read using Serial.read, they are interpreted as their equivalent integer value on the ASCII chart. This puts 0 to 9 in the range of 48 to 57, so to get them to the correct range, you simply subtract 48 from the reading.

```
    int bitToSet = Serial.read() - 48;
```

A custom function called registerWrite makes conversion of 0 to 9 to the relevant byte value simpler. The function is outside the main loop at the bottom of the sketch.

```
  // write to the shift register with the correct bit set high:
    registerWrite(bitToSet, HIGH);
  }
```

The two values that can be entered into `registerWrite` are declared at the top of the sketch as `whichPin` and `whichState`. These variables and any within the function are local and cannot be referenced in the main `loop`.

```
void registerWrite(int whichPin, int whichState) {
```

A byte variable is declared and set to 0.

```
// the bits you want to send
  byte bitsToSend = 0;
```

As in the previous example, the latch pin is set `LOW` before the bits are shifted.

```
// turn off the output so the pins don't light up
// while you're shifting bits:
digitalWrite(latchPin, LOW);
```

This time, a new function called `bitWrite` is used. It has three parameters: the variable that you are writing to, in this case `bitsToSend`; which bit of the byte to write to, from 0 (least significant bit, rightmost bit) to 7 (most significant bit, leftmost bit); and the state, either HIGH or LOW.

```
// turn on the next highest bit in bitsToSend:
bitWrite(bitsToSend, whichPin, whichState);
```

For example, if byte `bitsToSend` is equal to 0, it equals 00000000 in binary. When you use the `bitWrite` function with `whichPin` equal to 4 and `which-State` equal to HIGH (or 1), `bitsToSend` equals 00010000.

After `bitWrite` updates the value of the byte `bitsToSend`, `bitsToSend` is put through the `shiftOut()` function to update the register.

```
// shift the bits out:
shiftOut(dataPin, clockPin, MSBFIRST, bitsToSend);
```

Finally, the latch pin is set `HIGH` and the results are updated on the LEDs themselves.

```
// turn on the output so the LEDs can light up:
digitalWrite(latchPin, HIGH);

}
```

Doing more with the same circuit

This last example allows you to communicate values over serial, but you could just as easily automate this process using a `for` loop to count from 0 to 7 and back again. The value could also respond to a sensor, such as a potentiometer, using the `map` function to give you a power bar as you turn it. The possibilities are endless. There are many other examples on the Arduino site for increasingly complex functionality (go to `http://arduino.cc/en/Tutorial/ShiftOut`) including cascading multiple shift registers.

After you go past two shift registers, you're well-advised to power the LEDs externally to reduce the amount of current passing through the Arduino. When you're using lots of LEDs, you can easily go over the 200mA max current draw, so use your multimeter to check the current draw of the circuit and stay safe.

This chapter's example described just one chip that is available. You can find many other chips, such as the TLC5940, which can control 16 PWM outputs and works on a very similar principle. The Google Code page contains many details as well as a library contributed by Alex Leone (`http://code.google.com/p/tlc5940arduino/`). You can also reverse the principle of shifting out with a different chip and read lots of inputs. More details on shifting in are available on the Arduino site at `http://arduino.cc/en/Tutorial/ShiftIn`.

Chapter 15

Multiplying Your Outputs with I²C

This chapter tells you all about working with I²C (pronounced *eye-squared-see* or *eye-two-see*), giving you another way to control lots of outputs. As an example of this great communications protocol, instead of just controlling LEDs (described in Chapter 14), you learn how to control an army of servo motors. With the potential to control hundreds of servos comes the need to power them all so this chapter also talks you through the various options when choosing a power supply.

What Is I²C?

I²C is a great communication protocol that is ideal for getting signals to lots of outputs (I also talk about other ways to control multiple outputs in Chapter 14). Luckily, I'm not the only one who thinks so. There's an excellent product that uses the I²C controlled PCA9685 chip, a PWM driver that lets you drive up to 16 servo motors with a single board. The 16-channel 12-bit PWM/Servo Driver (see Figure 15-1), I²C interface (http://www.adafruit.com/products/815) from Adafruit Industries is a partially assembled kit that makes it easy to control lots of motors, LEDs, or even other circuits.

The board is designed around controlling *servos*, which have three pin connections (ground, 5V, and the signal wire), so there are 16 groups of three to allow you to easily plug your servos in using the standard three-pin socket. Physically, these pins are in groups of four, so the header pin is three deep and four wide (3 x 4). On either end of the board is space for a six-header pin to communicate with the PCA9685 chip.

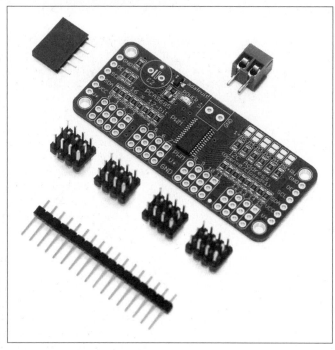

Figure 15-1:
I²C PWM/
Servo Driver
board.

A servo, as mentioned in Chapter 8, is a DC motor packaged with an encoder that allows it to keep track of its position. Standard DC motors are work-horses that are great at speeding up and continuously rotating in one direction, as they do on remote control cars and planes. Servos, on the other hand, are for precision movement; some servos continuously rotate (or can be hacked to do so), but generally they move to a specific degree within their range and are excellent for all sorts of applications, from walking robots to electronic sail winches on boats.

The pins from top to bottom are

- **GND:** Ground
- **OE:** Output eEnable
- **SCL:** Serial clock
- **SDA:** Serial data
- **VCC:** Power line for the PCA9685
- **V+:** Power line for the servos

Of these pins, all you need to use are VCC and GND to power the PCA9685 chip, and SCL and SDA to let I²C talk with the Arduino and other boards. Because the board has the same pins on each side, you may rightly assume that these boards have the ability to be daisy chained together. Each board is given a physical address using the little golden terminals to the top right of the board, known as solder jumpers. These allow you to set the order of the boards by connecting the relevant jumpers to give each board a binary value. Board 0 has no terminals connected, so boards are addressed from 1 onward by soldering the terminals together, using the same principles of counting up in binary that Chapter 14 covers. This arrangement is semi-permanent but can be undone with use of a solder sucker or solder braid.

The V+ pin is linked to the last component, the screw terminal that sits at the top of the board. This is an important feature of this board. Although it is possible to power motors and their controllers using the same supply, doing so is rarely advisable. Motors often need very large amounts of current and voltage to rotate and move loads. Sometimes, current spikes or drops depending on the number of motors and the load on them. Such spikes can be extremely hazardous for the low-voltage PCA9685 control chip, so on this board, the voltage supply has been separated, meaning that the servo motors (or LEDs) can be run from a separate high-voltage, high-current power 12V supply, and the PWM driver chip can operate from an Arduino's low-voltage, low-current, 5V power supply.

Unlike the 74HC595 shift register and the TLC5940 PWM driver, the PCA9685 has a built-in clock, so your Arduino doesn't need to constantly send messages to update it, leaving it free to do other things.

In the following example, you learn how to assemble and control an I²C PWM/Servo Driver to make your own mass motor project.

Assembling the I²C PWM/Servo Driver

All the tricky components on the I²C PWM/Servo Driver board have been assembled for you, but you need to know a trick for doing the final bits of soldering. Doing a dry run and laying out the components is a good idea, so do that first.

In the kit, you have:

- One I²C PWM/Servo Driver board
- Four 3 x 4 header pins
- One length of header pins
- One screw terminal

Follow these steps to perform your dry run of the assembly:

1. **Using a pair of wire cutters, cut the length of header pins so that you have two lengths of 1 x 6 (see Figure 15-2).**

   You use these at either end to connect your first board to the Arduino and any daisy chained boards.

2. **Place all the parts loosely in the board to make sure they all fit.**

   The header pins should have the long side pointing up, and the screw terminal should be facing away from the board, to make it easier to connect cables. When you're happy with where the pins are, it's time to get soldering.

3. **Ensure that you have a clear workspace (as described in Chapter 5), power up your soldering iron, wet your sponge, and find your solder.**

   Making a cup of tea or coffee is optional, but always advised.

Figure 15-2:
Cutting the headers to length.

Before you start soldering, note that the data pins on the board are the most sensitive to heat, and if they get too hot, they can be damaged. These are the single rows of headers at either end and the signal pin on the servo headers. I recommend using a high heat on your iron to allow the solder to melt quickly. This means that the solder melts around the joint before it can be conducted and spread all the way down to the chip, by which time you have finished the joint and it is already cooling down. If you are uncomfortable with this level of soldering, practice first on a piece of stripboard with some spare header pins.

The 3 x 4 header pins are the most difficult, so you do best to start with them. The aim is to get the plastic bit level on the board. You can do so by pressing adhesive putty onto the component and board or by using a third hand clamp. I find third hands and other clamps useful for holding boards, but more trouble than they are worth for holding components. They can also sometimes scratch the delicate circuitry, so be careful with them and avoid dragging boards out of their teeth. Using Blue Tack, you can safely secure the component until you have a couple of solder joints. Then you should secure the header pins. I recommend connecting the GND and V+ first, because these can handle more heat than the data line can.

When soldering the inside connectors of the 3 x 4 headers, it can be awkward to get the soldering iron in position. Try holding your iron at an angle across the rows and working from one side to the other, such as left to right if you are right handed. Doing so avoids working over your previous solder joints and lessens the chance of the individual joints becoming connected. If they do connect, simply use a solder sucker to remove the excess and reapply solder if necessary.

After you have the 3 x 4 header pins soldered in place, move on to the header pins at each end. These should be a lot simpler in comparison, and with luck, your technique improves after the repetition of the previous task.

Finally, connect the screw terminal. Notice that the holes and pins are a lot wider than the header pins. This is because this connection is used for supplying power to every motor connected, so a thicker piece of metal is needed to cope with the amount of current. If the connection is too small, it builds up heat until it melts, so it's important to always have thick wires and connectors that are rated for more than the current that you are expecting. Because of this thicker connection, you may notice that the screw terminal takes a little longer to heat up and melt the solder. If it takes too long, the plastic part may melt, so be sure to turn up the heat on your iron if it's taking a while.

That's it. Simple, isn't it? You now have an I²C PWM/Servo Driver board ready for use. Make sure to check over your connections for any short circuits, and use your multimeter's continuity checker when the board isn't attached to a power source to check connections if you are unsure. The V+ and GND lines for the servos should be connected in two rows because they all draw power from the same source. For now, you should leave the addressable solder jumpers unsoldered because you are starting with the first board, board 0.

Using the I²C PWM/Servo Driver

In the previous section, you find out how to assemble an I²C PWM/Servo Driver. In this section, you see how to make it perform. The example in this section shows you how to send a signal to the board to control servos on each pin. You can test this functionality with a single servo, which is included in most Arduino kits, but after you have it working, you want to order other servos to get the full effect.

For this project, you need:

✔ An Arduino Uno

✔ A servo motor

✔ Jump wires or pre-crimped wires

✔ An external power supply

✔ A precision screwdriver

The shield has header pins to connect to, but these pins don't slot directly into an Arduino. A good way to connect them is to use jump wires with sockets on one side and pins on the other (male to female), such as those from Cool Components (`http://www.coolcomponents.co.uk/catalog/jumper-wires-male-female-p-355.html`) or from SparkFun (`https://www.sparkfun.com/products/9140`), shown in Figure 15-3.

Figure 15-3:
Jump wires
with
sockets.

If you're a real connoisseur, you can make your own custom cables using pre-crimped wires and header sockets, such as these from Technobots (`http://www.technobotsonline.com/cable-and-accessories/cable/pre-crimped-wires.html` and `http://www.technobotsonline.com/connectors-and-headers/cable-assembly-housings.html`) or Pololu (`http://www.pololu.com/catalog/category/71` and `http://www.pololu.com/catalog/category/70`). These leave you with one connector at each end and look super professional when bound up using spiral cable wrap, available from RS Components (`http://uk.rs-online.com/mobile/p/cable-spiral-wrapping/6826842/`).

Bench-top power supply

Bench-top power supplies (shown in the following figure) are good for testing circuits quickly, allowing you to try a range of voltages with a high maximum current and (if you get a posh one) monitor the power consumption of your circuit. For comparison, you might check out a couple of varieties from Maplin in the United Kingdom. You can try cheap ones, such as a DC 3 - 12V 3A Compact Bench Power Supply available from Maplin at `http://www.maplin.co.uk/dc-3-12v-3a-compact-bench-power-supply-96963`, which has no feedback of the current consumed. Or try more expensive ones such as a Bench Power Supply with LCD Screen available from Maplin at `http://www.maplin.co.uk/bench-power-supply-with-lcd-screen-219129`, which can display the current consumed by your circuit. If you opt for a bench-top power supply, you can simply connect two lengths of wire to the positive and negative terminals and connect the other end to the screw terminal on the board.

Always disconnect the power supply before turning it on to check that the voltage is set to the appropriate level. It's easy to accidentally turn a dial too high when the bench top power supply is off and damage your circuit as the power comes on.

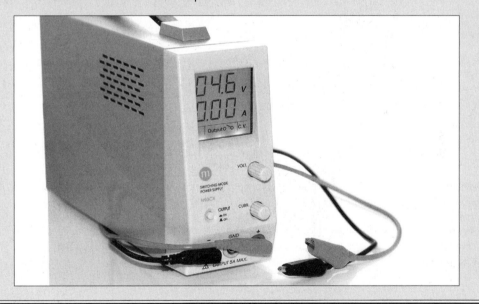

For the power supply, ensure that you have the correct voltage and current for the number of servos you are using. Some small hobby servos use 5V, but you can find much more variety after you get onto 12V ones. You have two easy options for a power supply: a bench-top power supply to quickly connect your board, or a modified external power supply like those used for charging phones, drills, or laptops. See the "Bench-top power supply" and "External power supplies" sidebars in this chapter for more information.

External power supplies

When shopping for external power supplies (shown in the following figure), you should always buy those that are regulated. Unregulated supplies don't have a definite voltage and so are cheaper, but more risky. Look on the box and the supply to find out which is regulated and which isn't. They can also be either fixed or multi-voltage. Fixed gives you the specified voltage and current; multi-voltage gives you a selection of voltages (such as 3, 4.5, 6, 9, 12) and, often, the current varies, allowing more current on the lower voltages.

A good example from Maplin in the United Kingdom. is the High Power Multi-Voltage Desktop Power Supply at http://www.maplin.co.uk/high-power-multi-voltage-desktop-power-supply-48517. It's expensive but can operate on a very useful range of voltages (5, 6, 9, 12, 13.5, and 15) and supply a maximum current of up to 4A, which is more than enough for most applications. You can find similar power supplies from RadioShack, such as the EnercellUniversal 1000mA AC Adapter (http://www.radioshack.com/product/index.jsp?productId=3875403).

These normally come with a variety of common connectors, such as the 2.1mm power jack connector on the Arduino. This is useful for lower amounts of current (up to 500mA), because it can be plugged into the Arduino to allow you to power things from the Vin pin. However, running lots of servos requires a significant current that could be over 1A, so I don't advise running this through your Arduino.

Instead, you can strip and tin the wires to allow them to be easily connected directly to the screw terminal on your servo driver board or to a choc block to extend the length of wire. First make sure that the power supply is unplugged. Cut the wire 10cm or so from the base of the connector (that way, you can always connect it back again). The wire on the power supply is most likely either *biaxial* — two multicore wire side by side — or *coaxial* — one multicore wire in the center and another surrounding it.

Biaxial is easy to bare using cable strippers and can then be tinned using a bit of solder. The positive is usually be marked in some discreet way, such as faint white or red dashes, but not always, so be sure to test with a multimeter.

Coaxial is a bit more difficult to work with. If you strip back the top layer of insulation on the wire with a cable stripper, you expose a mesh of wire. This can be straightened out and pulled to one side to reveal the central wire. Twist the now-straightened mesh of wire to one side of the central wire and then strip back the central wire as well, leaving enough insulation so that the two wires do not touch. You can then solder these two wires to keep the multicore wire together and connect it to a screw terminal. The ground wire is usually on the outside mesh of wire, but not always, so test it with a multimeter. When you're tinning, be careful not to melt the insulation around the center core because doing so could create a short circuit.

To test your power supply's polarity, secure the loose ends to your work surface so that they cannot touch; electrical tape is good for this. Plug in your power supply. Turn your multimeter to the DC voltage setting and place the probes on the ends of each wire. The probes are usually red and black for clarity. If you're reading a negative voltage, you are reading the power supply the wrong way around — switch your probes to find the correct positive and negative lines. Unplug the supply until the ends of each wire are secured on a screw terminal or tape them up with electrical tape when not in use to avoid accidents.

Always test the voltage of your external power supply with a multimeter before using it to power your project (as shown in Chapter 5). It can be easy to forget the voltage that your supply is supplying, and it is also good to practice to test older power supplies to ensure that they're up to scratch and supplying the full voltage for which they're rated.

If you have an external power supply or a bench-top power supply without a current display, link your multimeter in series with either the power or ground line to see how much current you're drawing as explained in Chapter 5. When you are sure of your positive and negative wires, turn the power supply off and attach them to the screw terminal using a miniature screwdriver. The polarity is marked on the top of the board, so make sure that the +5V and GND are the right way around.

The circuit diagram (Figure 15-4) and schematic (Figure 15-5) detail the wiring for the PWM driver board. The connections can be broken into three areas. First, to power the I²C chip on the board, the VCC and GND pins on the board must be connected to the 5V and GND pins on your Arduino. To send data to the chip, the SCL and SDA pins on the board connect to the SCL and SDA pins on your Arduino. If you are using an older board than the Uno R3, you won't be able to see these pins because they're a recent addition. Instead, use analog pins 4 (SDA) and 5 (SCL). The last bit of the wiring is separate from the others and is to supply the power for the servo motors. Connect your power supply to the positive and negative terminals using a precision screwdriver.

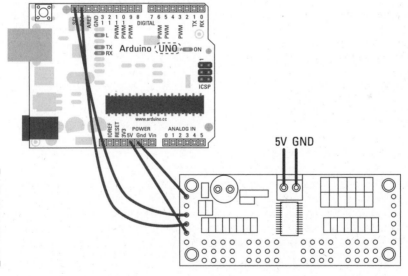

Figure 15-4:
Diagram
of a PWM
Driver board
wiring.

After your circuit is assembled, you need the appropriate software to use it. To get it, follow these steps:

1. **Download the Adafruit PWM/Servo Driver Library from Github**
   (`https://github.com/adafruit/Adafruit-PWM-Servo-Driver-Library`).

2. **From the project page, download the `.zip` file and unzip it to display the library folder.**

3. **Rename the library folder to Adafruit_PWMServoDriver, and place it in your libraries folder in your Arduino sketch directory.**

4. **Restart Arduino and click File⇨Examples to find the Adafruit_ PWMServoDriver sketch.**

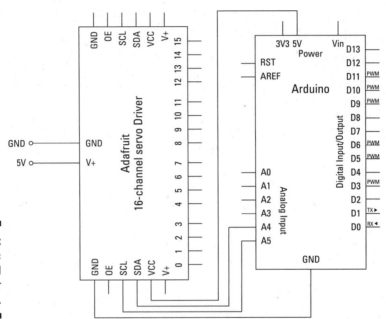

Figure 15-5:
A schematic of a PWM Driver board.

Following is the code for this sketch:

```
/*****************************************************
  This is an example for our Adafruit 16-channel PWM & Servo driver
  Servo test - this will drive 16 servos, one after the other

  Pick one up today in the adafruit shop!
  ------> http://www.adafruit.com/products/815

  These displays use I2C to communicate, 2 pins are required to
  interface. For Arduino UNOs, thats SCL -> Analog 5, SDA -> Analog 4

  Adafruit invests time and resources providing this open source code,
  please support Adafruit and open-source hardware by purchasing
  products from Adafruit!

  Written by Limor Fried/Ladyada for Adafruit Industries.
  BSD license, all text above must be included in any redistribution
  *****************************************************/
```

```
#include <Wire.h>
#include <Adafruit_PWMServoDriver.h>

// called this way, it uses the default address 0x40
Adafruit_PWMServoDriver pwm = Adafruit_PWMServoDriver();
// you can also call it with a different address you want
//Adafruit_PWMServoDriver pwm = Adafruit_PWMServoDriver(0x41);

// Depending on your servo make, the pulse width min and max may vary, you
// want these to be as small/large as possible without hitting the hard stop
// for max range. You'll have to tweak them as necessary to match the servos you
// have!
#define SERVOMIN  150 // this is the 'minimum' pulse length count (out of 4096)
#define SERVOMAX  600 // this is the 'maximum' pulse length count (out of 4096)

// our servo # counter
uint8_t servonum = 0;

void setup() {
  Serial.begin(9600);
  Serial.println("16 channel Servo test!");

  pwm.begin();

  pwm.setPWMFreq(60);  // Analog servos run at ~60 Hz updates
}

// you can use this function if you'd like to set the pulse length in seconds
// e.g. setServoPulse(0, 0.001) is a ~1 millisecond pulse width. its not
//              precise!
void setServoPulse(uint8_t n, double pulse) {
  double pulselength;

  pulselength = 1000000;   // 1,000,000 us per second
  pulselength /= 60;   // 60 Hz
  Serial.print(pulselength); Serial.println(" us per period");
  pulselength /= 4096;  // 12 bits of resolution
  Serial.print(pulselength); Serial.println(" us per bit");
  pulse *= 1000;
  pulse /= pulselength;
  Serial.println(pulse);
  pwm.setPWM(n, 0, pulse);
}

void loop() {
  // Drive each servo one at a time
  Serial.println(servonum);
  for (uint16_t pulselen = SERVOMIN; pulselen < SERVOMAX; pulselen++) {
    pwm.setPWM(servonum, 0, pulselen);
```

```
  }
  delay(500);
  for (uint16_t pulselen = SERVOMAX; pulselen > SERVOMIN; pulselen--) {
    pwm.setPWM(servonum, 0, pulselen);
  }
  delay(500);

  servonum ++;
  if (servonum > 15) servonum = 0;
}
```

Upload the sketch, and turn on your power supply. The servo moves to its maximum degree value and then back to its 0 position. If you have only one, there is a delay while it works through all 16 outputs. Monitor the current draw of your circuit, and if you are within the maximum current of the power supply, you can add more servos to the board to see the full effect. If you want to monitor the progression of the program, open the Serial Monitor to see the current motor as it works through each of them from 0 to 15.

If you don't see any movement or see erratic behavior, double-check your wiring:

- Make sure you're using the correct pin numbers.

- If you see a jerking movement from the servo(s), you are most likely not providing enough current. Monitor the current draw for any peaks in current and compare that to your supply.

- If you hear nasty grating noises from your servo, power it down immediately; you may have to adjust the SERVOMAX and SERVOMIN values. See how in the next section.

Understanding the I²C PWM/Servo Driver Sketch

Before setup, two libraries are included that are essential to use this hardware. Wire.h is included to allow you to talk I²C with the board, and Adafruit_PWMServoDriver.h is included to perform more specific functions relating to the design of this board.

```
#include <Wire.h>
#include <Adafruit_PWMServoDriver.h>
```

A new object, named pwm, is declared using a custom function from Adafruit_PWMServoDriver.h. This sets the address of the board, which defaults to 0x40 if omitted. This is used as the zero value for choosing a board. If you wanted to choose a board with id 1, you'd use 0x41, as shown.

```
// called this way, it uses the default address 0x40
Adafruit_PWMServoDriver pwm = Adafruit_PWMServoDriver();
// you can also call it with a different address you want
//Adafruit_PWMServoDriver pwm = Adafruit_PWMServoDriver(0x41);
```

The next two statements use `#define` to set the minimum and maximum pulse length. Practically, this sets the degrees of rotation of the servos, so if you find that your servo is rotating too far or not far enough, you can adjust this value to fine-tune it.

```
// Depending on your servo make, the pulse width min and max may vary, you
// want these to be as small/large as possible without hitting the hard stop
// for max range. You'll have to tweak them as necessary to match the servos you
// have!
#define SERVOMIN  150 // this is the 'minimum' pulse length count (out of 4096)
#define SERVOMAX  600 // this is the 'maximum' pulse length count (out of 4096)
```

The term `uint8_t` is a C datatype, which is an unsigned integer 8 bits in length. Unsigned means it uses only positive values, and 8 bits means it holds values between 0 and 255. In this case, it is used to declare `servonum`, the variable that stores the current servo as the program counts through them. A standard `int` in Arduino code is 2 bytes of data (-32,768 to 32,767), which can also be called an `int16_t`. You can find more details about `int` here: http://arduino.cc/en/Reference/Int.

```
// our servo # counter
uint8_t servonum = 0;
```

In `setup`, the serial port is opened with a baud rate of 9600, and the opening message "16 channel Servo test!" is sent to mark the start of the program. The object `pwm` (or board 0, as you know it) is initialized using `pwm.begin`, and the frequency of the servos is set to 60Hz.

```
void setup() {
  Serial.begin(9600);
  Serial.println("16 channel Servo test!");

  pwm.begin();

  pwm.setPWMFreq(60);  // Analog servos run at ~60 Hz updates
}
```

Next is the custom function `setServoPulse`, which sets the pulse length in seconds rather than hertz, but this function is not used in this example.

```
// you can use this function if you'd like to set the pulse length in seconds
// e.g. setServoPulse(0, 0.001) is a ~1 millisecond pulse width. its not
//              precise!
void setServoPulse(uint8_t n, double pulse) {
  double pulselength;

  pulselength = 1000000;   // 1,000,000 us per second
  pulselength /= 60;   // 60 Hz
  Serial.print(pulselength); Serial.println(" us per period");
  pulselength /= 4096;  // 12 bits of resolution
  Serial.print(pulselength); Serial.println(" us per bit");
  pulse *= 1000;
  pulse /= pulselength;
  Serial.println(pulse);
  pwm.setPWM(n, 0, pulse);
}
```

In `loop` the current servo number is printed to the Serial Monitor for you to see.

```
void loop() {
  // Drive each servo one at a time
  Serial.println(servonum);
```

Now that you know which servo you're on, it's time to move it. A `for` loop is used to move the current servo from its minimum value to its maximum. When that servo has reached its maximum value (`SERVOMAX`), it waits for half a second and then a second `for` loop returns its value back from maximum value to minimum (`SERVOMIN`). When at its minimum, there is another delay for a half second. The `for` loop increments the pulse one value at a time to give a smooth movement. Notice that `uint16_t` is used to declare the local variable `pulselen`; this is equivalent to an unsigned `int` in regular Arduino code. You can find out more about unsigned `int` values at `http://arduino.cc/en/Reference/UnsignedInt`.

```
  for (uint16_t pulselen = SERVOMIN; pulselen < SERVOMAX; pulselen++) {
    pwm.setPWM(servonum, 0, pulselen);
  }
  delay(500);
  for (uint16_t pulselen = SERVOMAX; pulselen > SERVOMIN; pulselen--) {
    pwm.setPWM(servonum, 0, pulselen);
  }
  delay(500);
```

After one servo has completed its movement, `servonum` is incremented by one. If `servonum` goes higher than 16, it is sent back to 0 because it has reached the last servo. There is another bit of C shorthand here, which is why the `if` statement can be written all on one line without curly braces({ }).

```
  servonum ++;
  if (servonum > 15) servonum = 0;
}
```

This is a great sketch for testing communication with the board and allows you to control your servos in any way you want by using pwm. setPWM(servonum, 0, pulselen). As with most libraries, this one is a work in progress, and you may find many questions without answers, as well see that many improvements and refinements could be made to it. The best place to ask further questions about this board and the library is on the Adafruit forum, where you can find other people asking the same questions and very helpful people trying to answer them. Head over to http://forums. adafruit.com and look in the Other Arduino products from Adafruit section to find out more.

Buying Servo Motors

Now that you have a way to control lots of servos, you need to know where to shop for them and what to look for. There are a variety of sites that sell servo motors online, so a quick Google returns lots of options. The two main applications for servos are in robotics and remote controlled aircraft, so any shop or site that supplies these is likely to have a range of servos that are specific to the application.

The strength of the servos, or the twisting force, is called *torque* and is usually measured in kilograms per centimetre (kg/cm) or pounds per inch (lb/in). Servos can range in torque from miniature servos designed to move the ailerons on a plane that provide around 0.2 kg/cm, to monster servos that can be used as sail winches on boats (9.8 kg/cm). Just for comparison, the torque created by an adult male hand is approximately 8 kg/cm (as NASA's human performance charts show at http://msis.jsc.nasa.gov/ sections/section04.htm).

Obviously, the amount of torque created depends on the strength of the servo motor and the quality of the parts. A wide variety of servo motors operate from 4V to 12V and cater to most needs. The main difference is the amount of current that is required when the servo is pulling or pushing, which is referred to as being "under load." When the servo is exerting itself, it can require much more voltage than when it has no load, so it is worth testing individual servos with a multimeter connected to the power line to monitor the current draw (as described in Chapter 5) and leaving a reasonable margin for any additional current. It's also worth noting that the average power supply is only 70–80 percent efficient, meaning that a 1A power supply may only really be supplying 700–800mA. Although it may be possible to get 1A out of it, it likely deteriorates quickly and so should be seen as the maximum and not the recommended supply under typical use.

Power doesn't always dictate price, and with servos, you find a great variety of seemingly less powerful servos for a high price. This is often because of the physical build of the servo itself. The gears inside the servo are of great importance, and depending on the material used, they can make a huge difference to the price and performance. Most hobby servos are for relatively small loads and use nylon gears. This is great because nylon exerts almost no wear on other nylon parts, even after thousands of uses. Nylon is self-lubricating, requiring no additional grease. More serious servos use metal gears. These can take much greater loads because they are not as flexible as nylon and are less likely to break if they are under an excessive load.

Servos can also either be digital or analog, which relates to the way the motor is controlled. Both types of servo have the same parts and the same three wires, but digital motors have a microprocessor that can analyze the signals sent to the servo and send pulses to the servo many times faster than a traditional servo with analog electronics. With more signals per second, the servo has a much faster response time. Because each pulse is a voltage, the servo consumes a lot more current per second and, therefore, also is capable of providing more torque and supporting a greater load. The drawback of digital servos is the price and power consumption, but if you can justify it, you won't be disappointed.

There are a variety of brands out there to choose from, so the best thing to do first is to research them. An excellent site that's aptly named www.servodatabase.com gives you a good idea of the cost versus performance of most servos, as well as a good indication of the most popular ones.

If you're looking for an affordable, basic servo that's a bit bigger than the hobby servos in most kits, you can't go far wrong with a Futaba S3003 found at http://www.gpdealera.com/cgi-bin/wgainf100p.pgm?I=FUTM0031). In this case, you cannot buy the motor directly from the manufacturer, so you have to shop around. Two such suppliers are Servo Shop in the United Kingdom (http://www.servoshop.co.uk/index.php?pid=FUTS3003) and Servo City in the United States (http://www.servocity.com/html/s3003_servo_standard.html). Happy shopping!

Other Uses for I²C

Servo motors aren't the only kind of object that you can control using I²C. Other products are ready to be hooked up to an Arduino to help you build a huge installation. One such product is the Addressable LED Ribbon (https://www.sparkfun.com/products/11272), shown in Figure 15-6. LED ribbon is a flexible tape of LEDs that can be stuck to a surface to allow lights to cover a huge area. The ribbon itself is a type of flexible PCB that has surface-mounted LEDs, resistors, and contacts, and has only recently become widely available for an affordable price. You may have seen it in venues that have mood lighting around the edges of the room.

Just like individual LEDs, this can either come as a single strip of an individual color or RGB, allowing you to tailor the color to the use. Most LED ribbon is a single circuit, meaning that you can change the brightness or color of the whole strip, but not affect the individual LEDs. Addressable LED Ribbon, however, is different because it allows you to control each LED individually, allowing full control of the brightness and color and creating a potential for very cool animation.

Figure 15-6:
A reel of addressable LED ribbon.

There are many great online tutorials for integrating addressable LED ribbon in your project. Check out the SparkFun (https://www.sparkfun.com/products/11272) and Adafruit (http://learn.adafruit.com/digital-led-strip) product pages for more details.

Part V
Sussing Out Software

The 5th Wave   By Rich Tennant

© RICHTENNANT

"Roger! Check the sewing machine's connection to the PC. I'm getting e-mails stitched across my curtains again."

In this part . . .

So, by this stage of the book, you must feel that you have a pretty good grip for the physical world, wiring, soldering, and uploading code. But what if I told you there was a whole other virtual world out there as well? Interested? It's possible to combine your (now copious) knowledge of electronics with software on your computer to create stunning interactive visuals in the virtual world that exists on your computer, or to use data from software, your computer, or the Internet to create light, sound, or motion in the real world.

Chapter 16

Getting to Know Processing

In This Chapter

▶ Getting excited about Processing

▶ Making shapes of all sizes and colors

*I*n the previous chapters, you learn all about using Arduino as a stand-alone device. A program is uploaded onto the Arduino and it carries out its task ad infinitum until it is told to stop or powered down. You are affecting the Arduino by simple, clear, electrical signals, and as long as there are no outside influences or coding errors, and if the components last, the Arduino reliably repeats its function. This simplicity is extremely useful for many applications and allows the Arduino to not only serve as a great prototyping platform but also work as a reliable tool for interactive products and installations for many years, as it already does in many museums.

Although this simplicity is something to admire, many applications are outside the scope of an Arduino's capabilities. One of these (at least for now) is running computer software. Although the Arduino is basically a computer, it's not capable of running comparably large and complex computer programs in the same way as your desktop or laptop. Many of these programs are highly specialized depending on the task that you're doing. You could benefit hugely if only you could link this software to the physical world in the same way your Arduino can.

Because the Arduino can connect to your computer and be monitored over the serial port, other programs may also be able to do this, in the same way that your computer talks to printers, scanners, or cameras. So by combining the physical world interaction capabilities of your Arduino with the data crunching software capabilities of your computer, you can create projects with an enormous variety of inputs, outputs, and processes.

Many specific programs are made for specific tasks, but until you want to specify, it's best to find software that you can experiment with — that is, be a jack-of-all-trades in the same way that your Arduino is for the physical world. Processing is a great place to start.

In this chapter, you learn about Processing, the sister project that was in the first stages of development around the same time as Arduino. Processing is a software environment that, in the same way that an Arduino is used to test circuits quickly, can be used to "sketch" programs quickly. Processing is a great piece of open source software to learn about, and because of its similarities to Arduino, learning it is even easier.

Looking Under the Hood

An Arduino can communicate over its serial port as a serial device, which can be read by any program that can talk serial. Many programs are available, but Processing is one of the most popular.

Processing has an enormous breadth of applicationsranging visualizing data to creating generative artwork to performing motion capture using your webcam for digital performances. These are just a few niches, but you can find a wealth of examples on the Processing exhibition to wet your digital whistle. Head over to `http://processing.org/exhibition/` to check them out.

Processing is a Java-based language that looks very similar to C (on which Arduino code is based) and C++. It is available for Windows, Mac OS, and Linux. Ben Fry and Casey Reas developed Processing to allow artists, designers, or anyone to experiment with code, rather than just developers and engineers. In the same way that ideas are sketched out, Processing is designed to sketch software. Programs can be quickly developed and adapted without a huge investment of time.

Processing is a text-based IDE very similar to that of Arduino (in fact, it was "borrowed" by the Arduino team when the Arduino integrated development environment [IDE] was in development). A window (see Figure 16-1) displays the Java applet that the code creates. As with Arduino, the strength of Processing is the vast community that shares and comments on sketches, allowing the many participants to benefit from a diverse array of creative applications Processing is open source and allows users to modify the software as well as use it.

In this chapter, you learn how to get started with Processing, but for more information, head over to the Processing site at `http://processing.org/`.

 Many other programming languages exist that can interface with Arduino. I describe Max/Pure Data and OpenFrameworks in sidebars in this chapter. For a list of even the most obscure, check the Arduino Playgound at `http://arduino.cc/playground/Main/Interfacing`.

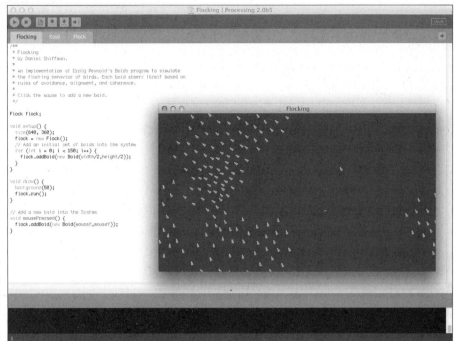

Figure 16-1:
A typical
view of
Processing.

Max/PureData

Max (also previously known as Max/MSP) is a visual programming language with a vast variety of uses but is most commonly used for audio, music and sound synthesis applications. It is available for Windows, Mac OS, Linux, and other, more obscure operating systems.

Unlike traditional text-based programming languages, Max uses a graphical user interface to connect visual objects to one another in the same way that traditional synthesizers could be "patched" using wires to connect the various functions of the instrument. Software company Cycling '74 released the commercial software Max in 1990 based on earlier work by Miller Puckette to create a system for interactive computer music. Although the software is

not open source, the application programming interface (API) allows third parties to make their own extensions to the software for specific uses. Miller Puckette also developed a free and open source, but completely redesigned, version of Max called PureData.

You can find more information about Max and PureData on their respective web pages: http://cycling74.com/products/max/ and http://puredata.info. To start communicating between Max and Arduino, check out the aptly named Maxuino (http://www.maxuino.org/archives/category/updates), and for PureData and Arduino, check out Pduino (http://at.or.at/hans/pd/objects.html).

(continued)

(continued)

Other helpful links are on the Arduino playground at (`http://www.arduino.cc/
playground/interfacing/MaxMSP`

and `http://www.arduino.cc/
playground/Interfacing/PD`).

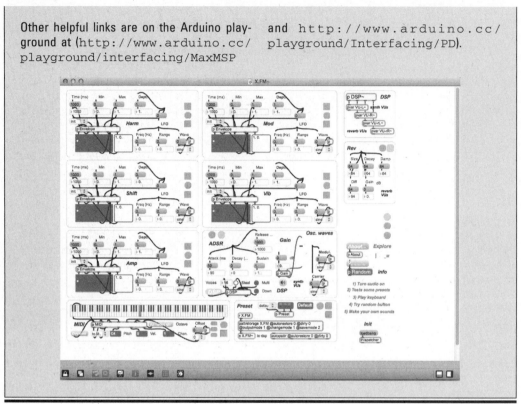

Installing Processing

Processing is free to download from `http://processing.org/`. To download Processing, go to the Download page and select your platform. At the
time of writing, Processing was version 2.0 Beta 5 and supported Mac OS X,
Windows 32-bit and 64-bit, and Linux 32-bit and 64-bit. Remember that things
may change between when I put these words down and when you get started.

To install Processing:

✔ **On a Mac:** The `.zip` file unzips automatically and can be placed in your
application folder at ~/Applications/Processing. Or you can place the
application on the desktop. From there you can drag Processing to the
dock for easy access or create a desktop alias.

✔ **On Windows:** Unzip the `.zip` file and place the Processing folder
on your desktop or in a sensible location such as your Program Files
folder: `C:/Program Files/Processing/`. Create a shortcut to
Processing.exe and place it somewhere convenient, such as on your
desktop or in the Start menu.

openFrameworks

OpenFrameworks, an open source C++ tool-kit for experimenting with code, is actively developed by Zachary Lieberman, Theo Watson, and Arturo Castro, as well as other members of the openFrameworks community. OpenFrameworks runs on Windows, Mac OS, Linux, iOS, and Android. OpenFrameworks is not based on Java as Processing is; it is a C++ library that is designed to be the bare bones for getting started with audio-visual applications.

OpenFrameworks is especially powerful with graphics, allowing you to use OpenGL easily for intensive rendering or video applications. In contrast to Processing, Max, and PureData, OpenFrameworks is not its own language; it is, in fact, a collection of open source libraries, known as a software framework — hence the name.

Because OpenFrameworks does not have its own IDE, the software used to write and compile the code depends on the platform. This feature can make getting started difficult because there is no centrally controlled IDE for continuity. The benefit is that the C++ is highly versatile and can be used on almost any platform you can think of, including mobile operating systems.

You can find more details and tutorials at `http://www.openframeworks.cc/` and `http://www.openframeworks.cc/tutorials/introduction/000_introduction.html`. SparkFun also has a great Arduino tutorial for using OpenFrameworks with Arduino on Windows at `http://www.sparkfun.com/tutorials/318`.

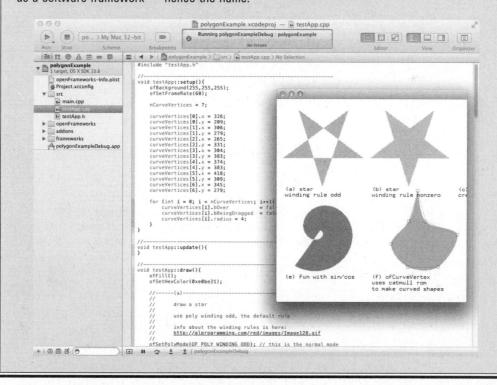

Taking a look at Processing

When you have Processing installed, run the application. Processing opens with a blank sketch (see Figure 16-2) similar to the Arduino window and is divided into five main areas:

- ✔ Toolbar with buttons
- ✔ Tabs
- ✔ Text editor
- ✔ Message area
- ✔ Console

The blank sketch also contains a menu bar for the main Processing application, which gives you drop-down menus to access the preferences of the processing application, load recent sketches and import libraries, and perform many other functions.

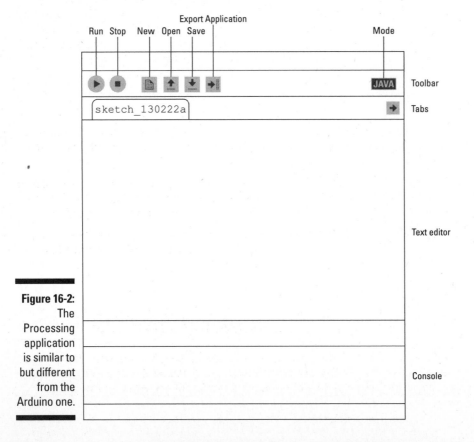

Figure 16-2: The Processing application is similar to but different from the Arduino one.

Here's an overview of the Processing toolbar:

✔ **Run:** Executes or runs the code in the text editor as an applet (small application) in a new window. The keyboard shortcuts for this is Ctrl+R for Windows and Cmd+R for Mac OS.

✔ **Stop:** Stops the code from running and closes the applet window.

✔ **New:** Opens a new, blank sketch with a dated name and a character to differentiate between sketches, such as sketch_121030a.

✔ **Open:** Lets you select from a directory, recent sketches, or the Examples folder.

✔ **Save:** Saves the current sketch. When saving, assigning a descriptive name rather than the preassigned name is best

✔ **Export Application:** Allows you to export your Processing sketch as a self-contained application. This is useful when you need to run the application at start-up or if you need to distribute the code to people who don't have Processing installed.

✔ **Mode:** Allows you to change mode between Java (standard), Android (mobile and tables), and JavaScript (online applications). This capability is a new development in the latest release. You can find more details on these modes here: `http://wiki.processing.org/w/Android` and `http://wiki.processing.org/w/JavaScript`.

✔ **Tabs:** Organizes multiple files in a Processing sketch. Use tabs in larger programs to separate objects from the main sketch or to incorporate look-up tables of data into a sketch.

✔ **Text editor:** Enters code into the sketch. Recognized terms or functions are highlighted in appropriate colors for clarity. The text editor is the same as that in the Arduino IDE.

✔ **Message area:** Displays errors, feedback, or information about the current task. You might see a notification that the sketch saved successfully, but more often than not, the message shows where errors are flagged.

✔ **Console:** Displays more details on your sketch. You can use the `println()` function here to display the values in your sketch; additional detail on errors is also shown.

Trying Your First Processing Sketch

Unlike with Arduino, you don't need an extra kit to get going with Processing, which makes Processing extremely useful for learning about coding because you can enter a line or two of code, click Run, and see what you've done.

Start your first sketch with these steps:

1. **Press Ctrl+N (in Windows) or Cmd+N (on a Mac) to open a new sketch.**

2. **Click in the text editor and enter this line of code:**

```
ellipse(50,50,10,10);
```

3. **Click the Run button.**

   A new applet window opens, showing a white circle in the middle of a gray box, as in Figure 16-3.

Well done! You've just written your first Processing program.

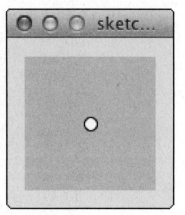

Figure 16-3:
A
Processing
sketch
that draws
an ellipse
with equal
dimensions,
also known
as a circle.

Done admiring your circle? That line of code draws an ellipse. An ellipse normally is not circular, but you gave it the parameters to make a circle. The word *ellipse* is highlighted in orange in the text editor, indicating that it is a recognized function. The first two numbers are the coordinates of the ellipse, which in this case are 50, 50. The unit of the numbers is in pixels. Because the default window is 100 x 100 pixels, coordinates of 50, 50 put the ellipse in the center. The 10, 10 values indicate the width and height of the ellipse, giving you a circle. You could write the function as

```
ellipse(x,y,width,height)
```

The coordinates for the ellipse (or any shape or point, for that matter) are written as x and y. These indicate a point in two-dimensional (2D) space, which in this case is a point measured in pixels on your screen. Horizontal positions are referred to as the x coordinate; vertical positions are the y coordinate. Depth used in 3D space is referred to as z. Add the following line of code, just above `ellipse()` statement:

```
size(300,200);
```

Click the Run button and you get a rectangular window with the ellipse in the top left of the window, as shown in Figure 16-4. The `size()` function is used to define the size of the applet window in pixels, which in this case is 300 pixels wide and 200 pixels high. If your screen isn't like Figure 16-4, you may have put the statements in the wrong order. The lines of code are read in order, so if the ellipse code is first, the blank window is drawn over the ellipse. And with a rectangular window, you see that the coordinates are measured from the top left.

Figure 16-4:
A resized display window shows more about the coordinate grid.

Coordinates are measured on an invisible a grid with the center point at 0, 0 for 2D (or 0, 0, 0 for 3D), which is referred to as the origin. This is based on the Cartesian coordinate system, which you may have studied in school. Numbers can be positive or negative, depending on which side of the origin they are on. On computer screens, origin is at the top left because pixels are drawn from top left to bottom right, one row at a time (check out Figure 16-5). This means that the statement `size(300,200)` draws a window 300 pixels from left to right on the screen and then 200 pixels from top to bottom.

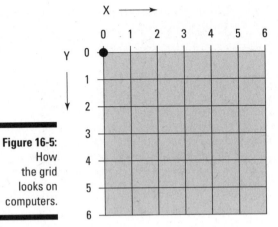

Figure 16-5:
How
the grid
looks on
computers.

Drawing shapes

To gain a better understanding of the possibilities you have in drawing shapes, look at a few basic shapes:

✔ **point()**

A single point is the most basic shape and is useful for making up more complex shapes. Write this code and then click the Run button. Look closely and you see a single black pixel in the center of the display window (see Figure 16-6). That is the point that your code drew.

```
size(300,200);
point(150,100);
```

Point can also be written as:

```
point(x,y);
```

✔ **line()**

A line is made by connecting two points, which is done by defining the start and end points. Write the code to generate a screen like the one in Figure 16-7:

```
size(300,200);
line(50,50,250,150);
```

You can also write a line written as

```
line(x1,y1,x2,y2);
```

Figure 16-6:
If you look closely, you can see the point.

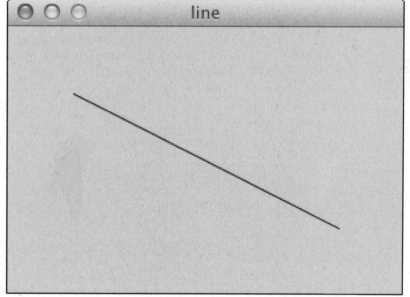

Figure 16-7:
A line between two points.

✔ **rect()**

You can draw a rectangle a number of different ways. In this first exam-ple, a rectangle is drawn by identifying the starting point and then the width and height of the rectangle. Write the following code to draw a rectangle in the center of your display window:

```
size(300,200);
rect(150,100,50,50);
```

In this case, you have a rectangle that starts in at point 150,100 in the center of the display window. That is the top-left corner of the rectangle, and from there it has a width of 50, which extends the rectangle to the right of the window, and a height of 50, which extends to the bottom of the window. This function is particularly useful if you want the size of the rectangle to remain constant but change the position of the rect-angle. You could also write this as

```
rect(x,y,width,height);
```

When drawing rectangles, you can choose among different modes (see Figure 16-8). If the mode is set to center, the rectangle is drawn centered around a point instead of being drawn from that point. Write the follow-ing code and you see that the same values display a different position when rectMode is changed to CENTER.

```
rectMode(CENTER);
size(300,200);
rect(150,100,50,50);
```

You can see that the rectangle is now centered in the display window. The shape extends equally from the center point both left to right and top to bottom. You can also write this as

```
rect(x,y,width,height);
```

You can also draw a rectangle by declaring two diagonally opposite cor-ners. Write the following code, this time with rectMode set to CORNERS.

```
rectMode(CORNERS);
size(300,200);
rect(150,100,50,50);
```

You see a rectangle that is quite different from the others because it starts at the same point in the center, 150,100, but ends at point 50,50, effectively doubling back on itself. You can also write this as

```
rect(x1,y1,x2,y2);
```

✔ **ellipse()**

The first item covered in this chapter was ellipse, which can be used to simply draw an ellipse. Write out the following code to draw an ellipse in the center of the display window.

```
ellipse(150,100,50,50);
```

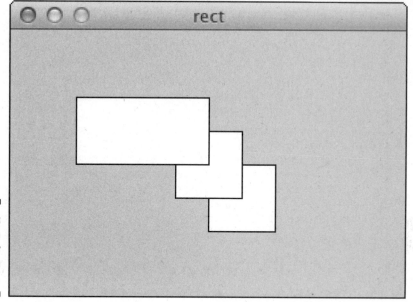

Figure 16-8:
A selection
of differently
drawn
rectangles.

It is clear that the default mode for `ellipse` is CENTER, unlike `rect`, which is CORNER. This can also be written as:

```
ellipse(x,y,width,height);
```

As with `rectMode()` it's possible to set different modes (see Figure 16-9) for drawing ellipses using `ellipseMode()`. Write out the following code to draw an ellipse from its corner instead of its center.

```
ellipseMode(CORNER);
size(300,200);
ellipse(150,100,50,50);
```

This draws an ellipse from starting from its top-left corner with a width of 50 and a height of 50. This can also be written as:

```
ellipse(x,y,width,height);
```

It is also possible to draw an ellipse by specifying multiple corners. Write out the following code to change the `ellipseMode` to CORNERS.

```
ellipseMode(CORNERS);
size(300,200);
ellipse(150,100,50,50);
```

Similarly to `rectMode(CORNERS)` you see that the ellipse doubled back on itself. The first corner is the center point of the sketch and the second is at point 50,50.

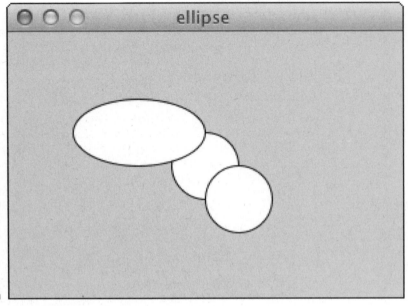

Figure 16-9:
A selection
of differ-
ently drawn
ellipses.

Changing color and opacity

Now that you have an understanding of shapes, it's time to affect their appearance. The simplest way to do this is with color and opacity. In fact, with this it is possible to see through each of the shapes and mix colors by overlapping shapes.

Here are the details:

✔ **background(0)**

This function changes the background of your sketch. You can choose grayscale values, or color.

• Grayscale

Open a new sketch, and simply type the following code to change the default gray window to black.

```
background(0);
```

Change 0 to 255 to change the color to white.

```
background(255);
```

Any value between 0 (black) and 255 (white) is a grayscale value. The reason that this range is 0 to 255 is that there are 8 bits of data in a byte (see Chapter 14), meaning that you need one byte to store a grayscale color value.

- Color

  To liven things up a bit you can add color to your sketch background. Instead of 8-bit grayscale you can use 24-bit color, which is 8-bit red, 8-bit green, and 8-bit blue. The color of the background is defined with three values instead of one.

  ```
  background(200,100,0);
  ```

  This gives you an orange background. The orange background is composed of a red value of 200, a green value of 100, and a blue value of 0. There are several color modes, but in this case this line of code can be interpreted as:

  ```
  background(red,green,blue);
  ```

✔ **fill()**

Want to change the color of the shapes you draw? Use `fill` to both set color and control the shape's opacity:

- Color

  `fill` sets the color for any shape that is drawn after it. By calling fill multiple times it is possible to change the color of several different shapes. Write out the following code to draw three ellipses with different colors, as in Figure 16-10.

  ```
  background(255);
  noStroke();

  // Bright red
  fill(255,0,0);
  ellipse(50,35,40,40);

  // Bright green
  fill(0,255,0);
  ellipse(38,55,40,40);

  // Bright blue
  fill(0,0,255);
  ellipse(62,55,40,40);
  ```

  The background is set to white (255), and the function `noStroke` removes border lines from the shapes (you can comment it out to see the effect). The first circle to be drawn is red. You can see this in the applet because the other two circles overlap it. The red value is the highest possible (255), as is the second for green and the third for blue. If another shape was drawn at the end of the code it would be the same strong blue as that is the last `fill` value.

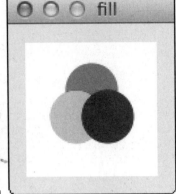

- Opacity

  It's also possible to affect the opacity of the colors, creating semi-
  transparent shapes. By adding a fourth value to the `fill` function
  you can set the opacity from 0 (fully transparent) to 255 (solid
  color). Update the previous code with the following values to give
  the circles transparency.

```
background(255);
noStroke();

// Bright red
fill(255,0,0,100);
ellipse(50,35,40,40);

// Bright green
fill(0,255,0,100);
ellipse(38,55,40,40);

// Bright blue
fill(0,0,255,100);
ellipse(62,55,40,40);
```

Playing with interaction

All of this is fun, but it's very static. In this example you learn how to quickly
inject some life into your sketches using your mouse as an input. To do this
you need to constantly update the sketch by looping through it over and
over again, sending new values in each loop. Write out the following code to
create an interactive sketch.

```
void setup() {
}

void draw() {
ellipse(mouseX,mouseY,20,20);
}
```

This code draws an ellipse centered on your mouse pointer coordinates, so when you move your mouse you leave a trail of ellipses behind, as shown in Figure 16-11. The functions mouseX and mouseY are highlighted blue in the text editor and take the coordinates of your mouse pointer within the display window. The values are the number of pixels horizontally and vertically.

With luck, this code looks familiar to you. Instead of Arduino's void setup and void loop, Processing uses void setup and void draw. These work in almost exactly the same way: setup runs once at the start of the sketch; loop and draw run forever or until they are told to stop.

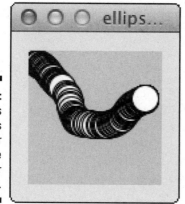

Figure 16-11:
Drawing lots
of ellipses
wherever
your mouse
pointer
goes.

Change the sketch slightly, and you can cover up all those previous ellipses to only show the most recent (Figure 16-12).

```
void setup() {
}

void draw() {
background(0);
ellipse(mouseX,mouseY,20,20);

}
```

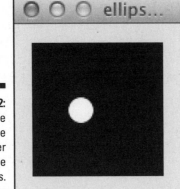

Figure 16-12:
Just one
ellipse
wherever
your mouse
pointer is.

There is much more to Processing that I can't cover in this book, but these few points should be enough to gain a basic comprehension of how code relates to visuals onscreen. You can find a wealth of examples, both on the Processing site and included in the Processing software. The best approach is always to run these examples and then tweak the values to see what happens. By experimenting, you learn what's going on much more quickly, and with no electronics, you are at much less risk of breaking things.

Chapter 17

Processing the Physical World

- -

- -

*I*n the previous chapter, you learn the basics of Processing and its similarities to and differences from Arduino. This chapter is all about combining both of these tools to integrate the virtual and physical worlds. These few exercises teach you the basics about sending and receiving data in both Processing and Arduino. You can build on this knowledge to create your own projects, maybe to generate some awesome onscreen visuals from your sensors or to turn on a light every time someone mentions you on Twitter.

Making a Virtual Button

In this example, you learn how to make an onscreen button in Processing that affects a physical LED on your Arduino. This is a great sketch to get started with interactions between computers and the real world, and between an Arduino and Processing.

You need:

   ✔ An Arduino Uno

   ✔ An LED

The setup is simple for this introduction to Arduino and Processing, requiring only a single LED.

As shown in Figures 17-1 and 17-2, insert the long leg of the LED into pin 13 and the short leg into GND. If you don't have an LED, you can simply monitor the onboard LED marked L.

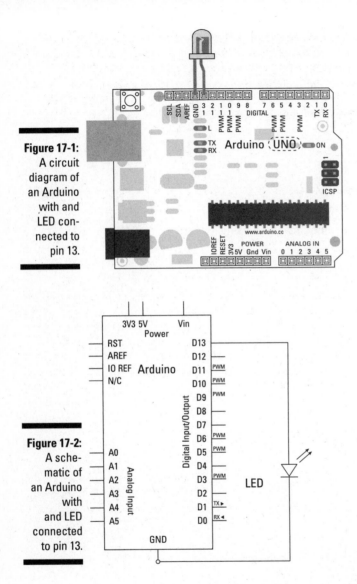

Figure 17-1: A circuit diagram of an Arduino with and LED connected to pin 13.

Figure 17-2: A schematic of an Arduino with and LED connected to pin 13.

Setting up the Arduino code

After your circuit is assembled, you need the appropriate software to use it. From the Arduino menu, choose File➪Examples➪04.Communication➪ PhysicalPixel to find the sketch.

This sketch contains both Arduino code and the relevant Processing code for the sketch to work (it also has a variation in Max 5). The code beneath the Arduino code is commented out to avoid interfering with the Arduino code.

In older versions of Arduino, the sketch files ended with .pde, which is the Processing suffix. This caused confusion, so now the Arduino suffix is .ino. Different suffixes make it possible to have the Arduino sketch and the Processing sketch in the same place. If you try to open a .pde in Arduino, the application assumes that it is an old Arduino sketch and asks whether you want to change the suffix to .ino.

```
/*
  Physical Pixel

An example of using the Arduino board to receive data from the
computer.  In this case, the Arduino boards turns on an LED when
it receives the character 'H', and turns off the LED when it
receives the character 'L'.

The data can be sent from the Arduino serial monitor, or another
program like Processing (see code below), Flash (via a serial-net
proxy), PD, or Max/MSP.

The circuit:
* LED connected from digital pin 13 to ground

created 2006
by David A. Mellis
modified 30 Aug 2011
by Tom Igoe and Scott Fitzgerald

This example code is in the public domain.

http://www.arduino.cc/en/Tutorial/PhysicalPixel
*/

const int ledPin = 13; // the pin that the LED is attached to
int incomingByte;      // a variable to read incoming serial data into

void setup() {
  // initialize serial communication:
  Serial.begin(9600);
  // initialize the LED pin as an output:
  pinMode(ledPin, OUTPUT);
}

void loop() {
  // see if there's incoming serial data:
  if (Serial.available() > 0) {
    // read the oldest byte in the serial buffer:
    incomingByte = Serial.read();
    // if it's a capital H (ASCII 72), turn on the LED:
    if (incomingByte == 'H') {
      digitalWrite(ledPin, HIGH);
    }
    // if it's an L (ASCII 76) turn off the LED:
```

```
    if (incomingByte == 'L') {
      digitalWrite(ledPin, LOW);
    }
  }
}
```

Now go through the steps to upload your sketch.

With the Arduino set up to receive a message from Processing, you need to set up the Processing sketch to send a signal message over the same serial port to your Arduino.

Setting up the Processing code

This code is available within multiline comment markers (/* */) at the bottom of the Arduino PhysicalPixel sketch. Copy the code within the comment markers, paste it into a new Processing sketch, and save it with an appropriate name, such as PhysicalPixel.

```
// mouseover serial

// Demonstrates how to send data to the Arduino I/O board, in order to
// turn ON a light if the mouse is over a square and turn it off
// if the mouse is not.

// created 2003-4
// based on examples by Casey Reas and Hernando Barragan
// modified 30 Aug 2011
// by Tom Igoe
// This example code is in the public domain.


import processing.serial.*;

float boxX;
float boxY;
int boxSize = 20;
boolean mouseOverBox = false;

Serial port;

void setup() {
size(200, 200);
boxX = width/2.0;
boxY = height/2.0;
rectMode(RADIUS);

// List all the available serial ports in the output pane.
// You will need to choose the port that the Arduino board is
```

```
// connected to from this list. The first port in the list is
// port #0 and the third port in the list is port #2.
println(Serial.list());

// Open the port that the Arduino board is connected to (in this case #0)
// Make sure to open the port at the same speed Arduino is using (9600bps)
port = new Serial(this, Serial.list()[0], 9600);

}


void draw()
{
background(0);

// Test if the cursor is over the box
if (mouseX > boxX-boxSize && mouseX < boxX+boxSize &&
mouseY > boxY-boxSize && mouseY < boxY+boxSize) {
mouseOverBox = true;
// draw a line around the box and change its color:
stroke(255);
fill(153);
// send an 'H' to indicate mouse is over square:
port.write('H');
}
else {
// return the box to it's inactive state:
stroke(153);
fill(153);
// send an 'L' to turn the LED off:
port.write('L');
mouseOverBox = false;
}

// Draw the box
rect(boxX, boxY, boxSize, boxSize);
}
```

Click the Run button to execute the Processing sketch, and an applet
appears. The applet shows a black background with a gray square in the
middle, representing your virtual button (shown in Figure 17-3). If you move
your mouse over the gray square (or pixel), you can see that its edges turn
white. If you then look at your Arduino, you see that whenever your mouse
hovers over the gray square, the LED on your board illuminates, giving you a
physical representation of your pixel.

If your LED doesn't light, double-check your wiring:

✔ Make sure that you're using the correct pin number.

✔ Make sure that the LED legs are the correct way around.

✔ Check that your Arduino code uploaded correctly and that your Processing code has no errors. Note that you cannot upload while the Processing sketch is communicating with your Arduino, so you need to stop the sketch before uploading.

Figure 17-3:
Your Processing applet displaying the virtual pixel.

Understanding the Processing PhysicalPixel sketch

Wherever possible, dividing projects into their elements is a good idea. You may have many inputs and outputs, but if you deal with them one at a time, they are easier to understand and easier to troubleshoot. Because the Processing side is the input, you're wise to start with that.

The structure of a Processing sketch is similar to Arduino. You include libraries and declare variables at the start of the sketch and set fixed values or initializations in setup. The draw function then repeats its process until told otherwise.

Processing uses libraries to add functionality in the same way as Arduino does. In this case, a serial communication library is needed to talk to the Arduino. In Arduino, this library is included by using #include <libraryName.h>, but in Processing, you use the import keyword, followed by the name and the syntax * to load all the related parts of that library.

```
import processing.serial.*;
```

A float is a floating-point number, one with a decimal place, such as 0.5, 10.9, and so on. In this case, two floating-point numbers are declared, boxX and boxY. These are the coordinates for the location of the box.

```
float boxX;
float boxY;
```

Next, boxSize defines the size of the box as an integer, or whole number. Because it is square, only one value is needed.

```
int boxSize = 20;
```

A Boolean (which can be only true or false) is used to communicate that the mouse is over the box. This is set to start as false.

```
boolean mouseOverBox = false;
```

The last thing to do is create a new serial port object. Many serial connections could be in use by your computer, so it's important that each one be named so that it can be used as needed. In this case, you are using only one port. The word *serial* is specific to the serial library to indicate that you want to create a new serial object (connection), and the word *port* is the name of the object (connection) used to refer to the port from this point on. Think of it as giving your cat a collar. If too many cats are in a room, they all look fairly similar and follow the same general rules, but they are still all individual. If you put a colored collar on each cat with its name printed on it, you can easily identify which one is which.

```
Serial port;
```

In setup, the first item to define is the size of the display window. This is set to 200 pixels square.

```
void setup() {
  size(200,200);
```

The variables for boxX and boxY are set to be proportional to the width and height of the display window. They are always equal to half the width and height, respectively. Next, rectMode is set to RADIUS, which is similar to CENTER, but instead of specifying the overall width and height of the rectangle, RADIUS specifies half the height and width. (CENTER could be interpreted as diameter in that respect.) Because the coordinates of the box are centered and are aligned to the center point of the display window, the box is also perfectly centered.

```
boxX = width/2.0;
boxY = height/2.0;
rectMode(RADIUS);
```

Your computer may have a lot of serial connections, so it's best to print a list of them to locate your Arduino.

```
println(Serial.list());
```

The most recent port usually appears at the top of this list in position 0, so if you've just plugged in your Arduino, the first item is likely the one you want. If you are not using the Serial.list function, you could replace Serial.list()[0] with another number in the list, which will be printed in the console. You can also replace Serial.list()[0] with the exact name of the port, such as /dev/tty.usbmodem26221 or COM5. Specifying the exact name is also useful if you have multiple Arduinos connected to the same computer. The number 9600 refers to the baud rate, the rate at which you are communicating with the Arduino.

If the baud rate number is not the same on both ends (the sending and receiving end), the data will not be received.

```
  port = new Serial(this, Serial.list()[0], 9600);
}
```

In draw, the first task is to draw a black background.

```
void draw()
{
  background(0);
```

Processing uses the same (or similar) conditionals as Arduino. This if statement tests the mouse value to see whether it is over the box area. If mouseX is greater than the box coordinate (center), minus the size of the box (half the box width), and less than the box coordinate (center), plus the size of the box (half the box width), the horizontal position is over the box. This statement is used again with the vertical position, using AND statements (&&) to add to the conditions of the if statement. Only if all these are true can the Boolean mouseOverBox be declared true.

```
  // Test if the cursor is over the box
  if (mouseX > boxX-boxSize && mouseX < boxX+boxSize &&
    mouseY > boxY-boxSize && mouseY < boxY+boxSize) {
    mouseOverBox = true;
```

To indicate that mouseOverBox is true, the code draws a white line around the box. Rather than requiring that another box be drawn, the white line appears simply by changing the stroke or outline value (*stroke* is a term common in most graphics software). The stroke is set to 255, which outlines the box in white.

```
  // draw a line around the box and change its color:
  stroke(255);
```

Fill is set to 153, a mid-gray, which colors the next object that is drawn.

```
  fill(153);
```

Then the all important communication is sent. The statement port. write is similar to Serial.print but is used for writing to a serial port in Processing. The character sent is H for high.

```
  // send an 'H' to indicate mouse is over square:
  port.write('H');
}
```

The else statement tells Processing what to do if the mouse is not over the box.

```
  else {
```

The stroke value is set to the same mid-gray as the box. The box fill color remains the same whether active or inactive.

```
// return the box to its inactive state:
stroke(153);
fill(153);
```

The character L is sent to the serial port to signify that the LED should be set low.

```
// send an 'L' to turn the LED off:
port.write('L');
```

The Boolean `mouseOverBox` is set to false.

```
    mouseOverBox = false;
  }
```

Finally, the box (technically a rectangle) itself is drawn. Its coordinates are always centered, and its size remains the same; the only difference is that the color applied by the `if` statement. If the mouse is over the box, the stroke value is changed to white (active), and if not, the stroke value is set to the same gray as the box and appears to not be there (inactive).

```
  // Draw the box
  rect(boxX, boxY, boxSize, boxSize);
}
```

Understanding the Arduino Physical Pixel sketch

In the preceding section, you find out how the Processing side works, providing a signal. The signal is sent over the serial connection to your Arduino, so in this section I explain what the Arduino code does with it. The Arduino code for this example is relatively simple compared to other examples in this book and is great for understanding how a serial connection is made. I always recommend starting with this sketch for any Processing-to-Arduino communication. It's great as a foundation to make sure that your hardware and software are working, and you can then build on it or adapt it as needed.

First, the constant and variable values are declared. The LED pin — pin 13 — is the LED output and does not change, so it is marked as a constant. The `incomingByte` value does change and is declared as an integer. Note that it is declared as an integer (int), not a character (char). I explain why a bit later.

```
const int ledPin = 13; // the pin that the LED is attached to
int incomingByte;      // a variable to read incoming serial data into
```

In setup, the serial communication is initialized and set to a matching baud rate of 9600.

Remember that in Processing and Arduino, if you change the speed of the device or application sending data, you also must change the speed of the device or application receiving. When communicating with a computer, you must choose from a range of values: 300, 600, 1200, 2400, 4800, 9600, 14400, 19200, 28800, 38400, 57600, or 115200.

```
void setup() {
  // initialize serial communication:
  Serial.begin(9600);
```

Pin 13, or ledPin as it is named, is set to be an output.

```
  // initialize the LED pin as an output:
  pinMode(ledPin, OUTPUT);
}
```

The first action in the loop is to determine whether any data is available. Serial.available reads the serial buffer, which stores any data sent to the Arduino before it is read. Nothing happens until data is sent to the buffer.

By checking that the value is greater than 0, you reduce the number of readings considerably. Reading lots of 0 or null values can considerably slow down the operation of your Arduino and any programs or hardware reading from it.

```
void loop() {
  // see if there's incoming serial data:
  if (Serial.available() > 0) {
```

If a value is greater than 0, it is stored in the int variable incomingByte.

```
    // read the oldest byte in the serial buffer:
    incomingByte = Serial.read();
```

Now you need to know if the data received is what your program is expecting. Processing sent H as a character, but that is just a byte of data that can be understood as a number or a character. In this case, you're treating it as an integer. This if statement checks to see whether the integer value is equal to 72, which is equal to the character H in ASCII. The inverted commas indicate that it is a character and not a variable. The statement if (incomingByte == 72) { would return the same result.

```
    // if it's a capital H (ASCII 72), turn on the LED:
    if (incomingByte == 'H') {
```

If the values are equal, pin 13 is set HIGH.

```
      digitalWrite(ledPin, HIGH);
    }
```

If the value is the character L, or the integer value 76, the same pin is set LOW.

```
  // if it's an L (ASCII 76) turn off the LED:
  if (incomingByte == 'L') {
    digitalWrite(ledPin, LOW);
  }
 }
}
```

This is a very basic Processing-to-Arduino interaction, but it works great as the basis for larger projects. In this example, the onscreen interaction is the input and could be swapped out for more useful or elaborate inputs. One such input is face tracking: so that When your face is at the center of the screen, the signal is sent. On the Arduino side of the code, as is true of Processing, a vast array of outputs could be triggered besides lighting an LED (lovely though it is). For instance, you could link optocouplers to a remote and begin playback whenever a high signal is sent, and you could pause playback whenever a low signal is sent. (See the bonus chapter at www.dummies.com/go/arduinofd for more about working with optocouplers.)

Drawing a Graph

In the preceding section of this chapter, you see how to send a signal in one direction. Want to learn how to send signals the other direction, from Arduino to Processing? In this example, you find out how to read the value of a potentiometer being read by your Arduino and and display it visually in a Processing applet.

You need:

- An Arduino Uno
- A breadboard
- A potentiometer
- Jump wires

This basic circuit uses a potentiometer to send an analog value to Processing that can be interpreted and displayed on an onscreen graph. Assemble the circuit connection the center pin of the potentiometer to analog pin 0, following Figures 17-4 and 17-5. The potentiometer is wired with the central pin connected to analog pin 0. Of the other two pins, one is connected to 5V and the other to GND. By reversing these pins it's possible to change the directions that the potentiometer counts in when turned.

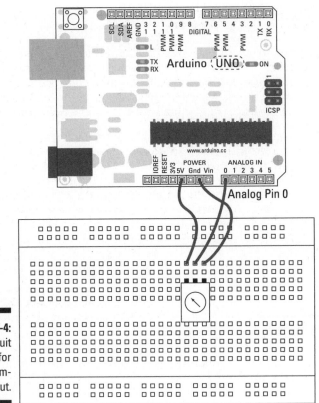

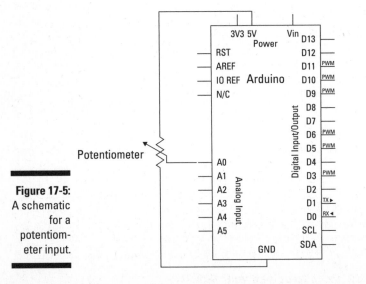

Setting up the Arduino code

After you assemble your circuit, you need the appropriate software to use it. From the Arduino menu, choose File⇨Examples⇨04.Communication⇨Graph to find the sketch. This sketch contains both Arduino code and the relevant Processing code for the sketch to work (and has a variation in Max 5 as well). The Processing code beneath the Arduino code is commented out to avoid interferenceing with the Arduino code.

```
/*
  Graph

 A simple example of communication from the Arduino board to the computer:
 the value of analog input 0 is sent out the serial port.  We call this "serial"
 communication because the connection appears to both the Arduino and the
 computer as a serial port, even though it may actually use
 a USB cable. Bytes are sent one after another (serially) from the Arduino
 to the computer.

 You can use the Arduino serial monitor to view the sent data, or it can
 be read by Processing, PD, Max/MSP, or any other program capable of reading
 data from a serial port.  The Processing code below graphs the data received
 so you can see the value of the analog input changing over time.

 The circuit:
 Any analog input sensor is attached to analog in pin 0.

 created 2006
 by David A. Mellis
 modified 9 Apr 2012
 by Tom Igoe and Scott Fitzgerald

 This example code is in the public domain.

 http://www.arduino.cc/en/Tutorial/Graph
 */

void setup() {
  // initialize the serial communication:
  Serial.begin(9600);
}

void loop() {
  // send the value of analog input 0:
  Serial.println(analogRead(A0));
  // wait a bit for the analog-to-digital converter
  // to stabilize after the last reading:
  delay(2);
}
```

Now go through the steps to upload your sketch.

With the Arduino now set up to send a message to Processing, you need to set up the Processing sketch to receive that message over the serial port.

Setting up the Processing code

This code is found within multiline comments markers (/* */) at the bottom of the Arduino Graph sketch. Copy the code within the comment markers and then paste it into a new processing sketch, saved with an appropriate name, such as Graph.

```
// Graphing sketch


// This program takes ASCII-encoded strings
// from the serial port at 9600 baud and graphs them. It expects values in the
// range 0 to 1023, followed by a newline, or newline and carriage return

// Created 20 Apr 2005
// Updated 18 Jan 2008
// by Tom Igoe
// This example code is in the public domain.

import processing.serial.*;

Serial myPort;        // The serial port
int xPos = 1;         // horizontal position of the graph

void setup () {
  // set the window size:
  size(400, 300);

  // List all the available serial ports
  println(Serial.list());
  // I know that the first port in the serial list on my mac
  // is always my  Arduino, so I open Serial.list()[0].
  // Open whatever port is the one you're using.
  myPort = new Serial(this, Serial.list()[0], 9600);
  // don't generate a serialEvent() unless you get a newline character:
  myPort.bufferUntil('\n');
  // set inital background:
  background(0);
}
void draw () {
  // everything happens in the serialEvent()
}
void serialEvent (Serial myPort) {
  // get the ASCII string:
  String inString = myPort.readStringUntil('\n');

  if (inString != null) {
```

```
    // trim off any whitespace:
    inString = trim(inString);
    // convert to an int and map to the screen height:
    float inByte = float(inString);
    inByte = map(inByte, 0, 1023, 0, height);

    // draw the line:
    stroke(127, 34, 255);
    line(xPos, height, xPos, height - inByte);

    // at the edge of the screen, go back to the beginning:
    if (xPos >= width) {
      xPos = 0;
      background(0);
    }
    else {
      // increment the horizontal position:
      xPos++;
    }
  }
}
```

Click the Run button to execute the Processing sketch, and an applet appears. The applet has a black background with a purple graph representing the analog Arduino input, as shown in Figure 17-6. As you turn the potentiometer, the purple graph changes to match it. The graph is updated over time, so as the reading progresses, the graph fills the horizontal space. When it reaches the edge of the display window, the graph resets to the starting point, starting at the left side again.

Figure 17-6:
A purple
graph
showing
your sensor
reading.

If you don't see a graph, double-check your wiring:

✔ Make sure you're using the correct pin number.

✔ Make sure that the potentiometer is wired the correct way around.

✔ Check that your Arduino code uploaded correctly and that your Processing code has no errors. Note that you cannot upload while the Processing sketch is communicating with your Arduino, so stop the sketch before uploading.

Understanding the Arduino Graph sketch

In setup, the code just needs to initialize the serial port. This is given a baud rate of 9600, which must match the baud rate in the Processing sketch.

The analog input pins are set to input by default, so you don't need to set their pinMode.

```
void setup() {
  // initialize the serial communication:
  Serial.begin(9600);
}
```

In the loop, a single line is used to print the value of the sensor to the serial port. The pin is directly named rather than being given a variable (such as analog Pin) because no repeat mentions occur. This pin is A0, or analog input pin 0.

```
void loop() {
  // send the value of analog input 0:
  Serial.println(analogRead(A0));
```

Analog readings are made extremely quickly, usually quicker than they can be converted to a digital format. Sometimes this speed causes errors, so a short delay of 2 milliseconds between readings can really help to stabilize the results. Think of it like a tap that limits the flow of water.

```
  // wait a bit for the analog-to-digital converter
  // to stabilize after the last reading:
  delay(2);
}
```

Understanding the Processing Graph sketch

When data is sent to the serial port, Processing reads that data and interprets it to draw the bar graph. First you import the serial library into the sketch and create a new instance of it. In this case, the new serial port object is called myPort.

```
import processing.serial.*;

Serial myPort;        // The serial port
```

One integer, defined as xPos , keeps track of where the latest bar in the bar graph is drawn (the x position).

```
int xPos = 1;          // horizontal position of the graph
```

In setup, the display window is defined as 400 pixels wide and 300 pixels tall.

```
void setup () {
  // set the window size:
  size(400,300);
```

To find the correct serial port, Serial.list is called and printed to the console with println. The function println is similar to Serial.println in Arduino but is used in Processing for monitoring values. These values print to the console rather than the serial port and are used for debugging rather than communication.

```
// List all the available serial ports
println(Serial.list());
```

Your Arduino is likely to appear at the top of the list, so myPort uses position 0 as the Arduino serial port. If you are not using the Serial.list function, you can replace Serial.list()[0] with another number in the list, which prints in the console. You can also replace Serial.list()[0] with the exact name of the port, such as /dev/tty.usbmodem26221 or COM5. Specifying the name is also useful if you have multiple Arduinos connected to the same computer. The number 9600 refers to the baud rate, the rate at which you are communicating with the Arduino. If this is not the same on both ends, the data will not be received.

```
myPort = new Serial(this, Serial.list()[0], 9600);
```

In this example, you have another way to sort out the good data from the bad. The function serialEvent triggers every time data arrives in the serial buffer. This line checks to see whether a character followed by a newline character is sent, such as Serial.println(100) on the Arduino side. Newline, or Return on a keyboard, has an ASCII character, which is referred to as \n. The line could also look for other special characters, such as tab \t.

```
// don't generate a serialEvent() unless you get a newline character:
myPort.bufferUntil('\n');
```

To start, the background is colored black.

```
// set inital background:
  background(0);
}
```

In draw, there is nothing to do because serialEvent is monitoring the serial port and triggering whenever a newline character is present. Which the comment in the code reminds you of!

```
void draw () {
  // everything happens in the serialEvent()
}
```

The function `serialEvent` is part of the serial library and triggers whenever data arrives in the serial buffer. Because the `bufferUntil('\n')` condition has been used, `serialEvent` triggers when a newline character is buffered.

```
void serialEvent (Serial myPort) {
```

A temporary string is declared to store the data read from `myPort`. This is also read until a newline character appears. Because the Arduino is sending an integer followed by a newline, followed by an integer, and so on, each value is read individually.

```
// get the ASCII string:
String inString = myPort.readStringUntil('\n');
```

An `if` statement checks that the string contains data and is not equal to 0 or null.

```
if (inString != null) {
```

To make sure that no anomalies exist, the `trim` function is used to remove spaces, tabs, and carriage returns from the string. The `trim` function effectively removes all formatting from the characters so that they can be read clearly.

```
// trim off any whitespace:
inString = trim(inString);
```

Now the clean string of numbers is converted into a float, called `inByte`. The float is declared on the left side of the equation and is made equal to the float conversion of `inString`. You can also use parentheses around the variable to convert it to other types of data, such as `int()` or `byte()`.

```
// convert to an int and map to the screen height:
float inByte = float(inString);
```

The newly declared `inByte` is then mapped or scaled to a more useful range. The range of the sensor is 0 to 1023, so `inByte` is scaled to a range of 0 to the height of the display window, keeping the display proportional without exceeding the height of the window.

```
inByte = map(inByte, 0, 1023, 0, height);
```

This bar graph is extremely detailed, with one bar represented by a column of pixels. These awesome visuals are created by using the `line` function. To change the color of the line to purple, the `stroke` value is set to its RGB components. The line is defined by its start and end point. Because it is displaying a graph, you want lots of vertical lines with varying heights. As you can see, the x or horizontal coordinates are the same variable. The height coordinate for one end of the line is equal to the height of the window, which fixes the height coordinate to the bottom edge of the window. The other height value is equal to the height minus the `inByte` value, meaning that the greater the value, the nearer the top of the line is to the top of the window.

```
// draw the line:
stroke(127, 34, 255);
line(xPos, height, xPos, height - inByte);
```

Note that if you're having trouble choosing a color, you can choose Tools⇨ Color Selector on the Processing menu. The Color Selector shows a color wheel that gives the red, green, and blue values of any color you select, as well as the hexadecimal value, as you can see in Figure 17-7.

Figure 17-7: The built-in color wheel can be really useful.

This next bit of code handles the movement of the `xPos` or horizontal position of the graph over time. If `xPos` is greater than or equal to the width, the line reaches beyond the edge of the display window. If this happened, the variable is returned to 0, and a new background is drawn to cover the old graph.

```
// at the edge of the screen, go back to the beginning:
if (xPos >= width) {
  xPos = 0;
  background(0);
}
```

If `xPos` is not equal to the width, it is increased by one pixel for the next reading.

```
else {
  // increment the horizontal position:
  xPos++;
  }
 }
}
```

This is a great exercise for getting familiar with communication between Arduino to Processing. The Arduino could easily be sending data from an analog sensor detecting sound, movement, or light. The Processing side things are a little more complicated, but largely because you are generating a complicated visual. The graph could just as easily be an ellipse that gets bigger or smaller as the values change. Why not try it?

Sending Multiple Signals

The only thing better than sending signals to Processing is sending multiple signals, right? Sending multiple signals is often a stumbling block, though, because although sending values from multiple sensors is easy, handling them in the correct order on the other end can often be difficult. In this example, you learn how to send data from three separate sensors attached to your Arduino to a Processing sketch.

You need:

- An Arduino Uno
- A breadboard
- Two 10k ohm potentiometers
- A pushbutton
- A 10k ohm resistor
- Jump wires

The circuit is a combination of three separate inputs. Although they all use the same power and ground, you can think of the inputs individually. Two potentiometers provide two values. These are wired in the same way as you would wire a light or temperature sensor, with one side wired to 5V and the other wired to the analog input pin that is reading it as well as to GND via a resistor. These could actually be replaced with any analog inputs with the appropriate resistors. The pushbutton provides a digital input as well. One side of the pushbutton is wired to 5V and the other is wired to the digital pin reading it as well GND via a resistor. Complete the circuit as shown in Figures 17-8 and 17-9.

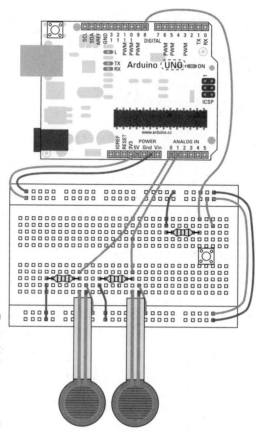

Figure 17-8:
A circuit
diagram for
two analog
inputs and
one digital.

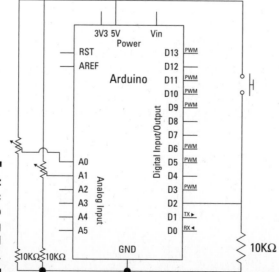

Figure 17-9:
A schematic
for two
analog
inputs and
one digital.

Setting up the Arduino code

After you assemble your circuit, you need the appropriate software to use it. From the Arduino menu, choose File⇨Examples⇨04.Communication⇨ SerialCallResponse. This sketch contains both Arduino code and the relevant Processing code for the sketch to work (along with a variation in Max 5 as well). The Processing code beneath the Arduino code is commented out to avoid interference with the Arduino sketch.

```
/*
  Serial Call and Response
  Language: Wiring/Arduino

  This program sends an ASCII A (byte of value 65) on startup
  and repeats that until it gets some data in.
  Then it waits for a byte in the serial port, and
  sends three sensor values whenever it gets a byte in.

  Thanks to Greg Shakar and Scott Fitzgerald for the improvements

   The circuit:
  * potentiometers attached to analog inputs 0 and 1
  * pushbutton attached to digital I/O 2

  Created 26 Sept. 2005
  by Tom Igoe
  modified 24 April 2012
  by Tom Igoe and Scott Fitzgerald

  This example code is in the public domain.
  http://www.arduino.cc/en/Tutorial/SerialCallResponse

  */

int firstSensor = 0;     // first analog sensor
int secondSensor = 0;    // second analog sensor
int thirdSensor = 0;     // digital sensor
int inByte = 0;          // incoming serial byte

void setup()
{
  // start serial port at 9600 bps:
  Serial.begin(9600);
  while (!Serial) {
    ; // wait for serial port to connect. Needed for Leonardo only
  }

  pinMode(2, INPUT);    // digital sensor is on digital pin 2
  establishContact();   // send a byte to establish contact until receiver
                        // responds
}

void loop()
```

```
{
  // if we get a valid byte, read analog ins:
  if (Serial.available() > 0) {
    // get incoming byte:
    inByte = Serial.read();
    // read first analog input, divide by 4 to make the range 0-255:
    firstSensor = analogRead(A0)/4;
    // delay 10ms to let the ADC recover:
    delay(10);
    // read second analog input, divide by 4 to make the range 0-255:
    secondSensor = analogRead(1)/4;
    // read  switch, map it to 0 or 255L
    thirdSensor = map(digitalRead(2), 0, 1, 0, 255);
    // send sensor values:
    Serial.write(firstSensor);
    Serial.write(secondSensor);
    Serial.write(thirdSensor);
  }
}

void establishContact() {
  while (Serial.available() <= 0) {
    Serial.print('A');   // send a capital A
    delay(300);
  }
}
```

Upload this code to your Arduino. Now that the Arduino is set up to send data to Processing, you need to set up the Processing sketch to receive and interpret the data over the serial port.

Setting up the Processing code

You find the Processing code within multiline comment markers (/* */) at the bottom of the Arduino SerialCallResponse sketch. Copy the code within the comment markers into a new Processing sketch and save with an appropriate name, such as SerialCallResponse.

```
// This example code is in the public domain.

import processing.serial.*;

int bgcolor;              // Background color
int fgcolor;              // Fill color
Serial myPort;                         // The serial port
int[] serialInArray = new int[3];      // Where we'll put what we receive
int serialCount = 0;                   // A count of how many bytes we receive
int xpos, ypos;                // Starting position of the ball
boolean firstContact = false;          // Whether we've heard from the
                                       // microcontroller

void setup() {
```

```
  size(256, 256);   // Stage size
  noStroke();        // No border on the next thing drawn

  // Set the starting position of the ball (middle of the stage)
  xpos = width/2;
  ypos = height/2;

  // Print a list of the serial ports, for debugging purposes:
  println(Serial.list());

  // I know that the first port in the serial list on my mac
  // is always my  FTDI adaptor, so I open Serial.list()[0].
  // On Windows machines, this generally opens COM1.
  // Open whatever port is the one you're using.
  String portName = Serial.list()[0];
  myPort = new Serial(this, portName, 9600);
}

void draw() {
  background(bgcolor);
  fill(fgcolor);
  // Draw the shape
  ellipse(xpos, ypos, 20, 20);
}

void serialEvent(Serial myPort) {
  // read a byte from the serial port:
  int inByte = myPort.read();
  // if this is the first byte received, and it's an A,
  // clear the serial buffer and note that you've
  // had first contact from the microcontroller.
  // Otherwise, add the incoming byte to the array:
  if (firstContact == false) {
    if (inByte == 'A') {
      myPort.clear();          // clear the serial port buffer
      firstContact = true;     // you've had first contact from the microcontroller
      myPort.write('A');       // ask for more
    }
  }
  else {
    // Add the latest byte from the serial port to array:
    serialInArray[serialCount] = inByte;
    serialCount++;

    // If we have 3 bytes:
    if (serialCount > 2 ) {
      xpos = serialInArray[0];
      ypos = serialInArray[1];
      fgcolor = serialInArray[2];

      // print the values (for debugging purposes only):
      println(xpos + "\t" + ypos + "\t" + fgcolor);

      // Send a capital A to request new sensor readings:
```

```
        myPort.write('A');
        // Reset serialCount:
        serialCount = 0;
      }
    }
  }
```

Click the Run button to execute the Processing sketch, and an applet appears. The applet has a black background, and whenever you press the pushbutton, a white dot appears. Move the potentiometers to move the dot horizontally and vertically. When you release the pushbutton, the dot disappears.

If you don't see the correct behavior, double-check your wiring:

✔ Make sure that you're using the correct pin numbers.

✔ Make sure that the potentiometers are wired the correct way around.

✔ Check that your Arduino code uploaded correctly and that your Processing code has no errors. Note that you cannot upload while the Processing sketch is communicating with your Arduino, so stop the sketch before uploading.

Understanding the Arduino SerialCallResponse sketch

At the start of the sketch, four variables are declared. Three of them are for the sensor values and one stores an incoming byte from the Processing sketch.

```
int firstSensor = 0;      // first analog sensor
int secondSensor = 0;     // second analog sensor
int thirdSensor = 0;      // digital sensor
int inByte = 0;           // incoming serial byte
```

In setup, the serial port is established with a baud rate of 9600. The while statement continually checks for the presence of a serial connection before proceeding. The statement is interpreted as "while there is not a serial connection, do nothing." This line of code is only needed only for the new Leonardo boards.

```
void setup()
{
  // start serial port at 9600 bps:
  Serial.begin(9600);
  while (!Serial) {
    ; // wait for serial port to connect. Needed for Leonardo only
  }
```

Pin 2 is the pushbutton pin and is set as an input using `pinMode`.

```
pinMode(2, INPUT);   // digital sensor is on digital pin 2
```

A special custom function called `establishContact` is called to signal to the Processing sketch that the Arduino is ready.

```
  establishContact();  // send a byte to establish contact until receiver
                responds
}
```

In the `loop`, an `if` statement checks whether any data being sent is greater than 0. If it is, that byte is read into the variable `inByte`.

```
void loop()
{
  // if we get a valid byte, read analog ins:
  if (Serial.available() > 0) {
    // get incoming byte:
    inByte = Serial.read();
```

The `firstSensor` variable stores the value of the potentiometer on analog pin 0 after dividing it by 4. This simple math reduces the range from 0 to 1023 to 0 to 255.

```
    // read first analog input, divide by 4 to make the range 0-255:
    firstSensor = analogRead(A0)/4;
```

A short break of 10 milliseconds occurs to give the analog-to-digital converter plenty of time to process the first value.

```
    // delay 10ms to let the ADC recover:
    delay(10);
```

The second sensor is read and converted in the same way and then the code writes to the `secondSensor` variable.

```
    // read second analog input, divide by 4 to make the range 0-255:
    secondSensor = analogRead(1)/4;
```

The switch is a little different. To scale the values, the `map` function is used. The first value inside the `map` function is the variable to be mapped. In this case, it is not a variable but rather a direct `digitalRead` of pin 2. Saving the `digitalRead` value to a variable first in this case is neither necessary nor beneficial. The range of the switch is 0 to 1, and it is mapped to the same range as the other sensors, 0 to 255. The converted value is stored in `thirdSensor`.

```
    // read  switch, map it to 0 or 255L
    thirdSensor = map(digitalRead(2), 0, 1, 0, 255);
```

Each of the sensor values is then sent one at a time to the serial port using `Serial.write`.

```
    // send sensor values:
    Serial.write(firstSensor);
    Serial.write(secondSensor);
    Serial.write(thirdSensor);
  }
}
```

At the end of the sketch is the custom function `establishContact` that was called in `setup`. This monitors the serial port to see whether a serial connection is available. If not, `establishContact` it sends a capital "A" to the serial port every 300 milliseconds. When a connection is available, the function stops.

```
void establishContact() {
  while (Serial.available() <= 0) {
    Serial.print('A');    // send a capital A
    delay(300);
  }
}
```

Understanding the Processing SerialCallResponse sketch

Now examine what's happening on the Processing side to establish contact, interpret the values, and display the data. The first action to take in the Processing sketch is to import the serial library.

```
import processing.serial.*;
```

Many variables need to be declared for this sketch. The first two are colors for the background and shapes.

```
int bgcolor;            // Background color
int fgcolor;            // Fill color
```

A new instance of serial port is created, called `myPort`.

```
Serial myPort;                          // The serial port
```

An array of integer values is created and declared to be three values long.

```
int[] serialInArray = new int[3];    // Where we'll put what we receive
```

An integer counter is declared to keep track of how many bytes have been read.

```
int serialCount = 0;                    // A count of how many bytes we receive
```

The integer values `xpos` and `ypos` store the coordinates of the dot.

```
int xpos, ypos;                    // Starting position of the ball
```

A Boolean stores a value that indicates whether contact has been made with the Arduino.

```
boolean firstContact = false;        // Whether we've heard from the
                 microcontroller
```

In `setup`, the size of the display window is set. The function `noStroke` ensures that no borders are on shapes drawn from this point on in the sketch.

```
void setup() {
  size(256, 256);   // Stage size
  noStroke();       // No border on the next thing drawn
```

The starting values for the dot are set to be the center of the display window: half the width and half the height, respectively.

```
  // Set the starting position of the ball (middle of the stage)
  xpos = width/2;
  ypos = height/2;
```

To make the serial connection, a serial list is drawn.

```
  // Print a list of the serial ports, for debugging purposes:
  println(Serial.list());
```

Your Arduino usually tops the list, so the temporary string `portName` stores the name of position 0 in the list, and `myPort` uses that connection when the serial port is set. Note that this could actually be written as `Serial(this, Serial.list()[0], 9600);`.

If you are not using the `Serial.list` function, you can replace `Serial.list()[0]` with another number in the list, which is printed in the console. You can also replace `Serial.list()[0]` with the exact name of the port. This is useful if you have multiple Arduinos connected. The number 9600 refers to the baud rate and must be the same on both ends.

```
  String portName = Serial.list()[0];
  myPort = new Serial(this, portName, 9600);
}
```

In `draw`, the background is drawn first. Because the background is undefined, it has a default value of 0, which is black. The fill color is also undefined for now, so the ellipse is black as well.

```
void draw() {
  background(bgcolor);
  fill(fgcolor);
```

The ellipse is drawn, centered on the display window, with a fixed diameter of 20 pixels.

```
// Draw the shape
ellipse(xpos, ypos, 20, 20);
}
```

Most of the action happens in `serialEvent`, which affects the ellipse being constantly drawn by the `draw` loop.

```
void serialEvent(Serial myPort) {
```

If data is sent over the serial port, it triggers a `serialEvent`. The first byte of data is read using `myPort.read` and stored to the temporary variable `inByte`.

```
// read a byte from the serial port:
int inByte = myPort.read();
```

If the Processing sketch is not already in contact with a serial device, it proceeds to the next `if` statement to see whether the byte is the character A. If so, the buffer clears and the Boolean `firstContact` is set to true and sends an A character back. Remember that `establishContact` function on the Arduino? It repeatedly sends the character A until the connection is made. When an A is sent back the other way, it triggers the `if` statement `if (Serial.available() > 0)`, which starts sending the data from the Arduino. This technique is called *handshaking*, a mutual negotiation between two parts of a system to establish a connection.

```
if (firstContact == false) {
  if (inByte == 'A') {
    myPort.clear();          // clear the serial port buffer
    firstContact = true;     // you've had first contact from the microcontroller
    myPort.write('A');       // ask for more
  }
}
```

If `firstContact` is true, the program reads bytes as they arrive and adds them in order to the array `serialInArray`.

```
else {
  // Add the latest byte from the serial port to array:
  serialInArray[serialCount] = inByte;
```

Every time a byte is read, the counter increases by one.

```
serialCount++;
```

When the counter is greater than 2, all three bytes have been read and assigned their tasks.

```
// If we have 3 bytes:
if (serialCount > 2 ) {
```

The potentiometer on analog 0 reflects the horizontal position of the dot; the potentiometer on analog 1 is the vertical position; and the button is the fill color.

```
xpos = serialInArray[0];
ypos = serialInArray[1];
fgcolor = serialInArray[2];
```

These values are also printed in the console for debugging, to check that everything is operating as intended. In Processing, you can combine many values in a print or println statement by using the + symbol. You can also use the symbol \t to put a tab in between each value to space them neatly.

```
// print the values (for debugging purposes only):
println(xpos + "\t" + ypos + "\t" + fgcolor);
```

Another capital A is sent to trigger the if (Serial.available() > 0) conditional and repeat the process.

```
// Send a capital A to request new sensor readings:
myPort.write('A');
```

The serialCount value is reset to 0 for the next set of values.

```
// Reset serialCount:
serialCount = 0;
    }
  }
}
```

This is a great way to get started reading multiple sensors into a computer program. Why not build your own giant keyboard to reenact a scene from the Tom Hanks film "Big"? Or, gather data from a variety of sensors to monitor the weather around your house? The output for this sketch is extremely basic but offers huge potential for amazing and creative ways to map data. A few Web searches for "data visualization" gives you an idea of what's possible.

Part VI
The Part of Tens

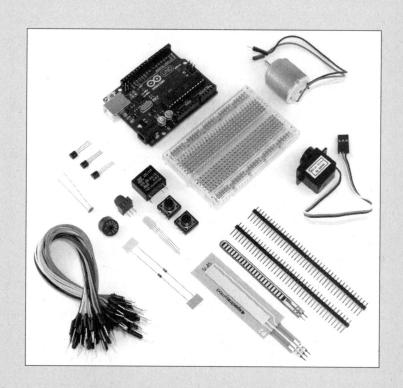

In this part . . .

This wouldn't be a *For Dummies* book without a *Part of Tens*. Here, I list lots of handy resources for aspiring Arduin-ists such as yourselves. These chapters list a selection of websites that are great for inspiring yourself as well as keeping up with all the new Arduino kit out there. I also introduce you to a few hobby shops that stock all sorts of Arduino-compatible components, and to a few larger electronics and hardware shops that are great to know about when you're looking for that special something.

Chapter 18

Ten Places to Learn More about Arduino

If this is your first step into the world of Arduino, you will be relieved to know that you have an abundance of resources available to you on the Internet. You can find new, Arduino-compatible hardware, projects, tutorials, and even inspiration. In this chapter, I offer ten popular websites to help you on your journey of discovery.

Arduino Blog

http://arduino.cc/blog/

The Arduino blog is a great source of all Arduino-related news. You can find news on the latest official hardware and software as well as on other interesting projects. Also found here are talks that the Arduino team wants to share with the community.

Hack a Day

http://hackaday.com

Hack a Day is an excellent resource for all sorts of technological magic. In addition to presenting a lot of Arduino-related projects and posts, the site offers equal amounts of just about any other category of technology that you can think of. This site contains an excellent collection of posts and information to fuel the imagination.

SparkFun

http://www.sparkfun.com/news

SparkFun manufactures and sells all sorts of products to make your projects possible, and many of these involve Arduino. SparkFun has an excellent and well-maintained newsfeed that always has some sort of interesting new product or kit to show off. The company also provides excellent videos that explain its kits and document any events that the SparkFun team hosts or attends.

MAKE

http://blog.makezine.com

MAKE is hobbyist magazine that celebrates all kinds of technology. Its blog covers all kinds of interesting do-it-yourself (DIY) technology and projects for inspiration. Arduino is so important to this community that it has its own subsection in the blog.

Adafruit

http://www.adafruit.com/blog/

Adafruit is an online shop, repository, and forum for all kinds of kits to help you make your projects work. Its blog announces the ever growing selection of available Adafruit products as well as other interesting tech news.

Bildr

http://bildr.org

Bildr is an excellent resource that provides in-depth, community-published tutorials. As well as providing clear tutorials, Bildr also has excellent illustrations, making the connections easy to follow. Many of the tutorials are Arduino based and provide all the code and information on the components that you will need as well as where to buy the parts.

Instructables

http://www.instructables.com/

Instructables is a web-based documentation platform that allows people to share their projects and step-by-step instructions on how to make them. Instructables isn't just about Arduino or even technology, so you can find a whole world of interesting material there.

YouTube

www.youtube.com

YouTube is a great place to kill time, but rather than watching cats do funny things, why not enter **Arduino** in the site's search box to discover new projects that people are sharing. YouTube videos won't always be the most reliable sources for well-documented projects, but they provide you with a broad look at Arduino projects in action. Watching videos is especially useful for seeing the proper result of projects.

Hackerspaces

http://hackerspaces.org

Hackerspaces are physical spaces where artists, designers, makers, hackers, coders, engineers, or anyone else can meet to learn, socialize, and collaborate on projects. Hackerspaces are found in a loose network all over the world, and a good place to start to find one near you is the map at http://hackerspaces.org/wiki/List_of_Hacker_Spaces.

Forum

http://arduino.cc/forum/

The Arduino Forum is a great place to get answers to specific Arduino questions. You often find that other people are working through the same problems that you are, so with some thorough searching, you're likely to find the answer to almost any problem.

Friends, Colleagues, and Workshops

Starting out in the world of Arduino can be difficult on your own. You can find many sources on the Internet, but one of the best ways to learn is with friends and colleagues, because learning together teaches you much more than learning on your own can.

Even better is to go to workshops and meet other people. You may find that they have exactly the same interests, allowing you to pool what you know; or they may have completely different interests, providing an opportunity to show you something that you never knew about. Arduino workshops are going on all over the world, so with some careful searching in the Arduino Forum, Hackerspace forums, and Google, you should be able to find a workshop near you.

Chapter 19

Ten Great Shops to Know

In This Chapter

▶ Finding Arduino stores in the United Kingdom

▶ Discovering suppliers that ship all over the world

*W*hen it comes to buying parts for your project, you'll find a huge and growing number of shops that cater for your needs. These stores also deal in other hobby electronics as well as Arduino, but they stock a variety of boards and components that you can use in your Arduino project. This chapter provides just a small sample of the stores out there, so shop around.

Shops in the United Kingdom

If you live in the United Kingdom, you're spoilt for choice! It's like the wild west of hobby electronics, and a vast number of smaller companies distribute Arduino-related kits. The ones mentioned here represent just a few of the stores out there; many more have varieties of Arduino-related stock, so don't limit yourself to these. Most of these stores also distribute to all corners of the world with the major courier services.

SK Pang

http://www.skpang.co.uk

SK Pang is an electronic component supplier based in Harlow, Essex. The company supplies a variety of Arduino-related kits and the staff members designs their own products. Such products include the Arduino CAN-Bus, which allows your Arduino to communicate with other microcontrollers in vehicles, and the Arduino DMX Shield, which allows you to communicate with DMX-compatible stage lighting and effects.

Technobots

http://www.technobotsonline.com

Technobots was established 2001 and is a supplier of electronic and mechanical components based in Totton, Hampshire. These people supply a huge variety of electrical, electronic, and mechanical parts, with more than 8,000 product lines. I haven't found this company's variety of pre-crimped wires and headers — in all shapes and sizes — anywhere else in the United Kingdom. Pre-crimped wires and headers are very useful for connecting boards neatly and effectively.

Proto-PIC

http://proto-pic.co.uk

Proto-PIC is based in Kirkcaldy in Fife, Scotland. The company is owned and operated by RelChron Ltd, which started with the much more serious job of developing "a software system to assist with the pressure testing process in the subsea-oil manufacturing industry," according to the company's website. Starting in 2006, the company developed in-house hardware and software, and using this base of knowledge, it started Proto-PIC for electronics hobbyists and enthusiasts. One of the best things about Proto-PIC is that the company doesn't ship items in jiffy bags but rather in reuseable plastic boxes, which you can never have enough of.

Oomlout

http://www.oomlout.com

Oomlout describes itself as a "plucky little design house" with offices in Leeds, Yorkshire (design), Point Roberts, Washington (shipping) and Vancouver, British Columbia (manufacturing). The store produces a variety of open source products as well as its own Arduino kits, such as the ARDX kit, which is great for getting started with Arduino.

RoboSavvy

http://robosavvy.com/store

RoboSavvy sells numerous Arduino-compatible products but caters more to the robotics crowd, providing support and distribution for a large number of robotics products imported from around the world. RoboSavvy was established in 2004 and is based in Hampstead, London.

Active Robots

http://www.active-robots.com

Active Robots is a leading supplier and manufacturer of robotics and electronics products based in Radstock, Somerset. As well as selling a range of Arduino-related products, the company has a great selection of more robotics-specific kits, such as relay boards (for driving lots of bigger loads safely) and linear servos.

Shops around the World

Arduino developers can find a great number of local distributors to choose from in almost any country. Here are a few that manufacture and distribute their products worldwide.

Adafruit (U.S.)

http://www.adafruit.com/

MIT engineer Limor "Ladyada" Fried founded Adafruit in 2005. Through its website, the company offers a wealth of resources, including products that company designs and makes itself; other products sourced from all over; tools and equipment to help you make them; and tutorials, forums, and videos covering a wide range of topics. Adafruit is based in New York, New York (it's a wonderful town!). It distributes worldwide and has distributors in many countries.

Arduino Store (Italy)

http://store.arduino.cc/

Arduino Store was official opened in May 2011 to sell Arduino products directly rather than solely through distributors. The store sells all the official Arduino branded products as well as a few select third-party ones. It also sells the TinkerKit that is designed to make Arduino and electronics even simpler for beginners by using plugs to connect inputs and outputs rather than requiring breadboards or soldering.

Seeed Studio (China)

http://www.seeedstudio.com/

Seeed Studio is based in Shenzhen, China, and is self-described as an "open hardware facilitation company." The shop uses local manufacturing to quickly make prototypes and small-scale projects that are distributed worldwide. In addition to manufacturing and selling products, the company offers a community area on its website where people can vote for the projects that they want Seeed Studio bring to fruition (http://www.seeedstudio.com/wish/).

SparkFun (U.S.)

http://www.sparkfun.com/

SparkFun sells all sorts of parts for every variety of electronics projects. As well as selling Arduino-compatible hardware, it designs and makes a lot of its own boards and kits. SparkFun has an excellent site that acts as a shop front, a support desk, and a classroom for Arduino-ists. SparkFun also has very active (and vocal) commenters on each of its product pages, which help to support and continually improve the company's products. SparkFun was founded in 2003 and is based in Boulder, Colorado.

Chapter 20

Ten Places to Find Parts and Components

In This Chapter

▶ Finding parts for your projects anywhere in the world

▶ Finding local shops

▶ Reusing old parts

*Y*ou can find many Arduino-related shops in the world, but there are also a number of suppliers that are good to know about when shopping for parts and components.

RS Components (World)

http://www.rs-components.com

RS Components markets itself as "the world's largest distributor of electronics and maintenance products," so it's a reliable source of products available in an extensive range and at low prices. RS also has a sister company that operates in the United States, Allied Electronics.

Farnell (World)

http://www.farnell.com

Farnell is a British suppler of electronics with an enormous range of components to choose from. It operates worldwide under the Premier Farnell Group. This company is made up of several sister companies that allow the group to distribute to 24 countries in Europe (Farnell), North America (Newark Electronics) and Asia Pacific (Element14).

Rapid (World)

http://www.rapidonline.com

Rapid is one of the United Kingdom's leading electronics distributors. Its main promise is to source components quicker than other suppliers. Among its stock is a huge selection of educational electronics kits, ideal for those who are just starting out with soldering.

Digi-Key (World)

http://www.digikey.com

Digi-Key is one of the largest distributors of electronic components in North America. The company originally started by supplying the hobbyist market of amateur radio enthusiasts, but it has since grown into the international electronics distributor that it is today.

eBay (World)

www.ebay.com

One person's junk is another person's treasure, and eBay is a great source of tech products that need a new home. Many parts are available through eBay — even quite specific ones. But better than that, you can find other bits of consumer electronics that you can hack to suit your own ends.

Maplin (U.K.)

http://www.maplin.co.uk

Maplin is a consumer electronics shop that can be found in most city centers across the United Kingdom, providing all sorts of electronic products as well as a fair selection of components, kits, and tools. Maplin can be a lifesaver for Arduin-ists when they're caught in a tight spot. The company has also recently started stocking a range of Arduino products that show off the new Arduino branded retail packaging.

RadioShack (U.S.)

http://www.radioshack.com

RadioShack sells a wide range of consumer electronics product accessories and has more than 7,000 stores in the United States. As well as stocking more conventional consumer electronics, it offers a selection of electronics components, kits, and tools.

Ultraleds (U.K.)

http://www.ultraleds.co.uk

Ultraleds is a U.K.-based specialist supplier of LED lighting products and other accessories to use them. Ultraleds stocks more conventional LED replacement bulbs for use around the house and offers a wide range of low-voltage DC LED ribbon and bulbs at extremely competitive prices.

EnvironmentalLights.com (U.S.)

http://www.environmentallights.com

EnvironmentalLights.com is a leading supplier of sustainable and energy-efficient lighting based in San Diego, California. It offers a huge variety of LED lighting that can be used for an equally huge number of applications. The company may even give you ideas for new projects as well.

Skip/Dumpster Diving (World)

People are always amazed at the amount of useful stuff that's thrown away, but they rarely know what's useful and what's not. The key is to know what you're looking for and find out whether you can salvage the parts you need for your project. This may take a bit of Googling because there are so many products and components out there that could be of use to your project. The motor is one such component that can be extremely expensive if bought new but is used in a variety of consumer electronics that are often discarded without a thought. Printers and scanners use relatively complex and expensive stepper motors to work, which can be used again another day. Also, because these everyday objects are mass-produced, even the cost of a new printer with several motors can be cheaper than buying motors on their own.

Index

• M •

• *N* •